To my Mom and Dad,
Rose Sabellico (1925-1993) and
James Sabellico (1924-2000)

They gave me life, and a great model as to how to live
one. He gave me my love for baseball and many a
lesson on what it meant to be a man; she gave me my
love for books and reading and many a lesson on what
it meant to be a parent. Together they gave me all a son
could ever ask for: love, guidance, support, self-esteem,
and a life based in faith and family.

Tom Sabellico

TABLE OF CONTENTS

PROLOGUE

Many words we use to describe public figures, especially athletes, tend to be overstatements. The terms "star" and "superstar", once reserved for the likes of DiMaggio, Mays, Mantle and Aaron, seem to have lost their impact with overuse. I'd venture to say every current professional athlete, in this public relations world of ours, has been described as a "star" or a "superstar." While it is true that a player must have world-class talent to be a professional athlete, only reading the press clippings makes it difficult to distinguish the really great ones. So in trying to describe Ryne Duren I searched for the word that would convey the place he holds in baseball lore. To me that word is "legend." During their moment in time, no matter how long that "moment" actually lasts, legends are larger than life. Their actions, their persona, their style, their swagger, make them stand out from the crowd in such a way that stories about them multiply and disseminate far beyond just those who have seen them. Their impact endures past the "fifteen minutes of fame" afforded to most of us according to Andy Warhol. Their accomplishments, and how they went about them, become more and more grandiose each time their story is related from person to person, because the people who actually witness them feel compelled to share the experience and in trying to convey the impact feel a little exaggeration seems fitting. Maybe the best way to define a "legend" is just to say you know one when you see one.

Ryne Duren is an American Legend, make no mistake about it. During the period from 1958 through 1960, Duren captured the attention of the sports world. He excelled during that time as a relief pitcher – one of the first to appear mainly in situations where victory was so close his team could taste it, yet defeat was also possibly imminent, requiring his heroics to shut down the opposition to secure the tenuous victory. Today, that position is called a "Closer" and the most notable is Mariano Rivera, of the New York Yankees. No name existed for Ryne's role in 1958, but the excitement was there just the same. He would usually come into a game in the last or next to last inning with the tying run for the opposing team either on base, at bat, or on deck, and the victory, so close, or the loss, so dreaded, rode on his back. Since Ryne's day, the relief pitcher has become much more widely used and now every team has a closer.

What made Ryne especially tough to hit was that from 1958 to 1960 he arguably threw a baseball faster than anyone else in the Major Leagues – in excess of 100 miles per hour. Add to that lightning velocity his trademark dark sunglasses, his legendary poor vision, and a tendency to be sort of a maverick. Then place him on the showcase stage of Yankee Stadium, playing for the world-renowned, World Champion New York Yankees, and the result is LEGEND. To this day, I assure you that if you raise Duren's name in conversation with anyone possessing any knowledge of sports, mention will be made of his sunglasses, his poor eyesight, his wildness, his trademark first warm-up pitch into the screen, or how fast he could pitch. You will undoubtedly hear about his striking pose on the mound, the fear he struck into the hearts of opposing batters, and his off-field antics generated by the consumption of too much alcohol.

Yes, like just about every other great legend, Ryne Duren had a legendary flaw. It was clear to all who saw Ryne Duren during the height of his career that he had Hall of Fame potential, but the tremendous ability and promise they recognized were ultimately drowned in fear and alcohol. That is what makes Duren's story so compelling. From the time Ryne Duren was a teenager in Wisconsin, until beyond his thirty-ninth birthday, his greatest opponent was not sixty feet six inches away, nor swinging a bat, nor wearing the other team's uniform.

Ryne's enemy was in his own body and mind. Early in life, Ryne bought into the myth that in order to be a real man he had to be able to drink alcohol and plenty of it. His belief in that myth, together with the terrible fear and anxiety he harbored, that without his ability to throw a ball a hundred miles an hour he would not be accepted, fueled his alcoholic addiction. Ryne's panache was the type of thing sportswriters lived for. Typewriters clicked away at a furious rate as reporters filled newspapers with stories about the blind-as-a-bat 29 year-old rookie from Wisconsin who could throw the ball faster than any person had a right to expect. They sang his praises and predicted future glory. But eventually, all the stories began to focus not on Ryne's style but on his drinking and how it made him act. They recited all the opportunities lost and what could have been.

Ryne Duren's actions on the field until the time his career ended in 1965 could fill a volume by themselves. But what is ultimately more significant is that Ryne Duren eventually conquered his greatest enemy. In 1968, Ryne came to grips with his fears, his anxiety, and his alcoholism – too late to resurrect a baseball career, too late to save his first marriage, but not too late to go out and perform heroically again: this time, without the stage of Yankee Stadium and the World Series, and without the support of stars like Mickey Mantle, Whitey Ford and others. What he would do would show up in the lives and hearts of countless people in Wisconsin and beyond, who were helped by Ryne to deal with their fears, their anxieties and their battles with alcohol and other drugs.

Ryne Duren, at the age of 39, finally left his adolescence behind him. He had matured and was ready to make a difference. What he has done in the last 34 years is truly legendary. Ryne Duren no longer works on a pitching mound in front of thousands of fans and millions more at home on television. He now works in hospitals, clinics, classrooms, and on Little League fields, sometimes to an audience of one. What he throws at you now are not 100 mile per hour fastballs, but fast facts about alcohol, what it has done and what it is capable of doing. His saves are not recorded in baseball records and have nothing to do with baseball games. His saves are now counted in lives, saved through interventions and education. No plaques exist in Cooperstown for what Ryne Duren achieved on a ball field, although many a player will tell you he is the toughest pitcher they ever had to face. More importantly, many people hold a special place in their homes and hearts for Ryne Duren for having intervened and saved them or their loved ones and their family.

My first introduction to Ryne Duren came at a distance of approximately two hundred feet away, in Yankee Stadium. Along with the thousands of other fans there that day, I experienced Ryne as he strode in from the bullpen in right field and took over the pitching mound. It was an awesome sight, something I will never forget. He appeared bigger than his 6 foot 2 inch frame, and looked like he could spit nails. To a little kid, which I was, he left a strong impression, one I will always have.

Most kids my age got to meet Ryne Duren through the television screen of WPIX in New York. But thanks to my Dad and my Aunt Angie and Uncle Sal who were all very big Yankee fans, and took me to Yankee Stadium often, I got to see him perform in person, and there was no comparison. That little black and white television screen just didn't do justice to the feeling you got at the Stadium. I could only imagine the feeling going through the hearts of those guys who got to meet him by standing only sixty feet six inches away, and waiting to hit against him, or at least to try.

My second introduction to Ryne Duren came almost forty years later. As the Executive Director of Winning Beyond Winning, Inc., a charity whose mission is to help past and future generations of athletes by imparting the wisdom of the former to the latter, I was in the process of selecting a speaker for our next program. As I chatted with Phil Linz at a golf outing attended by members of the Major League Baseball Players Alumni Association, I heard a booming voice say: "Well, hell, why don't you ask me? I know more about those things than any of these guys." I looked up and saw Ryne Duren's face, only four or five feet away from me. It still had all of the strength that I remembered seeing as a kid, but now it also had an embracing smile and a glow earned through years of maturity and growth. I accepted Ryne's invitation, and am forever grateful. From that chance meeting, Ryne Duren became a member of the Board of

Directors of Winning Beyond Winning, Inc., one of our regular speakers, a trusted advisor, and more importantly a true and terrific friend.

The stories of Ryne Duren have widespread appeal. They are stories to be shared with sports fans and to be used as life lessons by parents, teachers and today's young adults. Whether or not you are old enough to remember a twenty-nine-year old, rookie Ryne Duren, confidently striding from the Yankee bullpen in rightfield to the mound in Yankee Stadium with sunglasses on and his warm-up jacket slung over his shoulder, you should find yourself standing up and cheering for him by the time you complete this book.

I would like to thank Ryne Duren and his wife, Diane, for the opportunity of getting to know them and their family. Thanks to Ryne's son, Steve Duren, for reviewing the draft of this book and for providing his candid memories of life with Ryne. The insights provided by reading Steve's recollections are powerful. I would also like to thank Ryne for trusting me enough to tell his story, and for all of his work as a member of the Board of Directors of Winning Beyond Winning, Inc., and for his agreement to donate profits from this book to Winning Beyond Winning, Inc. Thanks also to my dear friend, Rosendo "Rusty" Torres, for his constant friendship and for introducing me to the world of the professional athlete, and to the Baseball Assistance Team (B.A.T.), for introducing me to Rusty. I extend my thanks and appreciation to Ralph Houk, Johnny Blanchard, Whitey Ford, Phil Rizzuto, Gil McDougald, Yogi Berra, Bobby Richardson, Mudcat Grant, Tommy Lasorda, Roland Hemond, Jim Maloney, Paul Foytack, Sandy Koufax, Fred Valentine, Bob Newton, Chuck Schilling, Joe Ginsberg, J.C. Martin, Chuck Hinton, Moose Skowron, Jim Kaat, Chuck Tanner, Jim Landis, Lee Thomas, Frank Torre, Frank Malzone, Don Ferrarese, Jerry Casale, Roy Sievers, Ted Bowsfield, and to all of the other athletes who have contributed their memories of Ryne and their insights to this book.

Thanks to the reporters who wrote stories about Ryne that found their way into his sisters' scrapbooks. Their work, performed more than fifty years ago, written as events happened, has served to memorialize those events, paving the way for researchers and writers. Unfortunately, many of those stories did not contain a byline, or even the name of the paper they appeared in, making it impossible to properly credit the reporters. Likewise, Ryne has included in this book photos that were given to him over the years, but which did not indicate who the photographer was. I would like to thank Ruth Wingfield and Don Wingfield, Jr., the widow and son, respectively, of sports photographer, Don Wingfield, for graciously agreeing to allow us to include photos taken by the late Mr. Wingfield. I would also like to acknowledge Bill Burdick and the staff of the National Baseball Hall of Fame Library and Archives and thank them for their assistance and cooperation in researching this book.

Thanks to Patricia Innella, Donna Salonia, Dan Kornfeld, Dave Diamond and Laurette Listro, and to my children, Christopher and Gina for their assistance in researching and editing this book, and to my son James for his technical assistance and for designing the cover of the book. In total you were all a great help in bringing this dream to reality.

Special thanks to my wife, Paula, for having the understanding and patience of a saint, for giving me the support to attempt this project, and the freedom to complete it.

Tom Sabellico

INTRODUCTION

This is the second book centered around my life, which is pretty remarkable considering that most people do not get the opportunity to commit their life story to writing even once. But I have really had two lives. My first life, which I related in my autobiography *The Comeback*, was a wild ride. It was dominated by my fight with alcohol, which cost me my baseball career and my first family. My second life started on May 2, 1968, when I began the journey that allowed me to conquer my addiction.

Since the writing of *The Comeback* in 1977, I have continued to lecture throughout the country on the issue of alcohol education, use and abuse. I have worked in every way I can to help people understand what alcohol is, what it can do to them and how to avoid many of those problems. Knowing my history, not everybody wants to hear what I have to say. Many people think that there is nothing as insufferable as a reformed alcoholic, or that my message is that of a latter-day Carrie Nation. But that is not the case. I, for one, am not a person who is in favor of prohibition, but rather I am in favor of education. My concern is that many people, many young people, buy into the concept of alcohol without the proper education, and trying to educate people after they have bought into an addiction is a very, very difficult thing to do. But I have a strong feeling that if parents and teachers take the time to understand alcohol and its abuse, they will be in a much better position to help our youth avoid serious problems.

I consider myself blessed in that I was given a chance to live a second life. Many of the friends and teammates I had during my "first life" were not as fortunate as I have been. By my conservative count, more than 115 of the fellows I played professional baseball with have died from alcohol related diseases or injuries.

At the age of 73 I now have the benefit of seeing very clearly what I could not see for so many years. Revisiting some of the things that happened to me and some of my actions was not easy. Opening your private life for the world to see seldom is. To begin with, I needed the help of some of my friends to even remember things that happened in my life. I recently saw a piece of film that showed me pitching in the 1958 World Series and as I watched it I realized I had no independent memory of that moment at all. Imagine that, getting to a pinnacle of a ballplayer's profession - pitching for the New York Yankees in a World Series - and I couldn't even remember it. Many things I had done were lost to me because of "blackouts" caused by the alcoholism.

I see many things much more clearly now, and I have a greater appreciation for the life I had as a professional ballplayer. I've been quoted as saying "I never really knew what it was like to pitch a sober inning." What I meant by that is not that I was drunk when I pitched, or that I had been drinking prior to the game, but that until I finally kicked the addiction I was not "sober", really. I was in a state of addiction which made everything kind of blurry and out of focus. I couldn't really appreciate the game, my abilities, my career or my opportunities, and therefore couldn't make the most of myself. Now, I have come to realize how much I appreciate the game of baseball and those players who came before me, and played with me, making it possible for the great game to continue. This book will give you an inside look at the game of baseball during its golden age. But, it will also allow the reader, no matter what age, to learn about alcohol and its effects, my life, and life in general. I am a very fortunate man to still be alive today to tell this story. Hopefully, it will create a spark bright enough to help someone else find his or her way to a second life.

I would like to thank Tom Sabellico for the enormous amount of research conducted to make this book a reality. I know Tom contacted many of my former teammates and opponents and I thank them for their assistance and their contributions. He also read the scrapbooks maintained by my sisters and relatives, along with every other article, column, and book ever written about me. The result of his extensive research is evident in the realistic descriptions he paints with my thoughts and his words. I believe his efforts have resulted in the most accurate portrayal of my life ever written.

                                                        Ryne Duren

FOREWORD

Ryne Duren. I only need to say his name to a group of us old-timers and I can get the room buzzing. Every one of us who played with or against Ryne has a favorite story to tell about him. Usually it involves getting up off the ground and dusting your uniform off, or dragging your bat back to the rack after a whiff, or something crazy that Rhino did while he was under the influence of alcohol, which seemed to be quite often back then. But I believe the best Ryne Duren story is the one you are about to read – an honest, from-the-heart, account of Ryne's life, and his ultimate victory over alcoholism.

Ryne was always a hard working athlete and an intimidating competitor. Our paths first crossed in 1958, when we were both in our rookie seasons, Ryne with the Yankees and me with the Indians. In fact, by June of that year, Ryne and I were among the leading contenders for American League Rookie of the Year, but we both lost that one to Albie Pearson of the Senators. (Writers never seemed to appreciate pitchers over hitters.) But that was not the only thing Ryne and I shared in common, before or after 1958.

That sounds kind of funny at first, even to me, Ryne being as fair as an albino and coming from Wisconsin, while I was among the first black pitchers in baseball, and was born in Lacoochie, Florida. We were both hard working kids who grew up loving and playing baseball. We both had to forfeit baseball scholarships to college during our freshman year because of family finances, and we both signed to play minor league ball in the early 1950s for about $250 a month. At the end of his first full season, in 1958, Ryne starred in the World Series: that was something I got to do in 1965, and Ryne was already out of baseball by then.

But our most important shared experience had nothing to do with baseball, or whether we were black or white. It had to do with our ability to overcome adversity, to get back up after getting knocked down.

At the end of my baseball career, in 1971, I lost my life savings of over $85,000 to a dishonest business partner. When I called my mother and told her I lost everything, she asked me if I lost my hands, my feet or my ability to think. When I told her no, of course, she said, "Then we don't have anything to talk about" and she abruptly hung up the phone. I was mad. I called her right back and told her not to hang up on me. She said, "Then don't ever tell me you're ruined again." Before talking to my Mom, I thought my life was over. Now, thirty years later, it's hard to believe I thought I was finished. Her determination, her will, her spirit, forged by surviving the death of my father when I was only two years old, and raising us all, with very little money and a lot of faith, was an inspiration to me, and led the way for me to climb back up off the floor.

No less of an inspiration was Ryne's determination, will and spirit, to defeat the one opponent who had dogged him for over twenty-five years, alcohol, and had driven him to a point where he had lost everything. Years ago I wrote a poem called "Life", comparing life to two opposing baseball teams: one team comprised of the traits that strengthen you and the other team made up of those that weaken you. Two lines from that poem talk to Ryne's struggle and victory:

On Ryne's team:

Your pitcher's name is courage; you need him in this game.

* * *

Against him:

There's one more man you'll have to watch, he's always very near.

He's the pitcher for this team: I'm told his name is fear.

Fear of failure, fear of not being accepted, fear of fear, all of these gripped Ryne's life harder than he gripped a baseball, until finally one day, at his darkest hour, when all seemed lost, he found the courage to try one more time, and the courage to not only save his life, but to allow him to work at saving other lives.

Ryne and I started together as rookies, and today our paths cross even more frequently on the golf and charity circuit. He tells everybody he threw the ball faster than I did, but I get even by golfing better than him. (The truth is Ryne could really bring the heat.)

I know you will enjoy this book, which I have had the pleasure of reading. Ryne has captured the feeling of what a ballplayer's life was like in the 1950s and 60s. More importantly he gives you an inside look at the despair he felt and the struggle and determination it took to overcome his addiction, and he provides some excellent advice for parents, coaches and educators about the education necessary to prevent life-threatening addictions. I, for one, am glad Ryne survived to write this book and I survived to read it.

Jim "Mudcat" Grant

One

MY SECOND BIRTH

The year was 1968, a year of upheaval and change: for the United States, for the World, and for me. North Koreans captured the USS Pueblo, and held its crew hostage. The world's eyes were on the war in Vietnam, where the North Vietnamese ratcheted up the pace by launching the Tet offensive. Richard Nixon entered the race for President of the United States, and Lyndon Johnson exited, shocking the nation by announcing he would not seek reelection. Martin Luther King was murdered in Memphis, sparking race riots that rocked the country, from Boston to Los Angeles. It was monumental news that would shape the world, but I do not have any independent recollection of any of it.

I was thirty-nine years old and in the deepest throes of my alcoholic addiction. Everyday started for me with the same prospect: I would wake up hoping I could beat the alcoholism, thinking that I could not, knowing that by day's end, somehow, someway, I would fall victim to the contents of a bottle. Many of the details of my activities, and the news happening in the world, were obscured from my memory because of "blackouts" caused by the alcoholism, and have been told to me by my family and friends. What I do have a clear recollection of is the feeling of despair deep in my gut, and my yearning to end that ongoing misery. Although I was thirty-nine chronologically, I was still only fourteen years old psychologically, an age I had been trapped at for twenty-five years. I could not figure out how to handle life without alcohol, and I could no longer stand life with alcohol.

During the lucid intervals I did have, I tortured myself emotionally with the knowledge that I wasted my tremendous talents and I squandered opportunities others only dreamed of being given. I was out of baseball for three years already, although realistically my baseball career had been washed up since the end of the 1963 season, and I bounced around for another season and a half, clinging to the dream, and the high life, surviving on instinct, reputation, and desperation. My career was definitely shortened by my alcoholism and the good years I did have were affected by the mischievous conduct that accompanied my suspended adolescence.

My childhood love and wife, Beverly, had divorced me, and I hardly saw my only son, Steve. From my recollection, I had already been involved in about thirty different car accidents. I had been in jail numerous times, and in my uneducated attempts to get a handle on my drinking, on thirty-four different occasions I had been in front of some type of helping professional: priests, ministers, social workers and marriage counselors, and I'm not even counting judges and jailers. And nothing was getting any better.

Since leaving baseball, I had already been through several other jobs, including being a dishwasher and a mechanic, and had failed at all of them, and then I really went and did it. In 1967, International Harvester had hired me as a mechanic's helper, but when they discovered who I was, they moved me out on the sales floor – to use my name. By then, I secretly hated the name Ryne Duren and all I thought it stood for – a hopeless drunk, a man who had destroyed his family, who couldn't get control of himself. I was sick and tired of Ryne Duren. By April 1968 I had been given a brand new Harvester Scout to drive as a company car. The very first time I took the car out on the road I wrecked it. I wasn't falling down drunk, but I was under the influence of alcohol while driving. I came up on a stop sign, hit the brakes and the car flipped. In actuality, it was my whole world that I really turned upside down with that accident. The immediate injury was a torn muscle in my back that cost me a few days in the hospital. Then I returned to my room at the The Knickerbocker Hotel, in Milwaukee, down near Lake Michigan, to find that the accident also cost me my job. Wrecking the car was the last straw, even for my friends at International Harvester. I had just managed, once again, to turn a positive into a negative. I went from a sales representative with a brand new car to an injured, jobless, alcoholic, with no car, no family, and no friends. I turned to the only thing I knew how to do – I just stayed in that hotel room and drank solidly for a ten-day period. I would drink until I passed out. And I would come to long enough to find a few dollars, and get something else to drink until I passed out again. Slowly, life was closing in on me. I didn't have much money left. After paying my latest bill at the hotel, my life savings was able to fit in one pants pocket. I was down to only about a hundred dollars or so, but how long would that carry me? Another week or so? I didn't have much for clothes either. I didn't know where I was going to go or what I was going to do. I was sick of life, repulsed by my inability to escape the same old story every day. So, I got dressed up in the best clothes I had left, walked down to Lake Michigan, found a big rock and I started to walk into the lake with intentions to kill myself. When I was in far enough so that the water was over my head, I realized how cold I was, and I said to myself, "Stupid, go get a couple of Brandy Manhattans and warm up first." My unquenchable desire for alcohol had won out again. Even over my desire to kill myself, my body wanted alcohol. I came back from the lake and went to the hotel where I had those Brandy Manhattans, and more. Then I just wandered about aimlessly, stumbling from bar to bar. I knew it was all over for me, and I either had to die or …. I don't know what.

My brothers, Vince and Larry found out where I was and came to check in on me. Upon seeing my condition, they begged me to get some help. I didn't think help was possible, because I had been in different places before and I didn't think people like me got better. I thought death was the only answer. I told them, "This isn't about me getting help. This is about whether I want to live or die." They proceeded in an attempt to persuade me to check in to the alcohol treatment center at DePaul Hospital. I resisted and they persisted. Finally, I compromised into letting them have Father Arcadius Marotti, from DePaul, come and talk to me. After Father Marotti visited me I was still not convinced about going to DePaul. I needed another day or two of drinking to sense the utter hopelessness of my despair. At that point I guess I figured I was just about dead, and I didn't have enough money left to buy one more drink, or stay in the hotel one more night, so I called my old boss at Harvester. He came to see me at the hotel and we talked about what choices I had left. I said, "Well, I suppose, maybe I can go over to the hospital, to the treatment center." Without hesitation he took me over to DePaul Hospital, figuring it was the last chance to save my life. I walked in to DePaul, not with any real hope that this would be different than any other failed attempt I had made at sobriety, but it was better than dying in the street. In the intake ward a nun came over, and I was just lying there half in the bag, like most guys were when they showed up at DePaul. I said, "I'm just here. I don't want to live, but I guess I can't die." This nun, who was also a nurse, said, "Oh, you can get well." I said, "I don't even know how to pray anymore. God won't listen to me, so I don't pray." She said, "C'mon, we can pray. God'll help you if you ask him." and we prayed a little bit. Her sincere face and words, and that prayer, constituted the first real signs of light in my life in a long, long time. Like someone trapped in the bottom of a cave who sees a ray of sunlight from above, I knew I had a lot of work ahead of me to climb up from where I was, but at least there was a sign of hope and direction. That was the last day I ever drank, May 2, 1968, a day I now celebrate as my second birth date.

Two

CAZENOVIA, WISCONSIN

I hail from Cazenovia, a very small town in Wisconsin. In fact, the highest reported population number I ever saw on the sign that welcomed people into town was 410. There's a good chance the rabbits and other wildlife in the area outnumbered the humans. It was rural America at its best, as good as that could be during a period of time that included the Great Depression, Prohibition and the beginning of American involvement in World War II with the Japanese bombing of Pearl Harbor, all happening before I was thirteen years old. For a kid who hadn't known anything other than country life in Wisconsin, it was certainly a fun place to grow up – plenty of things to do: fishing, farming, hunting rabbits, hiking. It was a community where everybody knew everybody else, and because of my family's history in the town, I was proud to be a Duren.

The Durens were one of the "pioneer" families of Wisconsin. My great-grandfather, William Duren, came to Wisconsin in 1856. In 1868 my grandfather, who was a lumber baron, erected a sawmill on the shores of the Little Baraboo River, and actually owned seven miles of the railroad that connected Cazenovia to the main line of the Northwestern Railroad, between Minneapolis and Chicago. That mill stayed in the family for over seventy years, and was one of the places I worked as a young man. I had other sources of pride in being a Duren beyond the history of my ancestors. My Dad served as the local Postmaster, and as the Constable of Cazenovia, and one of the streets just outside Cazenovia proper is Duren Drive.

The home I was born in was located on about ten acres of land with a stream running behind it, fed by a big spring that came out from under the town of Cazenovia. There was a dam and the lakes that formed Cazenovia were about a quarter of a mile away. As a kid I used to play at that spring and fish just below that dam and in that stream down the line.

In 1941, my family moved to Main Street, a move of about a quarter of a mile, to a house the local carpenter had built for himself and his family. It was a beautiful, impressive house, one of the nicest in town, with big colonnades in front and the upstairs rooms were cantilevered over a porch. But, as pretty as it was, it did not have any indoor plumbing, as was the case with most houses at that time. So, the first thing we did when we got there was to put in our own plumbing, and at twelve years old, my job was to assist in building the cistern by digging a hole about twelve feet in diameter and ten feet deep.

The new house had about an acre of land, and was located right across the street from the high school. That was a break for me. I had been walking two miles twice a day to and from St. Anthony's Grammar School in Germantown, a two-room schoolhouse, run by Franciscan nuns. I can still picture it, and smell it - the old wood burning furnace in the basement, the big piles of wood outside and the outdoor toilets that always had that stink about them. I don't think they knew what lime was then. It was while I was there the nuns found out I needed help with my vision. I was in the first grade when I got my first pair of glasses. I remember having to sit in the very front seat to see the blackboard, and even then I didn't see it very well. I remember the ballgames out in back of the school, and Mass every morning. My heart still quickens a beat when I think about the threat of having to go see the priest if you did something wrong. I also remember just how hard it was for me to stay in the schoolhouse, how long the hours seemed, especially on those afternoons when the weather turned warm and inviting. It felt like school just dragged on. Finally, one day, I jumped through an open window and took off running through the wooded country around the lake. I raced into the safety of the house, only to really catch hell from my Dad. That's when they decided I should go to the public school, across the street from our new house.

Cazenovia, Wisconsin was about as middle America as you could get. I have kind of a very fond feeling for it, truly I do. When I think of my childhood years and surroundings, I consider myself blessed to have the opportunity to grow up so close to nature and to so much family. There was never a need to lock the doors on your house, or to have any fear of your neighbors. They were all good, honest people. You never had a problem unless someone got drunk and wanted to fight. I was too young to see the connection between the alcohol and the behavior. I hadn't realized yet how important alcohol was to everyone there, and how ignorant we all were to its power. Thinking back about Cazenovia now, I realize we had four taverns in town, and two more within a couple of miles of town. There were more taverns than schools or churches, and that should have told me something about the power of alcohol.

Three

FAMILY AND FARM LIFE

I grew up in a large family – eight kids, four boys and four girls. My Dad's family, the Durens, were German, and my Mom's family, the Murphys, were Irish. I always lean a little bit more toward the Irish part of the family, but my Dad and his folks were very German. I always thought it was ironic that my Dad, coming from German stock, wound up fighting the Germans in World War I, causing him severe injuries. He was wounded in the back by machine gun fire, and mortar fire got him in the shoulder, causing him to just about lose his arm. He was kind of a local hero in the first World War and always got a kick out of showing us a newspaper, from Minneapolis, that had his picture in it and reported that he was killed in action, because he was missing for quite some time after he got hurt. Lucky for us the paper was wrong.

When I think of my Irish heritage I can just see that Irish face of my granddad Murphy, and the Irish fiddle and the jig and all the Erin Go Bragh stuff and the Irish fun we always had. My grandmother's name was Honora Quinn. She was such a lovely, kind lady and my mother was a little left-hander with an Irish temper. I guess calling it a temper has a negative connotation; it's just that she was so full of life compared to the stoic, stern nature of my Dad. Mom was the "glue" that held our family together. She was the one who always stressed the importance of education, and instilled the basics of religion in us. Mom was the spiritual leader of the family and I truly believe her ability to keep us all together with the limited resources available was nothing short of miraculous. She was a very resourceful woman who began every day by attending Mass and then proceeded to go about the business of readying eight children and a husband for the various respective stages of their workdays or school days. In the 1940s, Mom became the Assistant Postmaster, working for Dad, and she held that job until just before her death.

It was my father's father, Joe Duren, who owned the sawmill. He also owned a farm, which he lost to the Northwestern Mutual Insurance Company. They held the mortgage and repossessed the farm when he couldn't make the mortgage payments. It was pretty much like the bank threatened to do in *Field of Dreams*, but my grandfather lost the farm because of the Great Depression, not because he built a baseball field. Later on, in 1934, the insurance company offered the farm back to my Dad on the condition that he assumed responsibility for the loan payments. Dad accepted the offer and that farm is still with the Durens, owned by my oldest brother's family.

Because of the rural nature of Cazenovia, the presence nearby of so many relatives, and the demands of farm-life on all of them, I spent a great deal of time on a farm, whether it was Mom and Dad's, or Grandpa Duren's or Grandpa Murphy's. When I was 13 or 14 years old, I was doing a man's work on the weekends and after school.

On the farm I had the team of horses and would haul hay, pitch it by hand and put it in the hay mound with a big hayfork. I also did a lot of hard work thrashing grain. I'd hook up the team and go to the neighboring farm where the thrashing was being done that day, and haul the grain to the thrashing machine. The thrashing process would result in the grain being propelled into strong grain sacks, which would each weigh in excess of a hundred pounds by the time you filled it. The machine did the thrashing but we did the physical part – the carrying. I would throw each bag over my shoulder and carry it to the grain bin, which was usually one flight up, and then empty the bags into the bin.

When the thrashing was done, there were usually a few cases of beer on the truck and everybody would drink a couple of beers. That was the man's reward for a day's work. There was a sense of belonging and the fourteen year old could have his beer if he did the same work as the men and nobody thought anything of it. There were other guys my age around, but I always got patted on the back for being a real man, because no other guy my age at the time was doing as many different jobs and chores.

One of the things I did just as a chore to help out at my grandparents' farm was milking the cows. We had about twenty cows and sometimes I'd do all the milking. That was all done by hand, without the assistance of any milking machines. I firmly believe that all of that milking was what developed the strength I had in my wrists.

The work in the feed mill started about the time I was about 14. Farmers would bring their corn and their grain to be processed into feed, and similar to the thrashing process, I got to do the carrying. I would pound a full bag down a couple of times, tie a slip knot around the top of the bag, and would stack about ten bags onto a dolly and bring them outside and pile them on the dock. There were days when I handled three or four hundred bags.

The part of it that was really bodybuilding was unloading railroad cars. My grandfather's portion of the railroad ceased to be in 1936 or 1937, when a big flood came that took out all the bridges. Without the railroad, we had to transport everything by truck between Cazenovia and LaValle, where the main line of the Chicago and NorthWestern Railroads went through between Chicago and Minneapolis. Ronald Long owned the feed mill, and he had a nephew, Don Klang, who was a good pitcher himself. He pitched in high school and for the town team before I did. We'd get an extra truck and we'd drive to and from LaValle, working from after school or after dinner until 11 or 12 o'clock at night. Part of that work was a competition with Klang, to see who could lift more, and who could throw full bags further. Each bag weighed between a hundred and a hundred fifty pounds. Sometimes, we'd double up to go faster. So we were lifting anywhere from one to three hundred pounds. When we got to the warehouse or the mill, we'd pick up a bag, then flip it just as far as we could. I'm sure it was muscle building. I remember one time I picked up 400 pounds and walked off with it. When you do that kind of thing, you are strong everywhere, because your legs come into it. We'd carry loads up the steps, and bend a lot, so in a sense we "pumped iron", but it wasn't iron. It's funny that my attitude to this day about running or pumping iron is that if I'm going to do that, I'd just as soon do so some kind work and get something accomplished. We had a hell of a work ethic.

Another muscle building job was piling and hauling wood. We would pile wood all day. It was our fuel supply for the farm and our home, but, if anybody wanted to buy wood, then Dad would sell it to them. Some of the sales, especially to our big customers, like the cheese factory, the church and the school, required us to haul the wood. Many times, on the weekends, or even after school, I would use Heland Lovell's ton and a half milk truck to haul wood. We'd usually haul six to eight loads of wood a day. Everybody was burning wood at that time, and I don't really remember if that was part of the War effort to conserve fuel or if the wood burning stoves were the state-of-the-art heating furnaces in our area at that time.

I had a lot of chores after school – the wood, the milking, the feed mill, I even had different jobs working over at the creamery for a while, including driving the milk truck. Most of the guys liked to hunt deer and went on hunting trips several times a year. Although I could work like a man, I wasn't allowed to go hunting with them until I was a little bit older. Since I was home and I knew where everybody lived in the countryside, that left me as the logical choice to make pick-ups and deliveries for the creamery and feed mill with that old Diamond T truck. Sometimes I had to carry a whole truck full of stuff upstairs in the shed or the grainery barn. I worked pretty hard as a kid, and when we were finished the older guys let me drink with them, like a man. I was building muscle, which eventually made me much stronger, but at the same time I was building up a taste for alcohol, which eventually was my downfall.

Four

MY INTRODUCTION TO ALCOHOL AND BIG GEORGE

When I was growing up, alcohol was not only a presence it was a force. To put it in perspective, the way it appeared to me, which is important, drinking was the main event and everything else was incidental to it. Whether it was a wedding, or just a night the boys got together and went out in high school, the first questions were where are we going to get the booze and what's it going to be. The closer to my senior year the more important alcohol became. We'd enlist one of the town drunks to buy our case of beer or our fifth of whiskey and we would cut him in for part of whatever it was that we got. If we went out for the evening to a dance or a party, we'd never go unless we first loaded at least a case of beer into the car.

I started drinking when I was about 13 or 14, and it started innocently enough. As part of the family's status in the neighborhood you had to have a bottle of liquor in the pantry, and beer would always be around. Whenever anybody in the house was drinking, I would steal a sip or persuade someone to let me taste a little.

My Dad drank, and drank quite a bit until he had a stroke, in his early forties. That nearly cost him his life and, luckily, only temporarily paralyzed his right side. He didn't quit smoking after that, but the stroke did curtail his abuse of alcohol. He

still drank, but nothing like when he was younger. Back then,
from what I hear, Dad was a wild, roaring drinker who loved
to fight. A number of uncles in the family did die as a result
of their drinking, and some of them were quite young. One
of them died during a grand mal seizure, and another one had
a condition commonly known as "wet brain" which led to his
death. I also had first cousins and a brother-in-law who hurried
their death along at an early age because of their excessive
drinking, and there were several others in town that also died
due to alcoholism.

"Wet Brain"

*Chronic abusive alcohol use can permanently damage
the frontal lobes of the brain and can cause an overall
reduction in brain size and an increase in the size of the
ventricles. Alcoholism also leads to malnutrition and
poor absorption and storage of thiamine (B1). Because
of the lack of B1, a syndrome known as "Wernicke's
Encephalopathy" may develop, and manifest itself by
impaired memory, confusion and lack of coordination.
Further deficiency of thiamine can lead to "Korsakoff's
Syndrome" evidenced by amnesia, apathy and disorien-
tation. The advanced stages of disease of the brain are
commonly referred to as a "wet brain."*

I recently saw a picture of my Uncle Harold Murphy, my
mother's brother and my favorite uncle. I loved him dearly. He
died from the effects of alcohol when he was fairly young – 56
years old. He, my Dad and my Uncle Rudy, who was also on
my mother's side, were drinkers and hell raisers. Uncle Harold
made a big thing about drinking, and Dad got such a kick out
of Uncle Harold, as everybody did. Harold would drive up
from Milwaukee to visit us, and Dad would have Harold's
drink ready about the time he thought he might be showing up.
From that big window in the house on Main Street, he'd look
down and when he saw Harold's car coming up the line, he'd
start out the door with a drink in his hand. When Harold would
roll into the driveway, Dad would grab the driver's side door,
open it up and hand Harold the drink, and Harold's reply was "I
wondered when we were gonna get a drink around here." That

was the way they treated alcohol, so it led me to believe alcohol was the main event and the weddings and the celebrations and get-togethers were only justifications for the alcohol. Because of the status alcohol had, we thought we were being cool and becoming men, actually we were becoming alcoholics.

The United States tried to restrict the use of alcohol from 1920 through 1933, by passage of the 18th Amendment to the Constitution. During this period of time, commonly referred to as "Prohibition", the manufacture, sale, import, export or transportation of alcohol for beverage purposes was prohibited in the United States. If the alcohol was being used for medicinal or scientific purposes, it could be obtained with a prescription. In 1933, the 21st Amendment to the Constitution was passed which repealed the 18th Amendment and made alcohol legal again as a beverage. I can't really state if the desire to drink was despite Prohibition, or increased by it, but the desire was there, and despite Prohibition the alcohol was there. My Dad often told me that when the town doctor, who was a very good friend of my Dad's, wanted to get some booze during Prohibition, he would wait for Dad to pass as he walked home from work and holler at him, "Rinold come up here!" So he'd get up there and the doctor would bandage Dad up and say, "Now, here's a prescription. Get on to Hess's Drug Store and get a pint of whiskey." Dad would go down and get the pint of whiskey and then he'd sit with the doctor and they'd polish off the pint together. That happened on a number of occasions until Hess started to question it, but they all laughed about it. Who was going to question the Doctor? They all knew what was happening.

When I stated that alcohol was a force, I was remembering that it touched everyone's life. One guy in town ran a speakeasy, and people were making whiskey around the area. Dad's brothers were making their own whiskey ("White Lightning") and I think they got tissue addicted or burned their guts out from drinking it. All of this behavior was ingrained as a part of our culture and our living, our masculinity and our fun, our good times and the rebel in all of us. The way we looked at booze it represented manhood, and in high school when you're trying to experiment with sex, the thinking was you'd get the girl a few drinks and then you'd get the girl. Alcohol was in every aspect of our lives, it just was. For instance, my high school basketball coach had a serious problem with alcohol, and it probably was a contributing cause of his death. Yet, our reward from him for beating the team from his hometown was a case of beer. In fact, after the game he invited the whole team over to his house and that's where we drank the beer. Somebody found out, and made a big issue of it and he lost his job. For a teacher not to really know or see anything wrong with that tells you how alcohol was accepted in that area at that time.

I remember, as a teenager, a freshman in high school, my friend and I had gotten somebody to buy a fifth of Muscatel Wine for us. We drank all of it between us, but my friend was letting me take the big swallows and was looking forward to getting a kick out of seeing me drunk. It was terrible stuff. I can vividly recall my mouth feeling so dry and awful the next day (a condition now commonly referred to as "cottonmouth"). I made repeated trips to the water cooler all day to try to rid myself of that taste of dryness. I got so sick and threw up so violently I didn't know if I was going to survive that day. Then I drank more water and I felt like I got drunk and dizzy all over again. If I had gotten that sick on any another substance, I'd never have gone near it again. You'd be crazy to get that sick on anything. But because it was alcohol and because that was such a must in our area and our lives, the thought of not drinking again never entered my mind. That was the first time I got drunk, ugh!

I remember taking a car for a joy ride once after drinking. Luckily I didn't kill myself. I also remember climbing up on the roofs of people's houses and playing the trombone at ungodly hours. All of that aberrant behavior, and more, was directly alcohol related. It was all a preview of what was to come. Unfortunately for me, I didn't know that then and I didn't heed it as a warning.

I also remember being in the senior class play and the script called for me to kiss a girl I didn't particularly like, and that was going to be tough for me to do. So about half way through the last scene, my friend and I got into the booze which we had smuggled backstage and drank to the point where I wasn't feeling any pain when I had to go out there and kiss the girl.

I never considered not being a drinking man. I bought into

the drinking man profile so much so early in life that to not drink would almost be rejecting who I was.

As youngsters we build a vision in our own minds of the person we will eventually grow up to be, and we live to that vision. I believe we adjust that vision as we go through life, but the original vision is a very strong influence on our life. Bishop Fulton Sheen, a famous cleric who understood the power of television and the impressionability of children, echoed the earlier teachings of St. Thomas Aquinas, in saying, "Give me your children until they are seven and I will mold them for life." I also believe those early years are very determinative of who we become. One factor which influences young children is the actions of the "big people" in their life, those we refer to today as "role models" – their parents, grandparents, people in authority, and popular figures like athletes and entertainers. Psychologists say as early as eighteen months we start to realize what turns Dad on and what Dad likes and doesn't like by just his reactions or his stories. I also believe young people are strongly influenced by who they perceive to be the role models of their role models. You see somebody else's face light up; you want to know what lights it up, so you can make him just as happy. My Dad was very important to me, and therefore if somebody was good enough to be his hero, then I should mold my life after that person.

I believe one of the things that influenced me the most, and persuaded me to buy into the drinking man profile, was my Dad's hero worship of his war buddy, Big George. When Dad was telling his war stories about the real men that he was with, he always brought up Big George. Dad described him as a great, big, raw-boned old guy who was a lumberjack at home and when the war called, he went with Dad. He was the biggest, strongest, toughest guy, but fair. Champion of the underdog. Dad would tell us about one of the soldiers who got shot and how Big George carried him ten miles, or however far, back to a base hospital, holding the guy's arms, keeping him from bleeding to death. Then he'd talk about a situation when his troop had to hike a long distance. Some guy would tire out from marching and Big George would throw the guy's pack on him, carry it and support the guy. You could just see him helping this guy along. He'd tell us about when the soldiers would have a rest and relaxation period, they'd be doing their drinking and hell raising, and different segments of the service or different outfits might run into each other and they'd have a rumble. Big George would just step out in front and beat up the whole other gang, if need be, and then when the drinking started Big George would out drink everybody. He was a monster of a man in a sense, but when Dad talked about him his face would light up. Some of Dad's other friends who were in the service with Dad and Big George would verify what Dad was saying, or would chime in with their own stories about Big George. I never actually met Big George. Dad and his friends always talked about him, and my brothers and I would always ask Dad about where he was and if we could meet him, but Dad was always evasive about that. I remember seeing how excited Dad got just talking about Big George and saying to myself, "God, wouldn't it be something to be like Big George." I figured that if I modeled my life after Dad's hero, then I would win Dad's approval. That, I think, had the deepest influence on me as a youngster. Well, here's the rest of the story:

Several years into my recovery, some time after I started the treatment program in Stoughton, I was in Michigan, looking to buy a four-wheel drive pickup truck. While I was at the State Department of Transportation to get the title certificate, the officer that came out to assist me had on a nametag, and I noticed his last name was the same as Big George's. I said to him, "Any chance that there was a guy in your family that would be about 80 something years old by the name George? He was quite a war hero." And he said, "Yeah, Ryne, that was my uncle." I said, "Well, God, my Dad used to tell war stories about him. What ever happened to him?" And the officer got a little bit red in the face. By then, stories had appeared in the papers about my running the alcohol and drug program and saying I had been an alcoholic, and detailing the work I was doing. He said "Ordinarily, I wouldn't talk to anybody about this, but I know about your work. He died back in the late '30s as an alcoholic on skid row in Los Angeles." So I had truly patterned myself, more than I thought, after Big George. Absolutely amazing to me.

"Skid Row"

"Skid Row" is a classic American term for the area that exists in almost every city, populated by people who are usually addicted to alcohol or some other drug, and who are out of work and out of money. Its origin dates back to the Pacific Northwest of the early 1900s. In order to expedite dragging trees which had been cut down out of the forest, loggers built roads paved with skids and then greased the skids to make movement easier. These roads, "skid roads", were often home to bars and cheap, seedy hotels and attracted poor, often alcoholic, transient workers who were down on their luck. Soon it became accepted slang to say they were "on the skids" or living on "skid road" or "skid row."

Five

BEVERLY

It was during my childhood days in Wisconsin that I met Beverly Collins. Our families were friends, so I was aware of her, but didn't really notice her from a boy-girl perspective, until I was in the eighth grade and she was in the seventh grade. It was my first year in that new school, and the first time I saw her day in and day out. I was also at the age where boys start to notice girls and you pick out which one you think is the prettiest. There were other girls there, but evidently Beverly stood out and I wanted to ask her to go out on a date. The problem was that despite wanting to do it, I was so afraid of how I would feel if she rejected my offer that I couldn't do it. In the movie, *Ordinary People*, Timothy Hutton portrayed a teenager facing that fear of rejection when asking a girl out for the first time. It was so real and so reminiscent of how I felt, it made my skin crawl a bit when I saw the movie.

At that time of my life, I looked upon alcohol as an enabler. Whatever I did not have the courage to do on my own I could do if I bolstered myself up with alcohol. What I didn't know then is that I wasn't "bolstering myself up" I was "dumbing myself down." I used alcohol because I thought it helped me overcome the anxieties I had about rejection and the fears I had about doing certain things, like the first time I asked Beverly out. I remember being at Duane Frey's house, where there was always wine and beer around because his father, Lester, made

his own. Duane's parents were out, so he and I drank some of
the beer, and then I got on that old crank telephone and I called
up Beverly and asked her to go out. The alcohol had dulled
out my fear of rejection. That was my first psychological
dependence, as far as I know, on alcohol, and from then on I
relied on it as a tool.

What I didn't know is that the front half of your brain, where
the frontal lobes are located, helps you make certain decisions.
By drinking alcohol I was incapacitating that part of my brain
– similar to when people rig a motor to bypass a safety switch
– and you know what usually happens then – trouble. I thought
the alcohol was helping me reduce my anxiety, actually it was
numbing me and letting me go through an experience without
gaining any experience, so that I remained an adolescent for as
long as I relied on the alcohol. It wasn't until after my recovery,
when I started to do things without being numb, that I allowed
myself to mature through my experiences.

Well, unaware if it was me or the alcohol asking her for a
date, Beverly said "Yes" and we started dating. Eventually,
Beverly and I became friends, and more, with the intention of
remaining that way for life. We had some really great times
together, because we truly enjoyed each other's company.
But there were also some pretty tough times, where we didn't
exactly look nor act like friends, and now I can see all of that
was my fault. She matured into an adult and I was still acting
like a kid, and that didn't make for a very good mix. She was
really the only girl I was ever serious about. She was a student
in Cornell College, in Iowa, a small arts and sciences college
and doing very well. She loved music, took piano lessons since
she was very young, and she was a good clarinet player. Our
love of music was one of the things we had in common. I had
played the bass drum in a marching band, until one day when
I dropped one of the drumsticks while marching, and leaned
forward to pick it up. I got wrapped up in the drum and it
rolled right over me. That was pretty embarrassing and led me
to switch to the trombone.

While Beverly was at Cornell College I started attending
the University of Wisconsin, and we took advantage of the
freedom of being away from home to experiment with sex.
Before very long, by October, I got Beverly pregnant. Getting

married was the right thing to do, we thought, and so we both quit college and we got married on December 28, 1948. It was a pretty rough start for any couple under those circumstances. We were nineteen years old, kids ourselves, about to have a kid of our own. Although we were married, Beverly was living with her parents at home and I was working 100 miles away in a factory to earn a living, which only allowed us to see each other on weekends. Marriage is a union that takes a lot of commitment and the decision to get married is one that should be made without pressure and under circumstances that create that unmistakable kind of excitement. Instead, I robbed Beverly of some of her youth, and of that excitement. I don't feel or think she ever held it against me, but there's no doubt in my mind it was part of the anger I harbored against life and myself. I think all of that probably cost me quite a bit.

Within months after our marriage, our son, Steve, came along, on July 9, 1949. We lovingly accepted him and went on, but having a child, and getting married under those circumstances is difficult enough for any young girl. Imagine adding to that a husband who has a problem with alcohol, and who is gone most of the year, in pursuit of a professional baseball career. Actually, during the first several years of our marriage our love for each other, our youthful enthusiasm, and our mutual instinct to survive got us past many problems. As you can see from this recollection of my son, Steve, we shared some very happy moments:

Steve Duren: "I can remember driving across the country on a road trip with Mom and Dad to wherever Dad's new team assignment was and feeling so completely secure and safe with my parents singing songs together and play-acting like they were Ralph and Alice Kramden, The Honeymooners, with all the silliness of the dialogue of that favorite TV sitcom of that time. It was obvious they loved each other and cared for each other, and it made me feel like we had a real family."

Truth be told, we were fine until alcohol, consciously or unconsciously, started to take on a more important place in my life than my wife and my family. From that point on, I wasn't much of a husband, nor a father, until after I got my alcoholism behind me. Fact is, Beverly tried very hard to make our marriage and our family a go, but I wasn't mature enough to figure that out, or to appear to care. My immaturity led to Beverly being one of the three people in the world who suffered the most as a result of my drinking – our son, Steve, and me being the other two.

Beverly endured my wildness, off the field, most of which was alcohol-driven, for longer than most women would have. We remained married through the unexpected pregnancy, five miscarriages, the death of an infant son, about a dozen different teams that I played for, (between the minors and majors), and dozens of other episodes that by themselves would have driven couples apart.

Steve Duren: *"The first time I remember seeing Dad drunk was in 1959. We had gone to a party at Yogi Berra's house – a huge place in Saddle River, New Jersey, which had an upstairs where us kids would stay while the grown-ups partied down-stairs. At the end of the evening, Mom came up and retrieved me and when we got in the car I noticed that Dad was acting funny and Mom was driving which was real unusual. I also noticed that Dad had a black eye. When we got home Dad got progressively stranger and I became truly frightened. I tried to lay still in my bed hoping that I wouldn't become the center of his wrath but feeling like a coward as he was acting crazy and I felt that Mom was in jeopardy. This scene would be played over and over again in the years to follow, as I became a teenager, until the fear was displaced with disgust and rage. Actually, I found for a number of years that I had a soothing effect on Dad and could usually get him calmed down and often to sleep. I used to rationalize that he was not my real Dad when he was like that and that he was having a sort of waking dream nightmare in which he was possessed by some kind of demonic spirit which was always gone the next morning – replaced by a sullen moodiness. Anyway, that first night Mom finally yelled at me to run out the front door and we escaped to the safety of the car out front and waited for Dad to come out and chase us (which he never did). It was then that Mom explained that Dad became like that from time to time when he drank and that up till then, she had been able to hide it from me. I remember some years later that Dad would not come home some nights,*

or worse, he would come home real drunk and ready to ter-
rorize us and the neighborhood. Dad used to get his deer rifle
out and brandish it outside and yell to the general populace and
the heavens at the top of his lungs. Fortunately, no one ever
came outside."

Finally, in November 1965, after I almost burned down
the house by collapsing drunk, with a lit cigarette in my hand,
Beverly carried through on her oft-repeated threat to divorce
me. At that time, losing Steve hurt more than losing Beverly.
However, I came to realize Beverly never stopped loving me,
and in fact loved me and respected herself and Steven too much
to continue in the hell of a relationship I had created.

Beverly passed away this past year. I visited with her during
the last week of her life, and sat with her at her hospital bedside
the night before she died. It has been 34 years since I obtained
my sobriety. During all of those years people have repeatedly
asked me if my alcoholism cost me a chance at greater stardom
or robbed me of a Hall of Fame career. While I believe that
to be the case, what I realized this past winter is that what my
drinking cost me was a whole lot greater than any of that: it
cost me a lifetime of Beverly's love, and the burden of carrying
with me the thought that I caused this woman, and our son,
more grief than I could ever convey.

I am grateful I had the opportunity to spend time with
Beverly just prior to her death. It was an experience I will
never forget. It gave me a chance I thought I would never have
– to speak with her as a sober man about so many things and to
reminisce on what was. I had never held the hand of a dying
person before, or been with them in the last breath. It was an
awful lot to deal with.

The smiles reveal the love Beverly, Steve and I really had for one another, and the good times we shared when alcohol didn't get in the way. (Photo source: National Baseball Hall of Fame Library & Archive)

Six

GETTING INTO BASEBALL

In March of 1945 I came down with fever. Medically, it was rheumatic fever, but emotionally it turned into baseball fever. The doctors told my family I had to be confined to bed or possibly suffer an enlarged heart, so bed it was and I didn't get up and around until October. That confinement actually resulted in opening doors for me. Television wasn't an option in Cazenovia in 1945 and video games and personal computers didn't exist, so as I looked for some way to pass the time I turned to radio, and what captured my imagination and my fancy was listening to the Chicago Cubs. I listened to every single Cubs game on radio that summer and besides getting me pretty into baseball I think that saved my health, or at least my sanity. Stories have circulated about the rheumatic fever being the cause of my poor vision, but that's not true. What the rheumatic fever did do though was make me a baseball fan, and a Cubs fan, for life. And that was an exciting year to follow the Cubs – they won the pennant but got beat by Detroit in the seventh game of the World Series, and they haven't been back to the Series since.

One of my Cub heroes was Phil Cavaretta, although I guess he was every Cub fan's hero in 1945. That year he led the National League in hitting and was the League's Most Valuable Player. Oddly enough, Cavaretta was the first hitter I faced in the big leagues. It was 1954, when I came up with

Baltimore and had my first "cup of coffee" in the majors. By that time Cavaretta had gone cross-town and was playing with the White Sox. I only got to pitch in one game, two innings. It was a pretty strange feeling to be on that mound. I was thrilled to finally get the ball in a major league game and there at the plate was a childhood hero. Quite a thrill. I really don't recall whether it was my nerves, the presence of Cavaretta, or my control, but I walked him. Three years later when I was with the Denver Bears we made it to the Minor League Championships, known as the Little World Series, and Cavaretta crossed my path again, as the manager of the opposing team, the Buffalo Bisons.

Phil Cavaretta (1916-present)
OF-1B 1934-55 Cubs, White Sox
Cavaretta, a Chicago native, joined the Chicago Cubs near the end of the 1934 season and as an 18 year old he became the starting first baseman for the NL champs in 1935. He became the team's player-manager in 1951 and in 1953 he completed his 20th straight season with the team. He might have ended his career with the Cubs, but in spring training of 1954 he upset Cubs owner Phil Wrigley by predicting that the Cubs would finish in the second division, causing Wrigley to fire him – the first time a major league manager had ever been fired during spring training. Cavaretta moved cross-town to play his last two seasons for the White Sox.

Getting back to the summer of 1945, I just couldn't get enough of the Cubs on the radio. I waited every day for the game to come on and listened to every pitch to every batter, except when it was interrupted by bulletins about World War II. Bert Wilson was the Cubs' broadcaster that summer and he said hello to me on air one time. I had written him and told him I was bedridden and listened everyday, but I never expected him to answer me on the radio. I was hoping for a fan mail picture at best. When I heard him say, "I'd like to wish a speedy recovery to this young fella up in Cazenovia, Junior Duren" it was great. I couldn't believe it. It gave me the feeling that from my little bedroom I was reaching the outside world, like my radio was now a two-way instrument, and I was connected.

That feeling of love for the Cubs and Wrigley Field stayed with me. It was a special day for me as a player when I first got to see the "friendly confines" and the ivy-covered outfield wall at Wrigley. Although I had seen pictures of it I had never been to it before I went there as a player. In those days, the only thing I can ever remember seeing of any of the major leaguers and how they played, were the newsreels, where everything seemed to move herky-jerky, like in a Charlie Chaplin movie.

I knew how much I loved baseball after 1945, and how much the Cubs meant to me, being bed-ridden and all, but it wasn't until years later that I really began to understand the true heart and mind of a fan. It was kind of a strange thing. I had accepted Dallas Green's invitation to attend a special event at Wrigley Field in the early 1980s, and one of the first people I met upon arriving at the stadium was Charlie Grimm, who managed the Cubs in 1945. Time has erased some of the names of the other players who were there, but I sure remember meeting Hank Borowy, Paul Erickson, Peanuts Lowrey and Lennie Merullo. I was sitting there and I felt a kind of anxiety attack come over me. I just felt kind of different and didn't really know what was happening. Finally it dawned on me: I was that sixteen-year-old kid there with his heroes. It didn't matter that I myself had become a major league player, had worn the uniform, and had been on the field. When it came to my relationship with the players who were my heroes forty years earlier, they still had a measurable impact on me. I never had a bad attitude about fans or interacting, but since that day at Wrigley I've reached out to the people a little bit more. If I see people talking baseball I won't hesitate to get into the conversation. I find that fans, especially those about my age, get a kick out of meeting me now and I'm very happy to accommodate them. It gives me pleasure to give someone an autograph or a picture card because I can tell it brings them back in time, to a time they remember and treasure, probably just like my visit with the old Cubs brought me back to my childhood.

My family was in love with baseball and many of them played on the local adult team. I was naturally familiar with the game, but didn't really fall in love with it until that summer of 1945. My sister reminded me that I would pretend to be a big league pitcher and would wind up and hurl rocks at a neighbor's chimney for hours at end. At age 14, I had tried out for my high school team. Ray Miller, who lived next door to Beverly, was the Baseball Coach. He was also the Band Director, the local carpenter, and the shop teacher. I made the high school team, but during pitching tryouts I threw a wild fastball that caught one of my teammates in the ribs and broke two of them. After that, Mr. Miller refused to let me pitch. He didn't want it riding on his shoulders if I hurt somebody else. The only position I could play was second base, where I couldn't hurt anyone, because I would flip the ball underhand to first. I couldn't see well enough to play the outfield, although he tried me out there. My grades improved during my last year of high school, but I wasn't good enough in sports to attract a scholarship and therefore I wasn't going to college.

Town ball, known in some areas as sandlot ball, or home talent ball, was very popular in Wisconsin. Donny Klang, who preceded me in high school, was the star pitcher for the town team, the Cazenovia Reds, in 1947. A team from Franklin, Minnesota, in the Industrial League, stole him away from Cazenovia in 1948, and that gave me a chance to pitch for my hometown. The year before, when Donny was pitching, I didn't play. Right after graduation from high school, I went to work in Beloit. When I would come home on weekends, I'd sit in the stands and drink beer. I'd catch the warm-up throws from Donny between innings and I'd throw it down to second base. I would give it the gas and the fans always got a kick out of that because the second baseman couldn't catch it, but that was the extent of my participation until 1948.

My brothers, Vincent and Larry, my Uncle Bill, and my cousin George were also on the Cazenovia team. My sister, Mary Helen, was the scorekeeper for the team, and Dad was one of the umpires in the League. The Duren family was a baseball family to the extent that the home talent club provided the main pastime in our town and our family always had several players on the team. Mary Helen maintained a scrapbook on the team and it was great fun to go back and read some of her entries. This was how she recorded my start with the team, as only a sister could:

**The joke was on us all that summer. He not
only was a suitable pitcher but he was more
than that. Before the summer was over, Ryne
had taken up a good deal of ink in the Wisconsin
newspapers. We did have a good laugh here at
home though about the first game Ryne pitched.
On the first pitch of the game he threw the ball
so wild you'd never know it was intended for
the batter. With the next pitch he hit the batter.
A mighty fine start, to be sure. After this???
He did manage to settle down quite a bit and
as time went on he developed more control and
still later on he began to get his face plastered
all over the sports page as a No-Hit pitcher, only
19 years old.**

Actually, I realize most of my success was the result of
rearing back and firing the ball as fast and hard as I could. And
that was overpowering the hitters in that league. I was nineteen
years old now and benefiting from all of that work I had done
around the farm. After all that lifting, the ball felt like a pellet
in my hands, and that's what it must have looked like to most of
those batters, because not many of them ever hit it.

That was mainly because the ball either whizzed by too
fast for them to see or hit it, or I threw it so wildly, they were
either too busy ducking to save their life, or they couldn't
reach it. Mary Helen's scrapbook contains copies of three
articles reporting on my pitching for Cazenovia. The first bears
the headline: 'Junior' Duren Hurls No-Hit Loop Victory for
Cazenovia, and states: "Duren struck out 21 batters and walked
four in recording his no-hitter." A week later, I duplicated a
feat accomplished only by Johnny Vandermeer in the major
leagues, back-to-back no hitters, beating Lavalle 15-3. I walked
eight batters and my fielders made 10 errors behind me. The
third article featured a game against Reedsburg where I threw a
shutout, recording 18 strikeouts.

Roland A. Hemond
*Roland was director of the Los Angeles Angels farm
system while I was with the Angels. He is a three time winner*

of Major League Baseball's Executive of the Year Award, and is currently the Executive Advisor to General Manager Kevin Williams of the Chicago White Sox

"*I remember scout Eddie Dancisak of the Milwaukee Braves talking about when he scouted and signed Ryne to his first pro contract with the St. Louis Browns. Dancisak told me that since Ryne threw so hard even in high school and was wild, that they built a high wooden backstop behind and close to home plate. So, if Ryne struck out the batter and the catcher couldn't catch the ball, the ball would bounce back off the backstop to Ryne coming off the mound and he could throw out the runner at first base.*"

We had a great season in 1948, winning the Sauk County Home Talent League pennant. In fact, I was the winning pitcher in the championship game against Loganville, and I broke the right arm of Loganville manager, Dee Wesenberg, by hitting him with a pitch. Possibly fueled by the team's success, my love of baseball blossomed that summer. Other than drinking, it was the one thing that gave me satisfaction and enjoyment, and the more I enjoyed it the better I played. Word was getting around about my success on the mound. The town people wanted me fresh to pitch on Sunday, so they paid my Saturday salary in exchange for me having the day off to rest. It was during that summer of 1948 that the college scouts felt they could harness my ability to throw so hard and turn me into a pitcher, so I was offered college scholarships purely as the result of my ability to throw a baseball, not because of any academic ability, although I had some.

Then strangers started showing up in the stands to watch the games. I didn't realize at first that among the strangers were major league scouts. I had no idea what big league talent was, and I had no way to gauge my talent. Although I had listened to an awful lot of baseball on radio, I had never seen professionals play. In fact, the first time I saw a professional team play I pitched for them, and the first time I saw a major league game I was on one of the teams.

A birddog is an advance scout whose job is to relay information to the scouts who make the recommendations to the team. Birddogs help the scouts cover more territory and utilize their time more efficiently by concentrating only on genuine prospects. During the summer of 1948, one such birddog, Ernie Rudolph, was driving across southern Wisconsin when a game in progress caught his eye. I happened to be the pitcher for Cazenovia in the game Rudolph decided to watch. He sat down next to my sister, Mary Helen, who was keeping score and he witnessed me striking out the first nine batters he saw me face. Now the game was already in the seventh or eighth inning and he asks my sister, "Does he always strike out this many?" She says, "Usually more" because in the earlier part of the game there were a couple of guys who didn't strike out. Ernie always laughed when he heard that story because he didn't see anything but strikeouts. I struck out 22 or 23 that day, which was about my average, and he gave my name to Eddie Dancisak, the scout that eventually signed me in January 1949. But there were other scouts around too. I had a tryout with the Chicago White Sox, and in the winter of 1948-49, the Fond du Lac Panthers, the Class D, Wisconsin League Affiliate of the New York Yankees, sent me a contract to sign, which I never did.

Johnny Antonelli had signed with the Boston Braves and reportedly received a signing bonus of $75,000. The buzz around the town was the possibility I could get something like that, but all of a sudden the scouts' investigation showed me as a drinker. I had already dropped out of college and got married, and they were looking into the unplanned pregnancy. (Conceiving a child prior to marriage was not as socially accepted in 1949 as it is in 2002.) It also didn't help that I was in need of money to support my little family. I wasn't in a position where I had any real bargaining power. So, in January 1949, when the Browns offered me a $500 bonus and a salary of $300 a month, I accepted. I was optioned from Springfield, Illinois (Class B) to Class D ball, because Class D was where I really belonged but they wouldn't pay a Class D player $300 a month. So, they signed me to a Class B contract at Springfield, Illinois, for $300 a month and they gave me three or four months salary up front, and when I actually came to play at Class D, with Wausau, in the Wisconsin State League, I only got $150 a month. I had a wife and child to take care of, so I couldn't afford to wait for a better offer, but neither could I return to the iron works and turn my back on the appeal of a baseball career. The small amount of money and the enormous amount of travel would create a very, very tough and difficult time. But, compared to what? I didn't know anything but tough and difficult, so that was normal at that time. I'm not saying it was totally normal. Sure I was different because becoming a professional ballplayer was something that no one else around home did, but overcoming adversity in that area at that time was fairly common. I figured, at least if I got a $150 a month job, playing ball, and I had $500 in the bank, that was better off than I had been. It's amazing how in retrospect I look at that and it wasn't so bad. And somebody would say, "Isn't that terrible?" Well, compared to what I had before that, no.

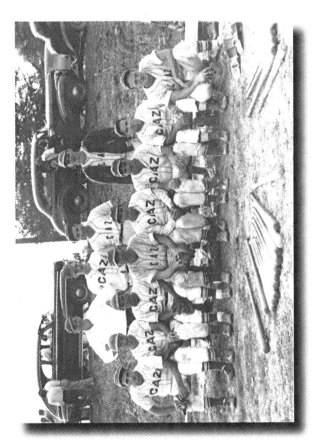

The "official" team picture of the 1948 Cazenovia Reds, Champions of the Sauk County Home Talent League. If you haven't identified me yet, I am the last one standing on the right (it wasn't often that I was the last one standing). My cousin, George, is standing next to me, and my brothers, Larry (third from right) and Vince (extreme right) are in the front row. (Photo source: Personal collection of Ryne Duren)

Seven

COLLEGE

My Mom believed that education was the key to life and had always hoped I would get a college education. She was disappointed at first when I went directly from high school to work as a waiter at a little restaurant in Rockford. I made an attempt at bettering myself by attending the Rockford School of Business, but it wasn't "college" and I knew Mom had been hoping for higher things for me. So, when my baseball ability earned me college scholarship opportunities, I took one. But I selected which college to attend based on my ability to drink and the opportunity to utilize that ability. My brother was attending the University of Wisconsin and he was the leadoff man on the chugalug team at his fraternity. I understood the fourth position on the team was up for grabs, and I knew I could out chugalug my brother. So I chose to attend the University of Wisconsin and joined that fraternity because I could be the number four man on the chugalug team. That's how much I bought into the drinking man's profile at that time. I could drink without breathing, but I couldn't think of living without drinking.

Chugalug
Chugalug is the act of swallowing a container of liquid, usually beer, in continuous gulps, without pausing to take a breath.

There are a number of things about my life I would change if I had the ability to go back in time, or if I had more time and energy left now. I know for sure one of them is I would have completed college, but at the time I quit I felt I didn't have any choice. Beverly became pregnant in October of my freshman year, and I was dropping out to become a wage earner and a father. I may be putting too much blame on the situation, because I don't think I was going to be able to handle college at that time anyway. I was already drinking quite a bit, and I wasn't academically prepared for college. I think my destiny as a dropout then was a question of "when" not "if", with my inability to study and to concentrate. I was over my head. The drinking was more important to me than the classes.

I didn't even make it to the first baseball practice of my first year at the University of Wisconsin. I don't know what would have happened to me at the University had I had a chance to try out for the baseball team, and I'll never know. After leaving the University, I went back to my job down at Beloit in the iron works to support my family. Then when the Browns signed me, I gave up thoughts of school altogether for the chance to get into pro ball, and I reported to my first professional training camp in the spring of 1949.

Although I blame my failure to obtain a college degree on getting married and having a child at such a young age, it didn't stop Beverly. She went back years later and finished her college education. That was another mistake I made – not continuing my formal education at a later date. As a result of running the program at Stoughton, I had faculty privileges at the University of Wisconsin, because I lectured there and monitored students who were candidates for degrees in social work. That gave me the opportunity to get grandfathered into some college degrees, but I failed to capitalize on that chance. I think I could easily have a Masters Degree today had I put my mind to it. It was definitely a mistake on my part not to finish. My lecture circuit schedule was so hectic and my life was so busy at the time I just didn't think I could squeeze it in. But I didn't even try.

Eight

MY VISION

As I said earlier, although many people have written that my poor eyesight was a result of the rheumatic fever I had as a teenager, I had vision problems well before that. I think it was a combination of my genetic make-up and the fact that as a kid one of my little buddies hit me in the eye with his popgun and cut my cornea. Whatever the cause, I was just near sighted, that was it, and more so in my left eye than my right eye. That defect in my vision would become the focus, pardon the pun, of more articles about me than my ballplaying ability, and even my drinking. Despite all the attention and all the medical attempts, my vision has never been corrected to 20/20. I think with glasses the closest they ever got it was 20/30, on my best day; without glasses I was 20/200 in my left eye and 20/70 in my right eye. In addition, I had a muscular imbalance that caused poor depth perception. That would cause an object to appear below the center of vision in my right eye and above the center of vision in my left eye. Since my recent cataract surgery, at which time they implanted lenses in my eyes, my eyesight has improved.

"20/20"
Visual acuity is usually measured with a Snellen chart. The chart displays letters of progressively small size. Normal vision is 20/20. This means that the person being tested sees the same

line of letters at 20 feet that a person with normal vision sees at 20 feet. 20/70 vision means that the person being tested sees at 20 feet what a normal person sees at 70 feet. A person with 20/ 20 vision is able to see letters 1/10th as large as someone with 20/200 vision. 20/200 is considered legally blind.

When I first started pitching professionally, the combination of my eyesight and the poorly lighted minor league parks made it very difficult for me to see the catcher's signs. I was in the St. Louis Browns' farm system at the time, and they sent me from Wausau to St. Louis to see an eye doctor. His report to the team was that with my vision I could easily be hit by a line drive and badly injured. With the doctor's report in his hands, Jimmy McLaughlin, a Browns executive told me, "The doctor advises you to give up baseball. But decide for yourself, if you want to quit." I was not going to let my vision stand in the way of my dream. I left St. Louis determined to not let my poor vision be a handicap.

I started wearing sunglasses as a result of my sensitivity to light. I was really very light haired as a kid, and probably a little bit more sensitive to light and sunlight than other people. Later on in life, in my studies, I found out that alcohol abuse also makes your eyes much more sensitive to light, so it might very well have been my heavy drinking as opposed to my light complexion. Either way, the sunglasses seemed to help. It wasn't that I could see better, but with the sunglasses on I didn't feel quite so agitated.

A lot of people thought the sunglasses were a style or image thing, but I never really bought into the image stuff. In fact, in those days, people were more team conscious with how they looked than they were concerned about individuality. The individuality thing didn't catch on until about the time I had gotten out of baseball, with the advent of the long hair and the moustaches and all that stuff. I guess that was part of the '60s rebellion that touched every facet of this country, not just baseball.

I actually needed the sunglasses to reduce the sensitivity and the glare. Over the years I played, I had seven differently tinted pairs of sunglasses that I wore. I had the really dark pair, a pair that were not quite so dark, the shooting type glass, a yellow lens, the rose colored lens for night vision, a pair with a gray tint, and just a regular pair of sunglasses.

An awful lot of ink was dedicated to stories about me and my sight, or lack thereof. Almost every article written about me, especially during my time with the Yankees, when I was a little more high profile, made mention of my eyeglasses or my eyesight. There were articles calling me "Four Eyed Flamethrower" and "Blind Ryne" and there were several stories circulating about my eyesight and resultant lack of control that were just pure myth. For instance, one story, which isn't true, but is pretty funny, has me staring into the plate from the mound and calling out to Yogi Berra to ask him if the batter was right-handed or left-handed. A true story that did involve Yogi is just as funny: I came in to pitch in relief, with Yogi catching, and Gus Triandos was the first batter I was going to face. I knelt down on the mound and started to move some dirt with my hands to fill in the hole that had been created in front of the pitching rubber by the previous pitchers. Triandos asked Yogi what I was doing and Yogi said I was trying to find the pitching rubber.

Joe Ginsberg
Joe's major league career spanned from 1948 to 1962, with seven different teams. Our paths crossed while Joe was with the Baltimore Orioles organization in 1956. Joe was the starting catcher in the New York Mets first home game.

"Sometimes Ryne would look at my signs and squint. The hitter would ask me if Ryne could see me. I would say, 'He can't see you or me, so be very careful up there.' Ryne would go on to pitch a two or three-hitter."

Jim Kaat
Jim pitched for 25 years in the major leagues, debuting in 1959. He won 283 games during his career. He was a twenty game winner with the Minnesota Twins and with the Chicago White Sox. Since there was no designated hitter back then, Jim faced me a number of times. He was a good hitting pitcher and hit 16 home runs in his career.

"The picture that was always in your mind when you faced Ryne as a hitter, was of Ryne wiping off his glasses and

*squinting at home plate like he didn't know exactly where it was
... very scary!"*

The reality was that I did have some trouble seeing the signs
the catchers were giving me, especially at night. The catchers
would indicate which pitch they wanted me to throw by ex-
tending a certain number of fingers, and they would do their
best to hide those signs from the batter, the base coaches and
any runners. They hid them so well that sometimes I couldn't
see them. I had a particularly tough time seeing Yogi's short
fingers during night games, and also Elston Howard's. I remember coming in off the mound after crossing up Ellie behind
the plate, and Casey Stengel yelled for the trainer to come over
and he ordered him to paint the fingers on Ellie's right hand red
with methyolate (mercurochrome) so I could see the signs.

One myth was that my eyesight caused me to be so blind
that I once hit a batter in the on deck circle. That is not true, but
what is true is that in one game while I was playing against the
Red Sox, in Boston, on a foggy night, I was called into the game
in the late innings and the first batter I was to face was Jimmy
Piersall. As I began to warm up, Piersall was doing what the
late, great Ted Williams would do when Williams was leading
off an inning, or was the first hitter up after a pitching change
or was on-deck: standing five or six feet from the plate and
studying and timing the pitches. I wouldn't dare hit Williams,
but Piersall was no Ted Williams, so I threw my first warm up
pitch at Piersall. It didn't hit him, but he fell down and started
hollering at me. I responded, "You've got yourself confused
with a hitter." It was reported in the Boston Globe the next
day that my glasses had fogged up just as I was about to throw
that first warm-up pitch, and it drilled Piersall in the ribs. I may
have helped fuel the fog theory, because after throwing the ball
I reached into my back pocket, pulled out a handkerchief and
cleaned my glasses. The Globe improvised and added the part
about the ball hitting Piersall.

Managers and reporters liked to perpetuate the story that
my success was based on my inability to see. When I got to
New York somebody asked Casey Stengel how the Yankee
organization got me pitching so well, and Casey said, "I'll
tell you how, we got this kid and he had a vision problem

and he could throw awful good, and then we brought him to these fancy New York doctors and they got him fixed up so he was seeing so good he was throwing that ball right down the middle all the time and by God they got to hitting him pretty good." Then there was the pause and then the question: "Well, what'd you do?" Casey said, "Simple, I just took him a dirty handkerchief to wipe his glasses."

Some of the writers called me "Coke Bottles" referring to the thick glasses I wore, or described me as blind or goggle-eyed. My teammates used to call me "Four Eyes", then the Yankee guys called me "Mr. Magoo." And I'd hear it from the fans, too. I remember Baltimore as the town where the fans gave me the most grief about my eyesight, and they didn't limit their comments to only my eyesight. They were at their worst when I came into town with the Yankees. If I had to single out one fan who was relentless in heckling me it would be the guy in Denver, who I finally hit with a pitch, and he was about thirty-seven rows up in the stands. That's a true story.

One story that you don't hear too often about my eyesight happened in spring training. It was a night game in Miami and I was pitching to Hank Foiles, who himself wore contact lenses. I threw a pitch up and in, and thinking it was coming at his head Foiles jerked out of the way and one of his lenses flew out of his eye. I stood on the mound for a few seconds watching as Foiles, our catcher, the umpire, and the batboy were all looking around home plate for the lens. Then I strode in to the plate reached down, picked up the lens and handed it to Foiles. The lens had caught a reflection off the stadium lights and shone right in my eyes. Nobody could believe that Blind Ryne found the contact lens. They all couldn't stop laughing about that.

Although a lot was made of my eyeglasses and eyesight, I was far from being the first pitcher to wear glasses in the major leagues. In fact, prior to 1921 the only players that had ever worn glasses on the field were pitchers: Will White (1877 – 1886), Henry Lee Meadows (1915 – 1929) and Carmen Hill (1915 – 1930). George Toporcer was the first position player to wear spectacles, in 1921. Either as a sign of the unimaginative players and press at the time, or the fact that ballplayers with glasses were such a rarity, Meadows, Hill, and Toporcer were all nicknamed "Specs." I imagine that Chris Berman of ESPN would be much more creative with those names today. It wasn't until 1951 that there was a catcher who wore glasses. That was Clint Courtney with the Yankees. That being said, even though I was not the first, I think my name has become the most synonymous with being a pitcher with poor eyesight and hence poor control.

Nine

THE MINOR LEAGUES

By the time I reached my early to mid-twenties, I started to think something was wrong, that drinking was becoming a problem. But that was such a deep secret, the possibility that I shouldn't be drinking, that I didn't even want to share it with myself, if you know what I mean.

I didn't like being the way I was. I went to marriage counselors, and psychologists, and psychiatrists. I heard all kinds of answers but none that helped me. What I would hear from a priest might be "Well you're not in a state of grace" or "You may be possessed by a devil." One psychologist told me I drank because I was "passive/aggressive" which I really never understood. One psychiatrist told me that all alcoholics were probably latent homosexuals. I wasn't sure what "latent" meant but I knew what "homosexual" was, and that kind of took me back. I also read a lot, searching in books for answers. But I was looking for an answer that didn't include requiring me to stop drinking, that's how important alcohol was to me. I reasoned that something was wrong with me, but it couldn't be the alcohol. I kept telling myself that the symptoms, the suspension of my emotional and psychological adolescence and my severe lack of social skills were the problems. But the reason for the symptoms was my abuse of alcohol and the style of life I had chosen, and although that would have been a problem no matter what I did for a living, being part of the baseball world made it worse. If you had already bought into the drinking before baseball and were not a person with great resolve and self-confidence, baseball at that time would wear you down and deliver you to seek comfort. By choice, many of us sought that comfort with alcohol.

My first minor league team was the Wausau Lumberjacks in the Wisconsin State League (Class D). There I did more drinking than anything else. And I developed a new nasty habit – chewing tobacco, taught to me by my manager, Joe Skurski. When I got to Wausau, they put my chances of succeeding, in my mind, in real perspective for me, giving me uniform number 385 in spring training. That just about shattered my fragile confidence right there. I doubted that they took me very seriously. The sheer degree of difficulty in getting to the major leagues made many guys doubt their ability. For a large number of guys the biggest blow to their confidence was their first farm team, when they saw what other professional players looked like. Even if they hadn't had a problem with alcohol or some other substance before they got there, some started to look to those substances for their courage and confidence. It got to the point where it was easier to just play and not even dream about going to the big leagues. Making it to the minor leagues in 1949 did not put a player as close to the majors as making it to the minor leagues today. At the current time the Atlanta Braves are the only major league team to have seven minor league affiliates. Most major league teams have six affiliated minor league teams, and a couple have five – all have one at AAA, one at AA, two or three at A, and one or two Rookie League Teams. At the time I signed with the Browns, they had **twenty** minor league teams.

It was when I got to the minor leagues that I became aware of what poor control I had. Thanks to the newspapers, a lot of other people became aware of it also. Consider these statements, which appeared in the local papers, about some of my earliest appearances in Class D ball at Wausau:

> May 9 – Duren was as swift as Mel Patton stepping off the 100 yard dash but had trouble locating the plate. In his 2 2/3 innings stint, Duren struck out six, walked six, hit three batters and tossed two wild pitches.

May 12 - Rinold Duren, the starting pitcher, was as wild as a March hare in streaks as he gave up nine bases on balls, and hit an alien. [visiting player]

June 25 - DUREN STRIKES OUT 11 BUT TOSSES OWN GAME AWAY - Duren bore down to strike out Tom Taube and retire Andy Marinko on a grounder, but then undid his good work by throwing wild over Scarpace's head after fielding Donahue's easy roller, Ackerman and Gross scoring on the wild heave. Duren racked up eleven strikeouts to go with his six bases on balls and chipped in two wild pitches.

July 7 - In between four walks and four hits Duren struck out 12 Cub batters in the five and one-third innings he toiled. The first eight outs were via the three-strike route and 10 of the first 11 men he retired went down on strikes.

July 15 – Duren's third wild pitch and his wild heave to first base, trying to pick Jenkins off the sack, contributed to the scoring.

July 30 – DUREN WALKS 3, WILD PITCHES IN WINNING RUN – Rinold Duren, the third and final Wausau pitcher, gave bases on balls to three White Sox players and then uncorked a wild pitch to let the winning run be coined in the extra inning of play. The inability of Duren to locate the plate cost the invaders [visiting team] the ball game.

August - Rinold Duren, who received credit for his fourth win of the year although he was jerked for a pinch hitter in the eighth, was almost unhittable, but he had so much trouble controlling his pitches that the game dragged along like a funeral procession.

To be fair, to the reporters and to me, the papers also gave
me credit when it was due:

> August 23 – Feature of the game was the brilliant
> relief hurling of Rinold Duren. Duren came into the
> contest in the eighth inning with the bases loaded and
> struck out the side, the second time this season he has
> performed the feat in an emergency role.

I finished that year having won 4, lost 5, walked 144 men
in 85 innings, fanned 145, hit 19 batters and made 18 wild
pitches. That averaged out to over 15 strikeouts, and 15 walks,
for every 9 innings pitched. I hadn't walked that many guys
back home in amateur ball, so my immediate response was to
blame the umpires. I told myself either they weren't giving the
calls to a new kid, or they couldn't really see the pitch because
it was too fast, or the strike zone was smaller here than in the
Home Talent League. While any or none of those things might
have been true, my trouble controlling my drinking and my
struggle to learn how to really pitch instead of just rearing back
and throwing, were probably the real factors. After all, the
umpires had nothing to do with the wild pitches or the batters I
hit. The effects of alcohol on my system kept me a teenager for
years and correspondingly kept me in the minors longer than I
should have been there. It wasn't until long after I started my
successful rehabilitation that I came to learn the effect of the
abusive use of alcohol and drugs on the central nervous system.
Alcohol is a central nervous system depressant. Some of the
effects of alcohol consumption, even at a "low level", without
addiction, are: reduced coordination, slowed reflexes, and
impaired reaction time. Consumption of additional alcohol
causes slurred speech and drowsiness and altered emotions, and
eventually vomiting, breathing difficulties, unconsciousness
and coma. Although at this stage of my life it was relatively
early in my addiction and heavy use of alcohol, in retrospect,
it definitely had already begun to affect my hand to eye
coordination, one of the most important assets of a ballplayer.
My minor league managers would get ticked off at me,
especially if a bad outing, or a bad night out, followed a good
outing. They would all say, "Just throw the ball over the plate

and you'll go to the big leagues. You'll be a big winner." They
had no idea of what it took to do that, for me anyway. That
was pretty frustrating. Understand that I had never seen a big
league team. I didn't know if I really had talent or not. I was in
the minor leagues, and I watched some of those guys play and
I thought, "Boy, can they play ball." So, in my mind, surviving
the next game and staying on the team were my immediate
goals, not the major leagues. When my confidence sagged, or
when I needed to numb pain, alcohol provided the answer.

In 1951 I got to see a major league team for the first time.
While I was with Dayton we played an exhibition game against
the Cincinnati Reds. I got the start, and I had pretty good
success against them. The pitcher for the Reds that night said
to me, "You'll make it." From then on, I thought, maybe I
will make it. That Dayton club, the Indians, went 87-50 and
won the Central League pennant, which earned us $2,000, for
the team, breaking down to less than $100 per player. I led
the league striking out 238 batters. Despite the youth of that
team, all of us between 22 to 25 years old, and our dominance
of the league, only one player besides me made it to the major
leagues: shortstop, Bud Thomas, played the last two weeks of
the 1951 season with the Browns and got 7 hits in 20 at bats,
but never got back to the majors. The rest of the players never
realized their dream. As a footnote, which underscores the
tenuous nature of the minor leagues, after the 1951 season,
despite winning the championship, the Dayton franchise was
closed. Baseball didn't return to Dayton until 2000 when the
Cincinnati Reds' Single-A affiliate Dragons played their first
season in a new ballpark in Dayton, Fifth Third Field.

In 1952, JoJo White sent me down from Double A to Class
B. He said, "I like you, you're a helluva guy. You've got an
outstanding fast ball, but I can't stand those hellacious 3 and
2 counts." The 3 and 2 pitch (3 balls and 2 strikes) is a crisis
pitch, for the pitcher and everybody else too. The batter can
delay the inevitable by fouling off a pitch or two, but with the
count 3 and 2, a batter could reach base or be retired without
swinging the bat. It has to go one way or the other, and the
pressure is on both the pitcher and the batter. Managers feel
it too, and they are not very comfortable with pitchers who
continually go 3 and 2 on batters. As you can tell from the large

number of strikeouts I recorded, and the equally large number of walks I was yielding, the 3 and 2 count was a predicament I found myself in quite often.

At the time I was working my way up in the St. Louis Browns organization, (1951 – 1954), Bob Turley and Don Larsen were also there. But to give you a better picture of what the competition was, we were only three of about ten or twelve excellent pitchers in their farm system at the same time. One guy by the name of Eddie Albrecht, who was exactly my age, got to start a game with the Browns at the end of the 1949 season and was the winning pitcher in a rain-shortened game, giving up only one hit in five innings. He appeared in only two more games for the Browns, in 1950, pitching a total of 6 2/3 innings, and you never heard about him again; and then there was Jim Upchurch, Bob Nordgren, Bill Pilgrim, Bob Harrison, Jim Post, and Bill Hyde. Those were really good arms, each one thinking he had a legitimate shot at the major leagues, yet there was a hole in their confidence because they weren't really making any progress. Then somewhere along the dusty bus trails of the minor leagues, the dreams of each of them were jostled from the bus and their tickets to the major leagues were cancelled. Except for Turley, Larsen and myself you've probably never heard of any of those guys I just mentioned, and they were excellent, better than excellent, ballplayers.

Frank Malzone
Frank was a Gold Glove third baseman with the Boston Red Sox, and a perennial All-Star while I was in the American League. We were teammates in Winter Ball.

"*Ryne and I were teammates for a very short period of time, down in Ponce, Puerto Rico, in the winter of 1954. What happened is typical of how the teams treated you and how it could affect your confidence. If a team would get off to a slow start down in Puerto Rico, the major league team would call the players back to the States, rather than spend a winter's salary having the player play on a losing team. We got off to a very bad start and after a real short time they called Ryne back. Hobie Landrith and I got to stay. Looking back on it, it is no re-flection on Ryne, and he shouldn't feel so bad - at the same time they recalled him, they called back Frank Robinson, although*

*when it happened he wasn't a star yet. He was 19 and didn't
debut in the majors until 1956 with Cincinnati."*

Every year in the minor leagues was a different town and
a different manager. That meant a new coach looking at my
speed, my wildness and my behavior, and trying to control all
three with a new set of tricks. Some coaches gave up on my
wildness and capitalized on my speed, my foot speed. They
used me as a pinch runner rather than as a pitcher. In one town,
the idea was to have me continually throw at a target, so they
stitched up a green canvas the size of the strike zone and had
me throw at it. After five minutes I had conquered the canvas.
The lacing gave way to the speed of the ball before the target
could do much to help me with my control. One spring training
in Florida, Burleigh Grimes worked with me all spring, thinking
he could cure my control problems, but didn't have very good
results.

What added to my frustration, and that of my minor league
managers, was that every so often I would throw a gem. For
just about every minor league team I was on I threw a game
where I struck out 17 or 18 batters or only yielded one hit. In
1953, while with the San Antonio Missions, a farm club of
the Browns, I threw my first professional no-hitter against the
Beaumont Exporters in the Texas League. I found out later that
United Press International picked up the story and it appeared
in the Stars and Stripes military newsletter. They mentioned all
the details, including the fact that I walked 11 batters, three in
one inning, and made an error to boot. Except for yielding no
hits, it was somewhat typical of my performance that year. I
finished the year having pitched 202 innings, in 33 games, with
a 12-12 record. I struck out 212 batters and gave up 159 walks
and 133 hits. That confirmed the opinion of some people that I
was a hard thrower, but I wasn't a pitcher yet.

By 1954 the St. Louis Browns had become the Baltimore
Orioles, and Jimmy Dykes was the manager. Towards the end
of that season, I was called up to the major leagues for the first
time. I had lived with Don Larsen during spring training so
when I joined the team I moved into the same rooming house
where he was, although we spent more time out of our rooms
than we did in them. Larsen and I would be out in the bars

every night and we had a running mate by the name of Vern "Junior" Stephens. When they called me up I had a broken bone in the back of my hand, so it was quite a while before they had me pitch in a game. But I do remember warming up in front of the dugout when Detroit was in town. Freddy Hutchinson was managing Detroit and one of his coaches was Schoolboy Rowe. Clint Courtney was catching me and he had a glove that would really pop. Batting practice was going on, but the main attraction was me cutting it loose on the sidelines and the guys all came over to watch. I remember Schoolboy saying, "Boy, just give me five of those a game", and Courtney was in his glory. He'd catch that ball and make it pop so loud. He was just so proud. He'd step out there with a satisfied look, like he pitched it himself. I'll never forget that. But, more importantly, during that time I was up with the Orioles I was more closely introduced to Larsen's style of life and Vern Stephens' style of life than I was to major league baseball, and, even worse, I thought their way of life *was* major league baseball.

Steve Duren: "Dad used to take me with him to work a lot when I was growing up and I felt pretty honored and special to get to hang out with the guys. Most of them were very genuine. They were playful with me and with each other and made a real effort to include me in their fun. I think baseball players of that era in general were a fun loving lot who had happened on a way to avoid "growing up" by doing what they love to do and get paid for it. So, they could relate to a ten year old pretty well. I can remember one guy we used to car-pool with – I think it was in Seattle or Vancouver – named Bulldog Drummond. He was a big, black guy who loved to laugh, and also loved to play blackjack on the way to the park when we got stuck in traffic. I remember one time I was out on the field before a game (I must have been about six years old at the time), Bulldog gave me a big chew of tobacco and told me to put it in my mouth and then find my Dad and tell him that I was chewing tobacco."

September 25, 1954 – My Major League debut. I made only one appearance in 1954, giving up 2 runs on 3 hits and a walk, and striking out 2 in 2 innings. I wouldn't pitch in the majors again until I was with Kansas City in 1957, spending 1955 and

1956 back in the minor leagues. And again alcohol would be my companion. I would look to it for answers to the questions I had as to why I wasn't in the major leagues, why I couldn't make it. The doubt I had in my own ability and the inability to stick in the major leagues didn't help my marriage much either.

During the entire spring of 1955, Paul Richards, the Baltimore manager, had me working on throwing sliders and hard curves, which irritated the nerve in my elbow. I had looked good in spring training and I expected to be traveling north with the team, for my first major league opening day. Then I got my annual bad news. Because of the inflamed elbow, supposedly, the Orioles shipped me out to their farm team in Seattle, where Fred Hutchinson was now the manager. I can't say that was a confidence booster – going back to the minors after having pitched only two innings in the major leagues. Besides my ego continuing to be bruised, my elbow continued to hurt me at Seattle. The nerve kept acting up, preventing me from being able to throw consistently. I could pitch and then I couldn't pitch again for eight to ten days.

Don Ferrarese
Don and I are the same age and he also came up through the Orioles organization. Later he went on to pitch for the Cleveland Indians and the Chicago White Sox, where I batted against him. He finished with Philadelphia and St. Louis in 1962.

"In the spring of 1955, the Orioles had the pitchers report to Spring Training one week early. We were taking bunting practice and they had Ryne pitching to us. Everybody was bailing out as the pitches were coming in fast and all over the place. Connie Johnson came up to bat with all the catching gear on, including the catcher's mask. We all laughed except Paul Richards, the manager. He didn't think that was funny at all. He picked up a bat and said he was not afraid and he'd show us the correct way to bunt. One of the first pitches Ryne threw to Richards almost hit him. He bailed out too, then he dropped the bat and we never heard another word from him about that."

I started a game in Los Angeles against the club that everyone thought was the best minor league team in the country: the Los Angeles Angels led by Steve Bilko. Their leadoff man was Gene Mauch and coming into that game Gene had a 16 game hitting streak going. In his first at bat, he hit a ball down to our second baseman, Monte Bascoll, who knocked it down, picked it up, and then made a poor throw, and they gave Mauch a base hit on it. I went on to pitch a complete game, and Mauch's "hit" was the only one they got. Hutch was ready to kill the scorekeeper after that game. He said to me, "You pitched a no-hitter. By God, I'm going to go get it for you. I'm going to go have him change that." I said, "Well, I already pitched one." or something to the effect that it wasn't important to me, because the way Hutch looked I thought he was going to kill John B. Olds, the scorekeeper, whose life I probably saved. I said, "It isn't that important to me Fred. You do what you want to do." You had to know Hutch, how he was. He looked so mean, you were afraid to sig him on anybody.

But after that outing, my elbow hurt so much I couldn't pitch again for ten days. There was no way I was going up to the majors if I could only pitch every two weeks. In fact, I was about to find out that not only was I not going to the majors, I was being shipped in the other direction. One day Freddy was throwing batting practice and I hit two balls out of the park against him. It was the only time in my life I ever hit the ball out of the park, any park, under any conditions. After the workout, he called me over and said, "Kid, you just hit me too good. I gotta send you out." He was trying to be humorous, but the club was moving me down from Triple A to Double A in San Antonio, Texas. Even though it was a step back, I put the best spin on it. I just thought that down there, where the weather was warmer, I'd come around. Neither my optimism nor the weather helped. The first start in San Antonio, on a lot of rest, I had 18 strikeouts. But the pain in my elbow kept me inconsistent. Over the winter the existence of that pain settled into my head. Subconsciously I was a little bit slower with my pitches the next year.

In '56 I was in spring training at Scottsdale, Arizona with Baltimore and despite another decent spring training they shipped me out to the farm team again. This time it was

Vancouver, where old Lefty O'Doul was the manager. He took me aside one day and talked to me about pitching. He said, "You know, Ryne, you ought to pay a little attention here. Now, look at this guy. He's an ass-puller. You can't pitch him inside. You pitch him away and he'll never hit you." O'Doul was a poor man's Babe Ruth – as a pitcher he became a great hitter. The only difference was Ruth was an effective pitcher in the majors. O'Doul was 59 years old when he managed me that year, and seemed even older, probably because of his drinking problem.

Francis Joseph "Lefty" O'Doul (1897-1969)
LHP-OF 1919-20, 22-23, 28-34 Yankees, Red Sox, Giants, Phillies, Dodgers
O'Doul pitched sparingly for the Yankees and then the Red Sox from 1922 to 1926, appearing in 34 games, totaling 77.2 innings and had a 1-1 record. After his arm went dead he returned to the Pacific Coast League and worked on his hitting and outfield play and returned to the majors in 1928 where he continued playing, for the Giants, Phillies and Dodgers, through 1934, finishing with a .349 career batting average. In 1929, with the Phillies, O'Doul appeared in 154 games and batted .398, with 32 home runs, 122 runs batted in and 254 hits. He won the National League batting championship in 1932, while with the Brooklyn Dodgers.

O'Doul thought he came up with the solution to my control problems, and he truly did help me. He had me throw to the extremes to the point where I threw the ball right out of the ballpark with his goading. We were out there warming up and he said, "Ryney, I want to show you something when you get warmed up." He said, "Throw one high and tight. No, higher and tighter!" And I kept throwing higher and tighter, and he said, "No, high and tight!" and the catcher is jumping more wildly with every pitch I offer, and Lefty kept yelling "No, higher and tighter!" and finally I threw the ball right out of the stadium. I said, "How do you like that?" He said, "That's it." Then I threw one low and away for him, and it hit the dirt long before it reached the plate. Then he said "High and away" and I threw it out of the stadium to the other side of the plate and

we both started laughing. Then he yelled, "low and in" and I
hit the wall of the stadium because I was right in front of the
dugout in the old Vancouver park. He was trying to give me a
sense of throwing to different parts of the plate and being able
to move the ball, developing a touch he felt I never had. He
sensed from watching me pitch that I couldn't distinguish – if
I missed trying to throw down the middle how do I adjust my
delivery to that? So he started me from the extremes and then
I learned the ability to move the ball. Now I didn't continue to
throw it out of the park, but I could go high and in or low and
away, and there was a difference in my delivery and footwork
and he'd show me and tell me, "Well, you stepped a little
different for this or for that. Your body has to do something
different to throw here or there." Out of that came the ability
to adjust and a feel for it. When I would miss my spot I could
feel it right away and that was the difference that enabled me
to get control. It took a little time but I mastered what O'Doul
was trying to teach me. That doesn't mean I had great control,
it just meant I always could adjust. And then adjusting to the
mound was another thing. Every time you got on a mound it
was a little different. So you also had to learn to adjust to the
mound you were on.

Lefty was one hell of a guy. I just loved him. Through the
first half of that '56 season I wasn't throwing full tilt because
I still had that elbow problem, or at least I had a mental block
about the elbow pain. Then something happened in a game in
San Francisco that broke the mental barrier. I was pitching a
pretty good game and we had a 7-2 lead in the eighth inning
when my fielders started making errors. We couldn't get
the third out in the inning. Lefty came out after a couple
of runs had scored and it's 7-4 now, and he said, "I thought
I'd just come out and break this thing up a little. We got to
do something different. The fix might be on. Do you know
anything about it?" At that point I thought he was kidding and
he probably was, because I remember laughing about it and
said, "No. If it is, I don't know anything about it." Then he
said, "Alright," and went back to the dugout. Then he came
back out after two more errors. Now we're winning by one
run still, and he said, "Well, I think the fix is on." This time
he wasn't kidding, or laughing, and neither was I. He said,

"Obviously, you're pitching your heart out but these guys don't care. I'm gonna get you out of here."

I said, "You're not getting me out of this game. I'm staying in this game. I'll get out of it. I don't know anything about any fix, but I'm not coming out."

"I gotta take you out, Ryne. I've been out here a second time."

"No you don't. You can take yourself out." I don't know why I knew that but I did. So I said, "Just ask the umpire." So the umpire came out and Lefty said, "Ryney tells me that I don't have to take him out if I take myself out. Is that right?" The umpire said, "Yep, that's right." Lefty looked at the ump, looked and me, shook his head and said, "That's a good idea. I'm kind of thirsty anyway." So he went up to the clubhouse and had a few beers. Now I'm so mad I could kill. I threw three strikes right by the next batter. I just gritted my teeth, not caring about nor giving in to the pain in my elbow. In the ninth inning I struck out the side to win the game. More importantly, I could feel that my arm was back to normal – I broke through that subconscious barrier or whatever it was that was holding me back, and from then on I was 9-4, and finished the season at 11-11, with a club that finished in eighth place (last), 11 games behind the 7th place team. I pitched more than 50 consecutive innings without giving up a run, a record at that time.

It was during that season that my son, Steve, was diagnosed with polio. At the time, he and Beverly had just traveled from San Antonio to Wisconsin to visit the folks, and I was in Vancouver. Steve's condition was very serious. He was drawn and tightened up. A doctor told us this was pretty typical of a person who was going to either be permanently crippled or die from it. They admitted him to the University of Wisconsin Hospital and called me in Vancouver to tell me. I said, "Is he going to die on us?" The doctor said, "No, but if it gets any worse Ryne I'll call you. But right now just hold tight." My first instinct was to get to Wisconsin as fast as I could, but finances and ballclub rules wouldn't allow that. A few agonizing days later, the doctors were telling me, "We got something strange going on here. All of a sudden the symptoms have let up a lot, and we think, maybe, he's going to be okay." I couldn't wait any longer and I prevailed upon

Lefty to let me go. When I got to Wisconsin we found out that Beverly had forgotten to tell the doctors about the Salk shots Steve had. He had received the first vaccine, but not the booster. Steve was suffering from polio, but the Salk vaccine had prevented paralysis. He was in the hospital about ten days before they felt he was well enough to be released and to travel. That was certainly a scare. One of Steve's legs atrophied a little bit, but he soon overcame that. As a result of his hard work and dedication, he went on to attend Southern Methodist University on a track scholarship. Not bad for a kid who was almost paralyzed. Not so much that he had great speed, but he had great endurance. He could run the 440s and the 880s. As a matter of fact he still runs. To give you an idea of how crazy the minor leagues were, when the doctors cleared Steve to travel I took Beverly and Steve back to Vancouver with me, driving non-stop from Wisconsin. When I got there Lefty told me to run into the clubhouse and get dressed because he needed me to pitch. I left Beverly and Steve in the car and someone else brought them to a hotel.

At the end of the minor league season, which is usually about September 1, the Orioles sold me to Kansas City. I'll never understand that. I spent all those years in the Browns/Orioles organization and I felt like they must have been dead or not paying any attention to me. I was a league leader in strikeouts, I put together that great string at the end of the '56 season, and my bases on balls were down. I had pretty good command of my pitches by then. I was ready for the big leagues, or so I thought, and the day the season was over they sold me. It was depressing and demoralizing to think the organization had given up on me.

However, I was traded to a major league club and I immediately started out for Kansas City with my hopes high. Before I got there I called the team to check in and they told me, "We've decided not to bring you in for this year. We'll just have you come to spring training." I felt bad about that, because I was busting my butt to get to Kansas City, anxious to put on a major league uniform again. There was also something inside me that hoped I would get to face the Orioles before the end of the year – to show off my newfound ability to adjust, a la O'Doul, and to make the Orioles sorry they traded me. But, that would all have to wait until at least next year. So, I went home to San Antonio and subsidized my meager minor league income by working in a clothing store. That fall I got further depressed as I listened to the World Series on radio and my old drinking buddy, Don Larsen, hurled a perfect game. All I kept asking is why him, and why am I still in the minor leagues. I kept draining alcohol bottles looking for the answer in the bottom of the bottle, but it was never there.

October 8, 1956: Don Larsen, my former Oriole teammate and drinking buddy earned baseball immortality when he pitched the only perfect game ever thrown in World Series history, beating the Dodgers 2-0 in the fifth game. Don was upset at having been removed by Casey Stengel in the second inning of the second game when the Yanks had a 6-0 lead. Larsen, like many of us, found comfort for his anger in drinking alcohol. Being upset at Stengel was reason enough to drink more heavily. The day of the fifth game, Larsen came to the Stadium and found a baseball in his shoe. I would later learn that was the sign from pitching coach, Jim Turner, that you were the starting pitcher that day. I heard the game on radio, but the picture of Yogi jumping into Larsen's arms at the end of the game is burned in my memory, and probably the country's memory.

After the 1956 season, the Athletics sent me to the Caribbean to play winter ball. That's where alcohol may have indirectly prevented me from pitching another no-hitter in professional baseball. Sandy Koufax and I were pitching against each other in Puerto Rico in the Winter Leagues. We were on different teams but were roommates because they housed the American ballplayers (the "imports") together. My manager was Joe Schultz. Koufax and I were both pitching no-hitters, and we were both going 3 and 2 on most batters, striking out a lot and walking a few. Joe Schultz comes to me at about 11 o'clock, after the seventh inning and he says, "Kid, I'd really like to see a no-hitter, but you're already an hour into my beer time. I'm taking you out." I don't remember what happened in the game after that. I think they took Koufax out also.

Sandy Koufax (1935-Present)
Left-handed Pitcher 1955-66 Dodgers
    At the time Koufax and I faced each other in the Caribbean, his major league record was 4-6 and he had only appeared in a limited number of games with the Brooklyn Dodgers. At that time he was a hard thrower who had not yet mastered the ability to pitch. But after he brought his fastball under control he had a five-year stretch like no other pitcher in the history of the game. During the period from 1962 through 1966, Koufax was 111-34 with 1444 strikeouts, winning 25 or more games three times. He was elected to the Hall of Fame in 1972 with 344 votes out of 396 ballots cast.

Here I am as a member of the Vancouver Mounties, at the side of manager Lefty O'Doul, who finally taught me how to adjust as a pitcher (Photo source: Personal collection of Ryne Duren)

Ten

THE NEW YORK YANKEES - ALMOST

My first major league start was in Kansas City against the defending World Champion New York Yankees on May 10th, 1957. Needless to say I was as excited and nervous as I can ever remember. My wife and son drove in for the game from San Antonio and we had just had one of the worst tornadoes to ever hit town, so I was also anxious about them getting there safely.

Hank Bauer was the leadoff man for the Yanks and I dusted him with the first three pitches to move him off the plate. The next three were strikes away on the outside corner, and he never swung the bat. He just went back to the bench shaking his head. Gil McDougald was next with the same result. Later on down the lineup came the fiery Billy Martin. I threw him a fastball, inside, that cracked his bat sending the ball back out to me and knocking him to the ground. He was still in the batter's box when I threw him out at first base. He got up, wiped the dirt off his uniform and walked back to the dugout where everyone was laughing at him. He covered his embarrassment with anger by yelling at me, "I'll get you, you four-eyed so and so!"

Bauer always tells the story this way: Casey looked at him and said, "What's wrong with you fellas?" Hank told him, "That guy is throwing it 100 miles an hour out there and he don't know where it's going. We're married with families. Get him over here or get him out of the league, one of the two." Well, they made the trade for me later that season *and* they got me out of the league. But that day they beat me 2-1. I drove in our only run on a two out drag bunt against Tom Sturdivant and both of their runs were unearned. On June the 15th we played the Yanks again in Kansas City and that was trading deadline. The A's showcased me by having me relieve. Sure enough, after the game they called me in the office and told me I had been traded to the Yankees.

At first I was elated because I was going to the Yankees, a team I always wanted to play for, and so did most of the other guys if they are honest. Lou Boudreau, my manager at Kansas City, told me. "I didn't have anything to do with this. I think you're one of the best pitchers I've got. But the Yankees have just traded for you." Going with me to New York were Jim Pisoni, Harry "Suitcase" Simpson, and Milt Graff. In return, the Athletics got Billy Martin, Ralph Terry, Woodie Held, and Bob Martyn. Martin had just been involved in the Copacabana incident and New York wanted to get rid of him. That's one of the tricks in baseball. They trade one headache for another – thinking the change of scenery will help everybody. Looking back on it I think of the trade that way, although many sportswriters say that Stengel really wanted Harry Simpson. In fact, Simpson was the only one coming from the Athletics who made it to the Yankees parent club in 1957.

Harry "Suitcase" Simpson (1925-1979)
Outfielder-First baseman 1951-53, 55-59 Indians, Athletics, Yanks, White Sox, Pirates

"Suitcase" Simpson was one of the first black players in the American League. He earned the nickname "Suitcase" by playing for 17 teams in 11 years. Casey Stengel thought very highly of him, once calling him the best defensive right fielder in the league. His best year in the majors was 1956, when he batted .293 with 21 HR and 105 RBI for the A's.

So I sought out the Yankee brass, thinking I'm a member of the World Champion Yankees, this is fantastic. I could hardly believe it was true. Then they threw a wet blanket on the party when I found out they were sending me to Denver, their minor league affiliate. Once again baseball had found a way to make me disappointed, discouraged and angry. Lee MacPhail, the Yankee Director of Minor League Personnel at the time said, "Ryne just go down there." and I told him "Boudreau told me I would be the last pitcher he would get rid of, and here I am going down to the minor leagues, I don't understand this." "Ryne, just go down there, get your feet on the ground and help us out down there a little bit and we'll have you right up in the majors, not a problem." I went down there. My very first start (June 23, 1957) I threw a no-hitter against the Louisville Colonels and it stands today as the only no-hitter by a home team pitcher in the history of Denver professional baseball. Hideo Nomo has since thrown one there for the visiting team. I went 13-2, I got beat 1-0 twice on unearned runs, one of them was my own error, and yet, according to the Yankees, I never "got my feet on the ground."

When I got to Denver, the season was more than half over and the team was in seventh place. I like to believe I was at least partially responsible for our rise to within a half game of the pennant and then winning the Playoffs and the Little World Series.

Johnny Blanchard
John caught my no-hitter for Denver in 1957, and was then a Yankee teammate from 1959 until I got traded in 1961. He is most remembered for his role as a pinch hitter in 1961, when he hit 21 home runs in only 243 at bats.

"I was with the Denver Bears in 1957, catching regularly, and I remember Ralph Houk coming to me and telling me that the Yankees had acquired a new pitcher, Ryne Duren, and they were sending him down to us, and that I would be catching his first game the next day. I asked Ralph, 'What pitches does he have?' and Ralph said, 'He's got a fastball.' I said, 'What else does he have?' and Ralph said, 'He's got a faster ball.' And I clearly remember saying, 'OK, well what else does he throw?' and Ralph looking me straight in the face and saying, 'He's also got one faster than the first two!' Well, Ralph was right. My left hand was never the same after catching Ryne Duren. We got off to a great start, because the first game he ever pitched

*to me was a no-hitter. But let me tell you. I have never caught
a pitcher, nor batted against a pitcher that threw the ball any
harder than Ryne Duren. I tried several different items for
relief from his fastball, including putting a raw steak inside my
catcher's mitt, and when that didn't work, I had my wife go out
and buy some falsies so I could put them in there."*

Ralph Houk was the manager in Denver. Despite stories
that have been circulated later on to the contrary, I liked Ralph
very much. Of course I wanted him as a friend. I thought it
was a big deal to be around him, because he had that tough guy,
service image. "Major" was what we called him. Houk was
pretty honest about things. The guys came to him and said,
"Duren's never had a year like this before, what the hell did you
do to make a great pitcher out of him?" He said, "I gave him
the ball. I never told him how to do anything." And that was
kind of true; I really had no business being in the minor leagues
at that time. Some years later, Ralph wrote a book, *Ballplayers
are Human Too*, where he said the one thing he changed
about my pitching was to give me more work, and work was
something I never shied away from.

My drinking, like that of most alcoholics, was getting
progressively worse, and I was definitely drinking while
I was with Denver. I became involved in an incident that
became known as the Little Copa, in reference to the scuffle
the major league Yankees had gotten into at the Copacabana
in New York. About a month after I had thrown the no-hitter
against Louisville, we were in Louisville as part of a road
trip. I had been drinking with my teammates at a nightclub
near the Sheraton-Seelbach Hotel, where the Denver team
stays in Louisville. With my brain's frontal lobes disabled
by the alcohol, I got a little too familiar with my words to the
bandleader's wife. The husband took offense to it and started
getting real nasty with me. Words were exchanged and Rance
Pless, one of my teammates, trying to avoid any trouble, said,
"Let's get the hell out of here." So we went to another bar.
Later that night, as we were leaving a coffee shop, I saw the
guy that had been giving it to me, sitting in a booth. He saw
me and said, "Well, well, if it isn't the baseball star" and kept
needling me pretty good. As I walked by his booth, I reached

in and grabbed him. About that time I got hit in the head with a blackjack. He had a plainclothes cop come in with him and it was a set up. I had my head split open and needed fifteen stitches. The topper was they arrested me for creating a disturbance, disorderly conduct, assault and battery, and Norm Siebern went to jail with me because he was trying to break it up. That little escapade set me back financially (they made me pay a fine and reimburse the guy for bleeding on his suit) and somehow I thought the Yankees always kept it in the back of their minds. For sure, even though it took place in the minor leagues in a small city, the episode got national attention because it involved the Yankees. About a week or so after it happened, Arthur Siegel, one of the sportswriters for the Boston Traveler, tied our arrest into the Copa incident by facetiously asking, in his column, if based on the incident in Louisville, the Yankees were ready to ship Siebern and me directly to Kansas City (like they did to Martin) or if they were sending us up to New York to take our "final exam" at the Copa. Life was different when you wore pinstripes, even minor league ones. You gathered more attention.

Most people assume that Houk, having been a Major in the military, was a disciplinarian. Actually, he was a fun guy. One night in Charleston, West Virginia, Jim DePalo and I were the scheduled pitchers for a doubleheader. It was Ralph's birthday, August 9th, 1957. DePalo pitched a beautiful game in the opener, tossing a shutout. Ralph, who always knew what to say to motivate and challenge you, said to me as I start the second game, "Well, big boy it doesn't look like your gonna get much ink tomorrow." because DePalo had done such a great job. Then I went out there and gave up one hit in eight innings. And that was a change up that I had a guy fooled on and he just soft touched the ball to left field. I'm walking out for the ninth inning, and Ralph looked at me, and said, "Looks to me like you're about out of gas. Should I get somebody up?" More motivation. I didn't respond, verbally. I just went on out to the mound and threw nine fastballs right on the letters striking out the side. Then I gave Ralph the ball and said, "Here's a birthday present from a guy who is about out of gas." That night was the biggest night of my life, because Houk and I went drinking together at a club. Ralph had a curfew, but on that night, I suppose, DePalo and I didn't have to pay attention to curfews.

Ralph Houk
Ralph was my manager at Denver in 1957. He was a coach while I was with the Yankees from 1958 to 1960 and then became the Yankee manager in 1961.
"Ryne had a very successful year for me in Denver. He had a tremendous amount of confidence. Really, of course, he had a little problem with the drinking at that time too, which he overcame now, which is great. He was probably my best pitcher when he joined the club. He was a little wild, but he had great confidence and he could throw the ball right by those Triple A hitters, and I recall two things that he did when I had him: we were trying to get in to the playoffs that year, which we did, and we were at Charleston, and at that time if we won a game I would buy the players a case of beer so that would give each guy a beer after the game, and of course Ryne was pitching and it was a real close ballgame, I think we had a lead of one run in the last inning and Ryne came up to me and said, 'Go ahead and order that beer. Don't worry about it.' And I was a little worried because I knew he was tired and the head of their lineup was coming up, and the other manager was all over Ryne during the whole game. Ryne went out and struck out the side. The other time I'll never forget is when we were playing the Little World Series and we had won two games and needed to win one more game and Ryne wanted to pitch out of turn to 'make sure' we could win that game. As it turned out he didn't start but he wanted the ball. He always wanted the ball."

I started and relieved for Denver. After it looked like we had a good shot at the pennant, I would start and two days later I would go to the bullpen. If there was any need whatsoever for a relief pitcher I'd come in and pitch the last inning or two. Houk, who had been a third string catcher with the Yankees, told me he had often caught Joe Page, the Yankee relief ace, and he felt I threw the ball just as hard as Page, and that was some compliment.

Phil Rizzuto
*Phil followed his fabulous career with the New York
Yankees, as one of baseball's great shortstops, as a broadcaster
covering the Yankees, from 1957 until 2000. The "Scooter"
was finally recognized for the great ballplayer he was by being
inducted into the Hall of Fame in 1994.*
*"Ryne was a great guy. I started covering the Yankees in
1957 and I covered Ryne's rookie year. You could tell he loved
the game. He threw a 'heavy' ball. Some other guys threw fast
also, but the ball would come in like a feather, but not Ryne's.
He was very hard to hit. Houk compared Ryne to Joe Page, but
I think Ryne was much tougher. Page threw a lot of sinkers and
screwballs. Ryne just threw it by you."*

In September of 1957, Associated Press ran a column under
the headline: *Houk Tabs Duren as 'Yank Great'*, where they
quoted Ralph as saying, "Ryne is the best pitcher we have had
in three years of Triple A ball here. Yes, even better than Don
Larsen I believe." Houk told me that he advised the people
in New York I would be the best relief pitcher they ever had,
which he also told Associated Press, and the Yanks should bring
me up for the stretch run in '57. Several times I was packed,
ready to go, and waiting for the phone call that never came.
The Yanks felt they had it covered with Bob Grim doing the
late inning work and notching 19 saves with a 2.63 ERA, and
when I read that the Yankees bought 40 year old Sal Maglie
for the stretch run I knew I wasn't going to see pinstripes in
'57. They told me I'd be a lot better coming to New York in
the beginning of the year. I don't know if I was better or not,
but the Yankees won the pennant again that year and it's hard
to argue with success. But even though I couldn't argue, there
I was again with my constant companions – disappointment,
discouragement and anger. And I did what every good drunk
does, I bought my steady friends rounds of drinks.

*ERA stands for Earned Run Average and is a widely
used statistic when comparing pitchers. A pitcher's
ERA is calculated by dividing the total number of
earned runs allowed by a pitcher by the number of
innings pitched and multiplying that number by nine, to*

determine the average number of earned runs he gives up per game.

For example, if a pitcher has given up 30 runs in 108 innings of work, his ERA would be 2.5. 30 divided by 108, times 9.

An earned run is a run scored by the opposition without benefit of an error, or that would not have scored if an error did not occur. For instance, if a batter leads off an inning by hitting a home run, that run is an earned run. However, if a batter hits a ground ball to the shortstop, who makes an error on the play, allowing the runner to safely reach first base, and that runner scores, his run is deemed an unearned run, and will not adversely affect the pitchers ERA.

With the Denver Bears in 1957. Looking at this picture I notice how confused I looked, probably wondering how come I was back in the minor leagues. (Photo source: Personal collection of Ryne Duren)

Eleven

THE NEW YORK YANKEES
– REALLY

During spring training of 1958 I worked harder than at any other time in my professional career. I knew I had to impress the Yankees with my work ethic, my performance and my behavior, if I was going to break their reluctance to bring me up to the majors. Ralph Houk wound up traveling with me to the big club from Denver, and served as one of Casey Stengel's coaches. Being a coach on the major league club helped Houk convince Casey that I should be used as a reliever. The confidence that Ralph showed in me, by touting me to the press as a potential "Yankee great" and comparing me to Joe Page, also served as a motivator. I wanted to belong, and I wanted to justify Ralph's confidence in me. When the press began to support me, it propelled me to work even harder toward success:

United Press, February 1958
DUREN IMPRESSES STENGEL AT CAMP
St. Petersburg – Manager Casey Stengel opened the New York Yankees' rookie school here Monday by singling out pitcher Rinold Duren of Cazenovia, Wisconsin as the chief reason the Yanks feel they can get along without Cleveland's Ray Narleski.

"This fella Duren can throw as hard as anyone on our club," Stengel said. "Narleski has a good fast ball too, but Duren could be the man for us."

New York Journal-American, March 7, 1958
DUREN'S ON BEAM ... AND CASEY'S BEAMING
St. Petersburg, Fla. – Rinold Duren, the one-time scatter arm, is proving daily he knows the exact location of home plate ... the right hander has been the most impressive pitcher in the Yankee camp.

Milwaukee Journal, March 8, 1958
Duren, up from Denver, allowed just three hits in his four inning term and looked very much like a worthy addition to the Yankee staff.

Sure enough, my hard work paid off. I got to go north with the team, and 1958 became my first full year in the major leagues – with the New York Yankees. When I finally got to New York, I spent a good portion of the first three weeks of the season sitting on the bench with Jim Turner because the Yankee way was not to rush into anything. I don't think I started doing any relieving that amounted to anything until the end of April.

I remember the first game I saved. I went to Ralph before a game against the Orioles at the Stadium, and said, "Why don't you grab that fungo stick and come out and hit some balls back at me on the mound?" and he did. In the game that night, we were winning 4-0 going into the ninth and with Bobby Shantz working on a three hit shutout it didn't look like I'd be leaving Turner's side or that bench again that night. But Shantz faltered, as did Bob Grim who relieved him, and Casey called for me to come in, with the score now 4-3, with one out and a man on first and third. On my second pitch to Jim Marshall who was a left-handed hitter for Baltimore, he hit a shot back at me. I grabbed that ball, wheeled around and threw it to Gil McDougald who tossed it to Moose Skowron. Game over. That was my first save, with my glove, and I remember Casey saying, "And he knew just what to do with it." Two weeks later Casey was still talking about it. On May 16, 1958, in a column in the Wisconsin State Journal, Casey was quoted as saying, "I'll never forget that double play he got us out of. He just fired to second and didn't watch the play. He just started for the dugout." More important than what Casey said to the press was what Casey obviously felt. After that first save, Casey used me when the game was on the line.

I wound up saving a league-leading 20 games and won 6 more. I had a 2.02 ERA and struck out 87 batters in 75 innings - a K/9 innings ratio of 10.44. Meanwhile, opposing batters only averaged 4.74 hits against me per 9 innings.

*A **K/9 innings ratio** is the average number of strikeouts earned by a pitcher for every 9 innings he pitches. The average is obtained by dividing the total number of strikeouts recorded by a pitcher over a period of time by the total number of innings pitched during that period, and multiplying the result by 9. My K/9 innings ratio for 1958 of **10.44** was an excellent ratio. Consider the career K/9 innings ratio of some of the top strikeout pitchers in the game:*

Nolan Ryan (5714 Ks/5386 innings)   9.52 K/9 IP
Roger Clemens (3717 Ks/3306 innings)   10.12 K/9 IP
Randy Johnson (3412 Ks/2748.3 innings) 11.17 K/9 IP

The totals for Clemens and Johnson are through the 2001 season. Both of them are destined to be enshrined in the Hall of Fame, and Nolan Ryan is already there.

*When Troy Percival, of the Angels, had such a dominant year in 1996, allowing only 4.5 hits per 9 innings pitched, baseball researchers checked the record books to put his performance in perspective. As a result, I found out that 38 years later **my 1958 record of 4.74 hits allowed per 9 innings was still the 6th lowest average in baseball history**, with Percival's being the best. At the time I accomplished that average it was the second lowest in baseball history. Only Mike Naymick of the Cleveland Indians had done better, allowing only 4.57 hits per 9 innings in 1943.*

The press corps, with inspiration from the Yankees, made me out to be the big, bad guy that the other team, and the opposing fans, hated to see come out of the bullpen. For instance, Milt Richman ran a story through United Press International, entitled *Fast-Balling Duren Has Hitters Shaking*, the gist of which was that I pitched faster than Herb Score and "might possibly maim someone for life" if I ever hit him in the head. And with the Yankees it was all choreographed. Jim Turner explained the "Yankee style" to me step by step: "We don't use bullpen cars for our men. You put your jacket over your right shoulder and hop the short fence sideways as you leave the bullpen. Don't wait for the grounds crew to open it. You walk with your head high; taking long, slow, determined strides. As you approach the infield, your turn your head over your right shoulder and glance at the scoreboard to read the situation. As you approach the infield grass, you hand your jacket to the batboy who is there waiting for you. When you walk onto the mound, you take the baseball from the man you're replacing and you pat him on the rump with your glove. You listen to Casey, nodding in agreement, but keep your head high and your focus on home plate. Then you take your warm-up pitches." In those days, the teams didn't pump up their fans with loud rock music and DiamondVision screens didn't exist yet, so the excitement had to come from the drama built up on the field.

It's been written so often that I always threw one of my warm-up pitches, mostly the first one, over the head of the catcher and the umpire into the screen, for effect. In truth, that is not how it started. Originally, there was no intimidation or any other motive in mind. What happened was I came out of the bullpen already throwing my last few pitches there as hard as I could, and it was my philosophy that when I got to the mound there wasn't any need of throwing three quarters speed. I'm already loose. So I used my warm up pitches to try and get a sense and feel of that particular mound on that day, and a sense of my own feeling on that day. It's kind of like playing golf, "What swing have I got today?" The way I looked at it was: I'll throw the ball as hard as I can, I'll try to throw it over the plate, see where it goes and then I'll adjust from there; because that's how I finally got to the big leagues. It was not my ability to throw the ball over, but my ability to adjust to the last pitch - the Lefty O'Doul theory. So now I come in to Yankee Stadium and, unbeknownst to me, Bob Turley had asked for the mound to be flatter. So I threw the ball as hard as I could and my knee almost hit my chin, and the ball had to go. You know, once that foot's down the ball's got to go. It left my hand early and it went way up on the screen. Well, everybody thought I did it on purpose and got a big kick out of it. That's not the first time it happened, because many of the actual mounds differed in slope from the bullpen mound, but that was the first time it happened while I was with the Yankees. Frankie Crosetti, in particular, thought that it was a good idea for intimidation, and Cro really was the power coach on that club. Crosetti told me "Don't be afraid to throw that ball up there." I never really felt that it intimidated the hitters after awhile because I figured they just thought I was being really bush about this. So it was more for the fans and the writers, really, than it was for the hitters. It was as close to show business as I thought you could get in those days.

Phil Rizzuto

"I used to get a real kick out of Ryne throwing that first warm-up pitch into the screen. He would always get the crowd going with that. And he knew just how often to come close with a pitch to make it scary for a batter to stay up there against him."

Lee Thomas

Lee played two games with the Yankees in 1961, and went with me to Los Angeles in a trade in May 1961. He was my teammate with the Angels, and helped me win several games. In 1962, Lee batted .290, hit 26 home runs and knocked in 104 runs.

"Ryne would come into the game and put on his funky, thick glasses while on the mound. He would deliberately throw his first warm-up pitch to the backstop and then proceed to throw a 95 – 100 mph fastball. He was very unhittable."

Russ "Dutch" Kemmerer

Russ was a right-handed pitcher with the Red Sox, Senator, White Sox and Houston Colt 45s. His big league career spanned from 1954 to 1963.

"When he came into a game in relief, his first warm up pitch landed half way up the screen behind home plate. It was a well-placed reminder to the hitters not to get too comfortable in the batter's box."

Bobby Richardson
Bobby was the mainstay of the Yankee infield, rising to prominence in 1959, batting .301. During his twelve years with the Yankees, Bobby was in seven World Series, and batted .305 in World Series play. He totaled thirteen hits against the St. Louis Cardinals in the 1964 Series, and eleven hits and twelve runs batted in against the Pittsburgh Pirates in 1960, becoming the only member of a losing team to be voted the World Series Most Valuable Player.

"As Ryne's teammate I laughed at the opposition as they tried to hit him in between an occasional ball off the screen, and he'd be sure to remind them that maybe he couldn't see them as he wiped his glasses."

Jim Turner, who was my pitching coach with the Yanks and then later on again with the Reds, was also instrumental in having me throw the ball out of the strike zone successfully. I know that sounds a little funny, but it was effective. Turner made me think about choosing my battles on the mound and who to throw strikes to. In the long run he may have increased the number of walks I gave up, but improved my effectiveness as a pitcher. His theory was: what's the difference if I walk a very dangerous hitter and then get the next guy who I know I can retire. Turner also tried to get me to avoid another battle I couldn't win – the one with the bottle. He told me to stay away from Mantle and Ford, that I shouldn't be drinking and running around with them. Unfortunately for me, I understood and accepted Turner's pitching advice, but not the advice he was pitching me about drinking and life. Turner was very unselfish about taking any credit for my success, although he might not have been too original. In 1958 when Newsweek asked him if he had given me any special instruction on relieving, he pretty much used Ralph's line from 1957 in answering, "Sure, I told him, Ryne, here's the ball."

Jim Turner (1903-1998)

Right-handed Pitcher 1937-45 Braves, Reds, Yankees
As a 33-year-old rookie, in 1937, he won 20 games for the fifth place Boston Bees and led the NL with a 2.38 ERA. He got the nickname "Milkman" because during the off-season he worked for his family's dairy. He was part of the starting rotation for the World Champion Cincinnati Reds in 1940, going 14-7. He was the pitching coach for the Yankees from 1949-59 and then again from 1966-73, and served in that capacity for the Reds from 1961-65.

Frank Crosetti (1910-2002)

Shortstop - Third baseman 1932-48 Yankees
Was a defensive standout as a Yankee infielder for seventeen seasons. In 1938 and '39 he led the American League shortstops in putouts and double plays. He was a great sign-stealer, and also mastered the hidden ball trick. During his playing years he won nine AL pennants and eight World Championships. He coached for 20 more seasons with the Yankees, participating in another 15 World Series. His longevity in the game earned him the nickname "The Old Cro." Cro passed away on February 12, 2002.

Turner and Cro were the disciplinarians on the coaching staff, but the star attraction, as far as on the management side, was Casey Stengel. I liked Casey, because I knew he was a character and I kind of played the game with him. He sought me out which made me feel pretty good, especially as a rookie. He would come and ask me to have dinner with him and the feeling of acceptance was something I really needed. He just had a way about him. He was more than a baseball manager. He was part showman, part psychiatrist, and part motivator, just a jack-of-all-trades. I remember one particular time he called me into his office. I didn't know what to expect and he said, "Mr. Duren, have a seat over here. I need to talk to you a little bit. Sometimes, you know, I get awful busy around here and there's lots of things going on, but that doesn't mean that I don't appreciate what you're doing for us." Things like that, especially to someone craving acceptance as much as I was,

made you feel more loyal to Casey, and that was one of the
secrets of his managerial success.

Charles "Casey" Stengel (1890-1975)

*Outfielder 1912-25 Dodgers, Pirates, Phils, Giants, Braves
Manager 1934-36 (Dodgers), 38-43 (Braves), 49-60
(Yanks), 62-65 (Mets)
Long before Casey Stengel was mesmerizing people with his
special style of speech known as "Stengelese", and long before
he had a second career as a manager, Casey was a pretty decent
ballplayer. Over a fourteen-year career, he played in 1277
games and knocked in 535 runs, while batting .284. He is most
widely remembered for two particular incidents: 1) on May 25,
1919, while Casey was with the Pirates playing the Dodgers in
Brooklyn, someone handed him a bird, which he secretly placed
under his baseball cap; when he came to bat, he tipped his cap
to the crowd and out came flying one very relieved bird; 2) on
October 10, 1923, in Game One of the World Series. Casey
broke up a 4-4 tie in the ninth inning by hitting an inside the
park homerun and struggling around the bases with one spike
that was falling apart. The famous "Casey" nickname was a
phonetic derivation in honor of his hometown: Kansas City.
None of the major league teams managed by Stengel, before he
managed the Yankees, ever finished the season any higher than
fifth place, and during the four years he managed the Mets they
finished last every season. But while managing the Yankees,
Stengel enjoyed the greatest managerial run in baseball history,
winning ten pennants and seven world championships in twelve
seasons. One of Casey's famous sayings is often used to describe his own career: "There comes a time in every man's life
and I've had plenty of them."*

I don't think Casey ever called me Ryne. I don't know if
he knew my first name, or anybody's for that matter, because
he called everybody by their last name. And he did that thing
like he didn't remember your name. Did you ever have a
conversation with someone you know didn't know your first
name? And that Stengelese, well, when you sat down to dinner
with him, then you didn't have that, but the rest of the time he
was on stage.

But he did know how to handle the fans and the press and the bigger picture of how to build up his ballplayers. Just two months into my rookie season with the Yankees, people were speculating on my pitching speed and comparing me to Bob Feller, Herb Score and Walter Johnson. Stengel gave his opinion:

"I did not like to stand up against Walter's speed, and if I were a batter I would not admire hitting against Duren, which if he ever hit you in the head, you might be in the past tense.

"The kid throws hard enough to suit me. The ball makes a strange sound, like a small jet, as it travels toward the catcher and lodges, kerplunk, in Yogi's mitt. Duren is a splendid product of the Atomic Age.

"I think he has it in him to be one of the great relief specialists of all time, another Johnny Murphy for the Yankees."

Johnny Murphy (1908-1970)
Right-handed Pitcher 1932, 34-47 Yankees, Red Sox
Nicknamed "The Fireman" for his excellent relief pitching, Murphy's main pitch was the curveball. He began as a starter with the Yankees; starting 20 games in 1934, and only started a total of 20 games the rest of his career. His 12 relief victories in 1937 and again in 1943 were records at the time. His best season was 1941, when he compiled an 8-3 record with an ERA of 1.98, while collecting 15 saves. Murphy went on to become the General Manager of the New York Mets, and died only three months after the Amazin' Mets won the 1969 World Series.

During that first year, we were in Washington, D.C., playing the Senators in the old Griffith Stadium, where the dugout was actually in two pieces. In the middle was the runway back to the clubhouse. Casey always sat in the corner and anybody might be sitting on the other side. I relieved in the first game of a doubleheader, and did a good job. As a routine, ballplayers on the bench would keep our jacket handy or on, and our glove was always underneath the seat or near us. About the sixth or seventh inning of the second game, Casey said "Mr. Duren"

"Yeah, Casey, what is it?"

"Where's your glove?"

"Right under the seat here, Casey."

"Would you mind removing your jacket? And take your glove and your jacket and walk down to the bullpen."

I thought "What? I've already relieved today." and they had never pitched me twice in the same day. "Oh," he said "don't get excited, I'm not gonna use you, but you have become a big star around here and a lot of these people have not seen you or even know what you look like. Now go down there and take a walk. I'm not gonna use you, but let these people see what a big star looks like." That's a Stengel story.

In the middle of the 1958 season he told a reporter, "Duren, I don't have to tell you about him. He'll win 65 games, but they don't give him credit for all of them and he strikes them out wonderful so I like to put him in whenever we're ahead or tied and it's just been half a year but he's done the best relief pitching which I have seen since I been managing here. Ten years." Sometimes I think Casey invented the run-on sentence.

My favorite story about Casey was when they got Johnny Kucks and Virgil Trucks confused. Whitey Ford was pitching against the Red Sox and was beginning to tire in the ninth. Casey wanted Johnny Kucks to warm up. Darrell Johnson was the bullpen catcher at the time, and he didn't interpret the phone call right. The guys in the dugout said, "Get Kucks up." and Johnson was supposed to answer "Getting Kucks up." Whether it was the old guy's hearing or the distortion, he thought he was understood, but instead they got Trucks up. Now, with nobody out and one on, Virgil was cranked up ready to come into the game and Casey, before going out to the mound, just told them to call the bullpen and tell him that he's coming in. That's what they did but they didn't say who, they said "he." Trucks walks onto the mound and Casey doesn't pay any attention to who's walking in until he gets there. Virgil tells the story: he gets out there, Casey takes a look at him and says, "What the hell are you doing here?" Virgil says, "Well, you called me in the game." Once he's there he's got to pitch to the hitter. Casey came back to the dugout as fast as he could move with those old gimpy legs, muttering, "What the hell is this guy doing here, Turner?" He jumped all over Turner about it, then Turner called the bullpen and they're hollering and screaming down at the bullpen, and about then, Virgil has struck this guy out, whoever it was, on three pitches. The next hitter hit into a double play, game over. When the Yanks are playing Boston you can't tell by the noise whether it was good or bad. With that noise, Stengel turned around and started out toward the field and here comes the whole team running in at him. He didn't know what to think. The next day Stengel was a genius in the paper again. I'll never forget it.

I have included an Appendix to this book, where I provide more detail about my pitching experiences and philosophy, for those more interested in that area of my life. But I cannot omit from this portion of the book my experience of being hit in the head as a batter. On July 24, 1958, in Detroit, with the Yanks losing 5-0 to the Tigers in the sixth inning, I was brought in to relieve Virgil Trucks. The Yanks scored four runs in the seventh inning and two more in the eighth, to take the lead, 6-5, and I came to bat in the ninth inning against Paul Foytack. The excitement started after Foytack got two quick strikes on me. They say you'll never remember what happened a second before you get hit real hard in the head. True to that, I have no real recollection of ever seeing the pitch but, evidently, it was right at my head and I couldn't get out of the way of it. Helmets didn't have the protective flap over the ear and temple area back then. The ball hit the edge of the helmet where it met my cheek. The pitch broke my cheekbone and also cracked the helmet, which deflected the blow, but I went down to the ground, bleeding and dazed. My mind went reeling, but I don't recall being unconscious. I received immediate attention on the field to stop the bleeding, and I was removed on a stretcher and taken to Detroit Memorial Hospital. The cut required several stitches to close it and I suffered a concussion, resulting in dizzy spells and headaches. Tests revealed no brain damages as first thought but I spent several days in the hospital and about a week recuperating with my folks in Wisconsin. Some people speculated that Foytack purposely threw at me because in the 8th inning I brushed back Al Kaline, sending him sprawling. Gil McDougald, to this day, maintains that he saw Bill Norman, the Tiger manager, wave a towel at Foytack, giving him the signal to deck me. In an article that appeared in the Detroit Times, on July 25, 1958, Hall of Famer and teammate Enos "Country" Slaughter, who just passed away this year, noted that he too saw Foytack look into the Tiger dugout just before delivering the pitch that decked me. There was no designated hitter in 1958, and I had to bat, giving the Tigers a chance to exact their revenge. Foytack came to visit me in the hospital to explain to me that he did not hit me on purpose. Knowing how conscious I was, as a pitcher, of the damage I could cause to a batter's health, career and life, I believed Foytack was trying to send me a message. I didn't believe he was trying to hurt me, and I don't think he ever intended to give me a concussion or make me bleed. That's the same way I felt about the now famous Roger Clemens – Mike Piazza incident. Roger is a power pitcher and will claim the inside of the plate, with the intent of moving that batter out of there. I truly do not believe a pitcher would try to hit a batter in the head with a 90+ mile per hour pitch.

As for the game when Foytack hit me, play resumed after they got me on my way to the hospital. Casey put Bobby Richardson in to run for me and McDougald hit a home run, as did Mantle, and to my knowledge I became the first winning pitcher while in an ambulance. The Tiger pitcher we beat that day was Hall of Famer, Jim Bunning, who had pitched a no-hitter in his previous game, and who is now a United States Senator from Kentucky. Obviously, Jim had a lot on the ball, no matter how you read that, and was more prepared for life after sports than I was.

Paul Foytack

To me, the mention of Paul's name will always bring me back to that pitch in Detroit in 1958, but Paul was a mainstay of the Tiger rotation for several years. He enjoyed an 11 year big league career with Detroit and Los Angeles, joining the Angels after I left in 1963.

"*I remember that I was told to throw inside to send a message to Ryne, because he had knocked down one of our batters. The pitch should have either knocked him down or hit him in a harmless spot, like his butt, or thigh, but the ball got away from me. When I saw Ryne go down I was stunned myself. It was never in my mind, nor I think in any pitcher's mind, to hurt a batter.*"

Gil McDougald
Gil was the American League Rookie of the Year in
1951, and played 10 seasons for the Yankees, at second base,
shortstop and third. In 1957 he led the American League
in triples and sacrifice hits. He was a great teammate and
friend.

"I saw Tiger manager, Bill Norman, wave a towel from the
dugout and I knew Foytack would be throwing the ball inside at
Ryne; at least making him hit the dirt. I was on deck when Ryne
was at the plate. When the ball hit him I heard the crack and
saw Ryne go down in a heap. When I saw the blood flowing
from the side of his head, as he lay there motionless, my first
thought was that he was dead. It was very scary. I knew Paul
Foytack very well. He was a good friend. He never meant to
hurt Ryne, and he was very shaken by the incident."

One of the greatest things about being on the Yankees was
the opportunity to be around some of the legendary players
in the game: Mantle, Maris, Ford, Howard, Berra, etc. It was
unbelievable. When I got there Mantle had already had his
Triple Crown year (1956), and to me, during the years I was
there, 1958 through part of 1961, the best all around ballplayer
I played with, day in and day out, was Roger Maris. I feel that
way because of his consistent play and his ability to make good
plays in the outfield, run the bases, do the right thing. He was
just absolutely amazing. Actually, 1960 was the year I thought
he was so great. How many home runs did he hit in 1960?
How many runners did he throw out? How many game saving
catches did he make? How many times did he take the extra
base and score the run, or sacrifice, or hit the opposite way? He
was amazing.

Roger suffered an injury to his wrist that really robbed him
of some great years. Also, because the doctors couldn't initially
determine the cause of the pain or the nature of the injury,
Roger's detractors started saying he wasn't really injured and
was just "dogging it." I do not believe that Roger was "dogging
it", but I do believe that, emotionally, the 61 home run season
changed Roger and it changed his desire to excel. I think Roger
had too much of stardom in 1961. He just wanted to be a
member of the team, to be there and play ball and not be in the

spotlight. Roger loved the game and loved playing the game, but playing in the pros, especially in New York for the Yankees was so much more than just baseball: the fans, the media, the pressure of chasing the cherished record and the legend who held it.

Roger Maris (1934-1985)

Outfielder 1957-68 Indians, Athletics, Yankees, Cardinals
Besides hitting 61 home runs in 1961, which is mostly what the pedestrian fan remembers, the baseball devotee and the guys who played with him and against him, will tell you that he was one of the dominant players of the 1960s. Roger could hit, hit with power, field, throw, run, move base runners, slide to break up plays. He was a complete ballplayer. He won the American League MVP in 1960, with 39 home runs (one behind Mantle who topped the league) and a league leading .581 slugging percentage. Then he won the MVP again in the home run year, 1961. In fact, he is one of only two people eligible for the Hall of Fame who won back-to-back Most Valuable Player awards who is not in the Hall, Dale Murphy being the other. After appearing in five consecutive World Series with the Yankees, Roger was traded to the Cardinals, where he appeared in two more. He appeared in seven World Series in the '60s and was on the winning team three times.

Mickey Mantle, needless to say, was an awesome natural talent. For that reason alone the other guys on the team would look to him for leadership. But it was also because Mickey was different. Mickey was a fun guy. He knew how to have fun and loved having fun, and the other guys loved being part of that. I idolized him and was in awe of the fact that I was his teammate. Mickey did such gigantic things, with his bat, and he could run so fast, and all the rest. Mickey was the hero, our hero, and the guys wanted to be around him.

Early on in my days as a Yankee, I learned how gifted a player Mantle was, and how great it would be to pitch in front of a defense that included him. In May of 1958, Casey brought me in to hold on to a 6-5 Yankee lead, after the Washington Senators had climbed back into the game on the strength of a 3 run pinch hit home run by Roy Sievers off Bobby Shantz, with one out in the eighth inning. I struck out two batters in the eighth and struck out two more batters in the ninth, but gave up a single to Albie Pearson in the bottom of the ninth and walked Clint Courtney to put the potential tying and winning runs on base. Julio Becquer, a lefty firstbaseman from Cuba, pinch hit for Eddie Yost and lined a shot into the gap in right center. From my vantage point the ball was going to the wall, and would allow both runners to score, making me the loser. I started to walk off the mound with my head down, when I heard the Washington crowd's roar started to sound more like a tremendous sigh. I looked over my shoulder to see Mantle's momentum have him still running full tilt, with his left arm fully extended and the ball sticking out of his glove like a big ice cream cone. I had walked off the mound a loser and, thanks to Mickey, before I made it to the third base line I got credit for the save in the box score, although the real save belonged to Mickey.

I was in heaven when I car-pooled with Mickey in 1960. We lived in the same area in Englewood, New Jersey, and during all those trips back and forth to the Stadium, I had him all to myself in a sense. Getting Mickey into the car at the Stadium was a bit tricky. The police would take my keys and when we'd leave the Stadium they'd have the car waiting right there within the barricades at the Press Gate. I'd go out to the car first and keep it running, and Mickey would exit the Stadium and run into the car, with the police holding the door open. We'd drive through the crowd and I always kidded Mickey that he owed me a paint job, because the right side of the car, where Mickey sat, was all scratched from the kids trying to get to Mickey. But once we were in the car, we usually had a great time together. We laughed and drank, and kidded and drank, talked (baseball and women) and drank; played golf and drank. Because of Mickey's stature as a Triple Crown Winner, a multiple MVP winner, and the way he played, even with a hangover, he was larger than life. You see, Mantle might get totally drunk one night and come up the next day and hit a home run, and everybody would say, "Boy, that Mantle, he is something else, to go out and do that." and that would make the legend grow. All of us who worshipped what he could do, out of human nature, wanted to be like him.

He became another Big George in my eyes. At that stage of my life, from external appearances, I was a major league ballplayer who could instill fear in the hearts of batters by staring in to the plate, and compound that fear by throwing a ball a hundred miles an hour; but, internally, I was still a little kid, awed by Mickey's heroic acts and I wanted to emulate all his traits, even though some were flaws, unrecognized by me as such because of hero worship. Tragically, just like Big George, Mickey would die from an alcohol related illness, and about just as tragically, I was well on my way to following both of them.

Mickey got awful down on himself and was moody a lot, kicking the water cooler and those kinds of things. That's what the public saw. But he also turned to alcohol for answers. A good example was the day he forgot to run out a double play ball because he thought there were two outs. Even though he was a star, Stengel took him out of the game because of that mistake. That's how the game was a little different then. Mickey was steaming and didn't say a thing to me in the car as I was driving home from the Stadium. We crossed the George Washington Bridge, and then he started barking directions: "In here, ...go in here, ...and here, ... and then there." And there we went into a bar that we had been in before, not a lot, and as I remember it I think he had four double shots before he said anything. He was so mad, so upset with that whole thing, with him not running it out and with Casey showing him up by taking him out of the game.

It's public knowledge that Mickey had a problem with alcohol, but there are a lot of things that the fans don't know about Mickey. He was a terrific teammate, and I was glad to see the Yankees acknowledge that when they erected the monument to Mickey in Monument Park at the Stadium. Another thing about Mickey, which he didn't want publicized while he was with the Yankees, is that he would spend quite a bit of time visiting kids who were hospitalized. Mickey felt that if those visits were made public they would turn into a media circus, and he was probably right. But I remember many days when I would drop Mickey off at a hospital so he could just go visit with some kids.

Mickey's favorite drinking buddy while I was with the Yanks was Whitey Ford. Mickey and Whitey were fun guys to be around. In those ways they were similar, but in other ways they were different. Where Mantle exuded natural ability, Ford was a flat out smart ballplayer. Well, I thought he had outstanding ability too, but his control was his biggest asset, and backing that up, his ability to change speeds and of course to know the hitters. The other thing about him was he knew his own limitations pretty well, and from that standpoint I think he did a great job of managing himself. He'd call the bullpen and he'd ask Darrell or Jim Hegan, if they thought I was throwing well, because I'd been up or he might call me before I even got up and said, "How are you feeling?" and, "Did you have a good night?" or something like that. Of all the pitchers I ever knew I think he managed himself the best and he called his own shots. He's the only one, to my mind, that ever called the bullpen during the game to see what kind of stuff we had.

He knew the politics of the team and the game and everything. Very smart man. Very smart. Whitey would use a batter's thinking against the batter. For instance, the first time around the lineup he might throw a guy four straight curves. Now he had that curve ball in the batter's mind. The next at bat that batter came up looking for that curveball. Whitey would throw a fastball right through the heart of the plate and the batter would just look at it. Strike one. Now, having just seen the fastball, the batter was sure the curve was coming. Fastball again down the heart of the plate. Strike two. Now the batter knows Whitey's ahead 0-2 and can afford to throw a curve and probably will. Fastball again. Strike three, and this guy would walk back to the dugout, mumbling to himself, never having swung the bat and he just watched three fastballs right down the pipe, as they like to say in baseball.

With all the veterans and stars on the team, there was a lot of leadership on the Yankees. Yogi Berra, believe it or not, had the most influence among the players and Casey deferred to him, a lot. Most people identify Yogi with some of those things he's said that seem so puzzling, Berraisms. I know a lot of people think they were all made up, but I witnessed an awful lot of them. I can't remember a particular incident, but every once in a while, Mickey would walk over or Whitey and they'd say, "Did you hear what he said?" and they'd have a big grin on their face. If a guy came walking away from where

Yogi was and he was cracking up, you knew Yogi came up with something funny, and it could be innocent. You didn't ever want to laugh back in Yogi's face, but he just would come up with the damnedest things. I'll give you an indication, though, of how Stengel deferred to Yogi. It didn't take me long to become very aware of the difference between how Yogi caught me as opposed to how Elston Howard caught me, remembering that I came in at the latter part of Yogi's playing days. Yogi had great judgment from behind the plate. A lot of the pitchers would rather have him back there calling the game for them than another catcher. So for me it was just simply based on Elston's ability to catch me and his arm, that I preferred to have Elston catch me. Elston also had a fast release, which helped me with base runners. Like most fastball pitchers, I used an exaggerated leg kick to generate power. That increased the time of my delivery and gave runners a head start, necessitating a catcher with a fast release to throw them out.   One day I told Elston, "You know, you catch me so much better than Yogi. If you'd come into the game when I'm pitching, I'd feel a lot more confident." He agreed, but when I suggested that he go tell Stengel, he said, "Are you kidding?" So I said I'd ask Stengel. I knew, weighing everything, the Yanks wanted to keep Yogi's bat in the game and I kept that in mind when I approached Casey and asked him, if we had the lead when I came in to pitch, would it be possible to have Ellie come in from the defensive standpoint and maybe move Yogi to the outfield. He seemed to be nodding in agreement as I spoke, and then he delivered the punch line: "I couldn't agree with you more, Mr. Duren, but who's going to tell Mr. Berra."   Nobody liked to upset Yogi, obviously not even Stengel. Despite all the press about his mixed up language, etc., Yogi had a great baseball mind and Casey wanted to keep him content. So I said, "I'll ask him." Casey said, "You'd do that?" "Sure." So I caught up with Yogi and went through the whole thing with him, reminding him about his complaining about my sinking fastball and how his hands would puff up after catching me for a few innings. He said, "I don't care. I don't like to catch you anyway."

Yogi Berra
I got to New York toward the end of Yogi's great career, but it was clear that Yogi's baseball knowledge and instincts were second to none. His leadership qualities were evident to all his teammates, and it was no surprise to me that Yogi went on to manage the Yanks and the Mets. I think Yogi is even more popular today than when he played. "Ryne was a heck of a reliever for us, especially in 1958, when we came back from 3-1 to beat Milwaukee in the World Series. Without him, we just don't win."

I recently heard a tape of an interview that took place in 1964, when I was with the Phillies, and I was asked if I was surprised that Yogi had been named as the Manager of the Yankees. I still agree with the answer I gave then: Yogi might not have expressed himself as well as some of the more learned men in the game, but he had a terrific knowledge of the game and what it took to win, and I always felt he would be a very good coach or a manager.

Getting back to 1958, it was my first full year in the majors and I felt my performance justified my earlier feelings that I had been ready for the big leagues for a while. As a rookie I had been selected to the American League All Star team, and it was a thrill to be included on that squad, although I did not get to play. At the end of the season *The Sporting News* named Albie Pearson and me as their American League Rookies of the Year. Later on in the off season, the baseball writers, who officially vote for Rookie of the Year, voted for Pearson, who got fourteen votes to my seven. In January 1959, *The Sporting News* reported the vote of the writers and offered an opinion on why I didn't win. Several writers didn't feel that I was really a rookie, since I had already played with St. Louis/Baltimore, and Kansas City, and I was 29 years old, despite the fact that I pitched two innings in 1954 and was only with Kansas City two months before going down to Denver. (I wonder if those same guys would have voted for Ichiro in 2001.) Also, as still exists today, there were some writers who were "Yankee haters" – a sort of backlash response to the fact that the Yankees were perennial winners.

A few weeks later The Sporting News ran the results of its poll of sportswriters as to who was the most exciting ballplayer of 1958. Willie Mays won that contest for the second year in a row, but I got the vote of at least one sportswriter, Dan Daniel of the New York World Telegram and Sun. Daniel explained why he voted for me: "Duren's every throw was watched with the keenest interest, almost with bated breath. He could fan the batter for the game, he could hit him for the day's irremedial misadventure. But, no matter what Duren did, he was the game's exciting fillip. ... from where I sat the guy with the spectacles and the hardest pitch in the majors was the apotheosis of high adventure." The way Casey described the excitement I brought to a game was to say, "When Duren came in to pitch people stopped eating their popcorn." He had a way with words.

So did some other people, who brought me right back down to earth, and reminded me that being a ballplayer was what I did, not who I was: During the period I was recovering from the beaning from Foytack, I visited my folks in Cazenovia and went to the stream that comes out below the dam where I used to fish as a kid. I had decided to just go back and re-live a little of my childhood. I was fishing and basking in the sun, leaning back against a rock on this beautiful day, and I saw this little kid whose father I knew pretty well. He was with his mother and he kept poking at her as they walked over the bridge above me, saying, "Momma, Momma, look that's Ryne Duren down there fishing. Ryne Duren's fishing down there Momma." She didn't say anything and he said it again, wanting a response. Finally, the mother, disgusted, said, "So what, the fish won't bite any better for him than they do for me."

Sitting on the bench with Casey. It looks like Casey is trying to figure out what to say next, and I'm trying to figure out what he just said. (Photo source: Personal collection of Ryne Duren, reproduced through the courtesy of the family of Don Wingfield.)

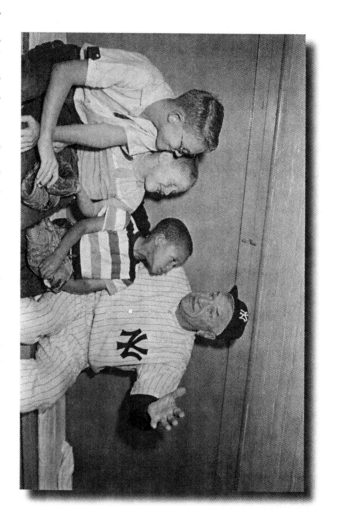

This photo brings back some of my fondest memories of my time with the Yankees. My son, Steve, on the left, Mickey Mantle, Jr., second from left, and Elston Howard, Jr., are entranced by Casey. (Photo credit: © Bettmann/CORBIS)

Don Larsen, a Yankee teammate in 1958, and I pose with Eddie Dancisak, the scout who signed me with the St. Louis Browns. This photo was taken in Milwaukee during the 1958 World Series. (Photo source: Personal collection of Ryne Duren.)

Twelve

THE WORLD SERIES - 1958

The World Series resided in New York full-time in the 1950s. Actually, beginning in 1949, straight through and including 1957, at least one of the teams in the Series was from New York every year. While the Yankees were the odds-on favorite to be in it almost every year, the Brooklyn Dodgers weren't far behind, and they faced each other six times between 1947 and 1956, insuring that all the Series games would be in New York City those years (although only once, in 1955, could the Dodgers best the Yankees). And when the Yanks and Dodgers took a year off from the fall classic in 1954 the New York Giants and Willie Mays not only made an appearance, they swept the Cleveland Indians who had won 111 games during the regular season behind the extraordinary pitching of Bob Feller, Bob Lemon, Mike Garcia and Early Wynn.

With that said, one might think that when the Yankees clinched another American League pennant, in 1958, the players would not have been so excited about it. One would have been wrong. For one thing, at the end of the 1957 season, both the Brooklyn Dodgers and the New York Giants abandoned their respective ballparks, and, worse yet, their fans, and headed to California. If there was to be a World Series in New York the Yankees were the only hope New Yorkers had, and we delivered. We clinched the 1958 American League pennant in Kansas City and I had the thrill of having pitched in the clincher, the second game of a double-header. The Yankees as a team were especially happy to get back to the World Series because they were looking to avenge their 1957 loss to the Milwaukee Braves. Also, the team had been losing more than winning since the middle of August, (winning only 19 of its last 44), giving rise to speculation that it was about to give up its birthright to play in October.

Personally, I was ecstatic upon clinching the pennant for several reasons. Some guys play in the major leagues for a very long time and never get to play in the post-season. Here I was, a rookie, getting to play in October with a chance for a championship ring. Secondly, it meant an additional check just for being in the post-season, with a chance for an even bigger winners' share check. Thirdly, and probably just as important at the time, it extended the "party" for at least another ten days or so.

Whatever everybody's reason for being happy, we all celebrated our joy at the victory dinner and on the train to Detroit, the next stop on our road trip as we played out the remainder of the season. It came as no surprise to anyone that I took the occasion of the long, happy train ride to overindulge in the alcoholic refreshments, including champagne, which seemed to be a whole new reason to drink. True to my nature, I didn't know when to quit, and I drank to the point of acting without any inhibition. My safety switches, those old frontal lobes, were awash in alcohol, and unable to warn me that it wouldn't be a good idea to crush Ralph Houk's cigar, even though my only intention was to be playful with him. Ralph instinctively reacted by swatting at me and catching me in the head with the World Series ring he was wearing. That ended the merriment for me, as Don Larsen and some of my other buddies escorted me to my sleeping quarters, despite my resistance, and tucked me in. The incident was written up by Leonard Shecter of the New York Post and predictably got blown out of proportion. To hear his account of the incident it sounded more like Rocky Marciano and Jake LaMotta doing battle than two friends horsing around. Whatever my intentions were that night, two things were certain: 1) my old friend alcohol had obviously made the trip with me from the minor leagues, and was proving itself to be a major problem; and 2) although I suffered embarrassment from the incident (and always thought that it stayed in the mind of Yankee management), it wasn't enough to get me to change my habits.

I survived that train incident with nothing more than a cut and a bruise, to my face and my reputation, for the time being. We all had bigger things on our mind, like beating Milwaukee in the World Series. After we played out the remainder of the season we headed to Wisconsin to play the Braves. Even though the opposition came from my home state it wasn't much of a rivalry for me. When I had been signed to play pro ball there was no such team as the Milwaukee Braves. At that time they were the Boston Braves, and only moved to Milwaukee at the beginning of the 1953 season. So, although the press found an angle to write about – Wisconsin Boy Coming 'Home' to face Braves – I really didn't even know the players on that team, except for the famous pitching duo of Warren Spahn and Lew Burdette, who beat the Yanks in '57, and, of course, Hank Aaron. What I also knew was that in my first full season I had reached a terrific milestone.

With all that anticipation, my introduction to the World Series was not a positive one. In Game One, at Milwaukee's County Stadium, Warren Spahn and Whitey Ford hooked up in a battle of lefthanders. Casey brought me in, with a 1-0 lead, in the eighth inning with nobody out and runners on second and third. I was in trouble before I left the bullpen. I was so excited about pitching in the World Series that I could not operate the simple latch to open the bullpen gate. After I fumbled with it for a few moments a member of the grounds crew released me. I liked it much better at Yankee Stadium where I could just hop the short fence. I struck out the first batter I faced, Joe Adcock, and then Wes Covington tied the game with a sacrifice fly. I wound up losing the game in the tenth inning, yielding singles to Adcock, Del Crandall and Billy Bruton, the last two coming with two outs. To be honest, I have no personal recollection of that game other than the incident with the bullpen gate. I recently saw film of it and found myself like a kid watching movies of his first birthday party: it's obvious I was there; I just didn't remember it. Maybe it was my nerves, as manifested by the problem with the gate, or whatever, but I had blocked that game from my memory. Looking back at newspaper accounts of the game, it sounded like "the operation was a success but the patient died." All the stories centered on the fact that I struck out five Braves in 2 2/3 innings, and how fast I was pitching, despite the fact we lost. Andy Pafko was quoted as saying he "nearly could feel the breeze" of my fastball over in the dugout, and called me the fastest pitcher he ever saw.

I didn't see any action in Game Two, a game that was over by the end of the first inning. The game started off by the Yankees loading the bases against Lew Burdette with no one out. Elston Howard hit into a force play, scoring Bauer, which broke up a string of 24 consecutive scoreless innings Burdette had hurled in World Series play against the Yanks. But Berra ended the rally with a double play. Milwaukee then went to bat, and put the game out of reach before they would take the field again, scoring seven runs in the first inning, three of them on a home run by Burdette. That cushion allowed Burdette to pitch a complete game, beating us 13-5. We were down two games to none and Milwaukee hadn't even used a relief pitcher yet. Needless to say, we were all very happy to be returning to Yankee Stadium.

Home cooking and whatever else combines to create the all-important "home field advantage" worked for us for in Game 3. Don Larsen, who I had finally rejoined on the '58 Yankees, pitched seven strong innings, yielding only six hits and no runs, and Hank Bauer knocked in all four Yankee runs. I came in to start the eighth and wasn't as sharp as I wanted to be. I walked three batters and threw a wild pitch, but didn't give up any hits, pitching two scoreless innings, to secure the shutout victory over the Braves. However, the euphoria was short-lived as Warren Spahn returned the favor in Game 4, pitching a two-hit shutout, putting the Yanks at a 3-1 disadvantage. To put what we were up against in perspective, only one team in World Series history had come back to win after being down 3 games to 1, the 1925 Pittsburgh Pirates.

In Game Five, the unfriendly, alternating zero returned to the Milwaukee side of the score sheet, as the Yankees won 7-0 behind Bob Turley's five-hit, ten-strikeout shutout effort. After losing four World Series decisions to Lew Burdette over a two year period, the Yankees were finally able to solve him, erupting for six runs in the sixth inning.

Having won two out of three at the Stadium, we were headed back to Milwaukee, down in games 3-2, needing to beat both Spahn and Burdette, who were a combined 7-2 against the Yankees in World Series play. The Yankees took some comfort in having won Game Five. Maybe, just maybe, momentum was on our side, although there is an old saying in baseball that momentum is only as good as tomorrow's starting pitcher.

That being the case, momentum took a back seat as two Hall of Famers, Spahn and Ford, went head to head again, in a rematch of Game 1. Like Game 1, Game 6 also went ten innings, and also ended 4-3, but the difference was this time the Yankees were on top, and I got a chance to contribute again. And I took advantage of the opportunity, but not without some controversy. Casey brought me in to start off the bottom of the sixth inning, with the score knotted at 2-2. I pitched a scoreless four innings, striking out seven batters and allowing only one hit. Meanwhile, the Yanks didn't score in the seventh, eighth or ninth inning either, but in the top of the tenth, McDougald led off with a homer, and three singles produced a 4-2 lead. I retired the first two batters in Milwaukee's half of the tenth and I was one out away from my first World Series win and getting the Yanks to Game Seven. On a three and two count, with Johnny Logan at bat, Umpire Charlie Berry called "Ball four" on a pitch I thought was definitely "Strike three." Disappointed at not ending the game and upset with the call, I instinctively reacted and gave the umpire the choke sign, which he didn't see. But Commissioner Ford Frick, who had just had an emergency appendectomy, was watching the game at home on television. The camera zeroed in on me and there was no doubt in his mind. That may have been the first use of television to enforce the rules. It cost me a $250 fine. Unaware of the fine at the time, I went after the last out. Logan's run didn't mean anything and since there were two out I pitched from the windup because I felt stronger that way. Logan took advantage of that and stole second and then scored on Hank Aaron's single. Joe Adcock followed with another single and Casey brought in Bob Turley who got pinch-hitter Frank Torre to pop up to Gil McDougald at second base for the last out. My first World Series victory was secure. I've seen several pictures that were taken in the clubhouse after Series games that year, and I notice that almost every one of them shows me and my teammates, whether it be Larsen or Whitey, or others, from the chest up with one arm draped over the other guy's shoulder. If the picture were enlarged, I can guarantee you that it would show my other hand holding a can of beer. It was just the way we cooled down after every game, with a couple of cold ones. The newspapers all heralded my relief performance, striking out eight batters in 4 2/3 innings while yielding three hits. Even I joined the parade and wrote a column for United Press International, which allowed the following sentiments to be preserved for history:

> I never worked so hard in my life and my only regret is that I couldn't finish.

* * *

> Striking out Wes Covington, Bill Bruton and Warren Spahn in the ninth must have taken more out of me than I thought.

* * *

> They asked me about some gesture I made to Plate Umpire Charley Berry when he called a fourth ball on Logan in the tenth. Frankly, I don't remember doing it. But I do know that I told him I thought the pitch was a strike, not a ball.

* * *

> Getting credit for the victory is about the biggest thing that's ever happened to me.
> When you're down in the minors you dream about something like this. But you never figure it will happen.

Bob Wolff

Bob is a winner of the Ford Frick Award and is in the Broadcast Wing of the Baseball Hall of Fame. I could not possibly do justice to all of Bob's years of excellent broadcasting in this short space, but suffice it to say that he has left his indelible mark on the world of sports journalism. Bob is the longest-running sports announcer in television and has broadcast the championship games in all four major US sports.

"I had the good fortune to call three World Series, including 1956 when Don Larsen threw his perfect game, but I still have vivid recollections of 1958 as I broadcast an exciting Yankees comeback to win the Series. With the Yanks down three games to two, Game Six was an elimination game for them, and what a tense game that proved to be. With no room for error, Stengel removed Whitey Ford in the third inning with the Braves ahead 2-1. After the Yanks tied the game in the sixth, Ryne Duren became the pitcher under pressure, brought in to keep the Yankee hopes alive. He put in 4 2/3 innings of terrific relief and picked up the vital win. I'll never forget Ryne's habit of wiping off his glasses, intimidating batters, hoping that Ryne could see where he was pitching. That was a meaningful extra touch, accompanied by his blazing fast ball."

Game Seven matched Don Larsen against Lew Burdette. Although I had pitched 4 2/3 innings the day before, I told Casey I was ready to go in, but when Larsen lasted only into the third inning, Casey called on Bob Turley for long relief to hold the Braves down. Turley went 6 2/3, giving up a game tying home run to Del Crandall in the sixth inning. The game remained knotted at 2 all into the eighth. Howard and Berra, who had killed the Yankee rally in Game Two, combined to put the Yankees ahead 3-2 in the eighth, and two batters later Moose Skowron deposited a three run homer into the grandstands, effectively ending the game and the Series. The Yanks became only the second team in baseball history to overcome a 3-1 World Series deficit.

All in all, I had a terrific Series, saving Don Larsen's 4-0 victory in Game 3, and winning Game 6. I ended up with a 1.93 ERA and 14 strikeouts in 9 1/3 innings. In all honesty, I think the key to our winning the Series was the job Stengel got out of me in Game 6, when we were down 3 games to 2. I know for sure it was my work in Game 6 that helped get me national attention as a ballplayer. Consider the high praise I received for my work in Game 6 from Roy Campanella in the column he wrote for the Hearst Service, which was carried nationwide:

PIN-POINT CONTROL

I thought Newk [Don Newcombe] could fire with pin-point control. But Duren really showed me something, especially in the sixth and ninth when he struck out the side.

We had some of the hardest throwing guys in baseball with us the past few years – fellows like [Rex] Barney, [Karl] Spooner, Stan Williams and [Sandy] Koufax. Only trouble with them was that half the time they never knew where the ball was going.

They never developed the real finesse that makes a great pitcher. That's what made Satch [Satchel Paige] so fabulous. He could almost thread a needle with his fast ball.

It seemed Duren threw harder today than Iron Mike. That's the automatic pitching machine we use in spring training to sharpen our batting eyes.

The Series ended in Milwaukee, which was just ninety minutes from my home. So, instead of traveling back to New York with the team, I headed home and we had a family celebration. I got a hero's welcome in Cazenovia, where the Durens predated the Braves by about a hundred years, and although Beverly also greeted me like a hero, it only took her a couple of days to give me a list of chores she wanted me to tend to during the off-season. Right after the Series, Beverly was quoted by reporter, John Trowbridge, as saying: "Oh, there's just so much to do around here. The lawn needs mowing. The garage needs cleaning out. You know when the man of the house is gone for such a long time things do pile up. We're not going to spend that world series money hiring any work around here. Ryne will do the work." So much for the fanfare of being a World Series hero.

This photo captures my trademark sunglasses, and me staring into the plate for a sign, fighting off the glare of the stadium lights. Notice that back then our gloves weren't embroidered with our names. We just used a felt marker to identify our equipment. (Photo source: Personal collection of Ryne Duren, reproduced through the courtesy of the family of Don Wingfield.)

After we beat the Braves in the 1958 World Series, I was given a hero's welcome back in Cazenovia. This photo was taken on October 28, 1958, a special day in my honor, and I was very happy to share that moment with my Mom and Dad. (Photo source: Personal collection of Ryne Duren.)

Thirteen

SEEKING ACCEPTANCE

I was past the point of "having a cup of coffee" in the majors, a term denoting a short stay. I was a full-fledged Major Leaguer, a member of the World Champions, and a World Series hero. But within my mind and heart I was still haunted by the adolescent feeling that most teenagers have, of not being accepted and liked by my peers. That was compounded by the fear I still harbored that I would be a failure, and that fear stayed with me my whole baseball career. The fact that many people thought I had the best "stuff" in baseball wasn't enough to shake it; in fact, that was part of it. I thought that whatever acceptance I felt at that time was directly connected to my ability to pitch, and if I didn't do well, then I was useless as a person. I had the feeling that people only liked me because I was a good baseball player, and once I couldn't throw people wouldn't like me, or if they really knew me like I knew myself they wouldn't like me.

I could throw three fastballs by somebody and amaze Mickey Mantle – he'd come over to my locker and say, "I don't believe what I just saw." And he'd shake his head and go get me a beer, and come back with it and with Whitey and they'd praise me. That was high praise and put me in pretty good company, sharing a post-game brew with Mickey and Whitey. What else did I need to tell my fragile psyche I was accepted as a member of the team, one of the guys? I knew my teammates and managers liked me when I was mowing down the opposition, but I never really felt accepted as a person, and I couldn't get past that.

I thought I was being a conformist, and I would be accepted more by my teammates by conforming to how a ballplayer lived, by drinking and living hard. I wanted to do the right thing and I thought the right thing to do was to be a real drinking man. When Ralph Houk said he'd rather have nine whiskey drinkers than nine milkshake drinkers, I said "Okay. There's my kind of man. I'll be happy to fill the bill." But Ralph didn't want nine alcoholics; he wanted nine men who were macho and tough, like whiskey drinkers were supposed to be according to myth, like the image of Big George.

The odd thing is that even when my teammates were probably trying to help me I interpreted it as rejection. For instance, when Mickey and Whitey suggested, after some incident, that I shouldn't drink, what I heard was, "We don't want you to run with us", because they were going to drink. This happened after a night out in Washington D.C. I got wild in a club where I had been drinking with them and the owner of the club wanted to throw me out. My feeling about that was that Mickey and Whitey just didn't want me hanging around with them and it really stuck in my craw. That winter, up in Dallas, I went out with Mickey one night, drank him drink for drink, and had to carry him home. Instead of taking their words as caution or advice I turned it into a challenge. And when I outdrank him that one night, I felt justified in having been ticked off. I reacted just like a teenager would react: I'll show you who can't drink, and so I got drunk one more night.

When I drank I became that wild Wisconsin teenager again. Back then your teammates didn't send you for counseling or really take an active part in your recovery. The most they might do is try to be humorous about it. They kind of laughed at my silly behavior and when I was sober enough to hear them, they'd shake their heads, say, "Boy, he really got fried." Then, if it was bad, they'd mock me a little bit. They'd say "Ry-hiccup-ne Dur-hiccup-en." Nobody told me I needed help, or suggested any help, they'd only make fun of me. And being sensitive and insecure, and never accepting drinking as a problem, I took that as rejection.

Gil McDougald: *"All the other players could sense that Ryne wasn't going to last long if he didn't overcome his problems with alcohol. When he drank it made his conduct different, and I just knew that the Yankees weren't going to stand for that for too long."*

Years later, when we were both sober, my old teammate Johnny Blanchard told me something very ironic. He said the guys on the team liked me the way I was when I wasn't drinking. What they didn't like was the person I became with a few drinks in me – argumentative, loud, boastful, adolescent. The very thing I was doing to gain acceptance from my teammates is what they found objectionable. I just couldn't get past my pre-conceived, ill-formed, definition of masculinity that included the consumption of alcohol as mandatory. I know now, that a true measure of my manhood would have been the ability to accept that I had a God-given talent and that I used it to become the hardest throwing, most successful, relief pitcher in the major leagues, and I really didn't need alcohol to prove anything or to achieve anything.

Bobby Richardson: *"I remember Ryne's feelings as being very fragile. After he was traded to the Angels, we were playing them with Ryne on the mound and I stole third base when the catcher threw the ball back, easy, to Ryne after a pitch because Ryne was nursing a hangover. The word was that Mantle had to go and drink with Ryne that night to convince him I wasn't in any way trying to show him up."*

Ralph Houk: *"The problem wasn't that Ryne drank, a lot of ballplayers drank. The problem was that when Ryne drank it changed his personality. It was like a Jekyll and Hyde story. Without alcohol, Ryne was a likeable guy with a good sense of humor and an intimidating pitcher. It wasn't so much that the alcohol made him drunk, it just made him a different person."*

Fourteen

1959-60

Going into the 1959 season, the Yankees had every reason to expect to repeat as American League pennant winners. After all, they had finished in first place in nine of the last ten seasons, failing to capture the American League flag only in 1954, and that year it took the Cleveland Indians winning 111 games to top the Yanks. Also, the Yanks came into 1959 as the reigning World Champs and the team was pretty much intact from 1958.

However, as the season progressed, it was evident that this year it would be different for the Bronx Bombers. Bob Turley, who had been 21-7 in 1958, fell to a record of 8-11 in 1959, and Whitey Ford led the team with a 16-10 record, a sub-par year for Whitey. The Yanks learned how much they had depended on Moose Skowron, who broke his arm in 1959, limiting his action to only 74 games. In that abbreviated time, he knocked in 59 runs, and still contributed enough to be an All-Star. Besides costing the Yanks his clutch hitting for half the season, Moose's injury forced Casey to use the less sure-handed Marv Throneberry and catcher Elston Howard at first.

I had come to appreciate the growing importance of Skowron's contributions to the success of the Yankees. Hank Bauer had turned 36 and Yogi turned 34 by the start of the 1959 season. Their ages were increasing and their offensive production was decreasing. Maris wasn't there yet, and with

Skowron out of the lineup, Mantle was the only legitimate power hitter, allowing opposing pitchers to pitch around him. The result was Mickey had only 75 RBIs and that led the team. The surprisingly strong Elston Howard was starting to come in to his own and contributed 73 RBIs, but the Yanks missed the Moose.

Bill Skowron (1930-Present)

First baseman, Third baseman 1954-67 Yankees, Dodgers, Senators, White Sox, Angels

Many people believe that Bill Skowron earned the nickname "Moose" in the baseball world because of his bulk and strength, but the name was started by his grandfather, who kiddingly referred to him as "Mussolini" because of his bulldog determination. It was his family who shortened the name to "Moose" which has stuck ever since. Skowron was an athletic standout at Purdue University, playing shortstop and pitching for the baseball team, and was a kicker and running back for the Boilermakers, when the Yankees signed him at age 19 in 1951. He came up to the Yankees in 1954 and was a steady contributor, being selected as an All-Star six times. Moose was the hitting star in the sixth game of the 1958 World Series, and maybe that's why I always loved him so. In 1963 the Yankees traded Moose to the Dodgers to make way for the upcoming Joe Pepitone. Although Moose didn't have a great regular season with the Dodgers, he went 5 for 13 in the World Series, helping the Dodgers sweep the Yanks. He split the 1964 season between the Senators and his hometown Chicago White Sox, staying with the White Sox until 1967, when he finished his career with the Los Angeles Angels. Moose lives in Chicago now where he does some work for the White Sox. He is a very popular player at card shows and fantasy camps.

On May 26, 1959, the Yanks traded Johnny Kucks, Tom Sturdivant and Jerry Lumpe to Kansas City for Ralph Terry and Hector Lopez. Casey used Lopez mainly to play third base, although he would later be used as an outfielder. With Skowron's injury, the increased age of some players and the mid-season trade, the Yankee infield in 1959 was hardly the picture of stability. The highest number of games played by any one player at the same position was 109 games played at second base by Bobby Richardson, who also played shortstop and third base that year, as did Clete Boyer and Jerry Lumpe. Five or six different players played every infield position. You definitely needed a scorecard to know who was playing where and when. For the Yankees, that was turmoil.

I had pitched through the 1958 season with a problem in my knee that grew worse as the season progressed. As a matter of fact, I pitched in the World Series with my leg wrapped from thigh to shin, what the players called a "Mantle wrap." In the off-season I had it operated on by Dr. Sidney Gaynor, but that didn't really help much. Despite the injury, I continued to pitch very well in 1959. In fact, I lowered my ERA, to 1.88, and struck out 96 batters in 76 innings of work. I led the team in appearances and saves, but together with the rest of the pitching staff, I fell victim to the team's weak offense and its inability to put away the opposition. I pitched more than 31 consecutive innings, over an 18 game span from April 30th to July 16th, 1959, without giving up a run, and, unbelievably, during that same stretch the fabled Bronx Bombers didn't score a run to support me. That was amazing to me. This was the New York Yankees in the late innings.

At the time the Yankees were eliminated from pennant contention, my ERA was 0.69. After the pennant was out of reach, really late in the year, the Yanks either started me or brought me into a game in the early innings, and I pitched way beyond the number of innings I was accustomed to. I got kicked around for a few runs and they just left me in there. I believed it was a bargaining tactic on the part of Yankee General Manager, George Weiss, and the Yankees, and a sort of punishment for losing the pennant. The game was meaningless since we were already eliminated. If my ERA became bloated by otherwise inconsequential runs, it was something they could throw at me when it came time to talk contract. That may sound like paranoia on my part, and maybe it was, but that is how I felt, and sure enough the Yanks reminded me about my ERA at contract time.

In 1959 Major League Baseball instituted a two-game per year All-Star Game format, and I was named to the American League All-Star Team for both games. I got to pitch in the first game, which was held on July 7, 1959 at Forbes Field in Pittsburgh. I pitched three scoreless innings, striking out four batters and allowing only one hit. I was facing Orlando Cepeda, and with a count of 3 balls and 2 strikes I let go of a pitch that was screaming toward Cepeda's body. Orlando managed to get out of the way and took first base. Many years later, a card show promoter asked me to go to the airport to pick up Orlando who was also appearing at the show. It had been a long time since I saw Orlando and I didn't know if he would remember me. That fear was quickly wiped out when Orlando stepped off the plane and upon seeing me bellowed out, "Duren! I ain't never gonna forget you, man!"

The end result of the 1959 season for the Yankees was an unfamiliar third place finish, 15 games behind the White Sox. This would be the lowest a Yankee team would place in the seventeen-year span from 1948 through 1964. And to make matters worse for the New York fans who had been spoiled for so long, the Dodgers, in just their second year in Los Angeles, not only won the National League pennant, but topped the White Sox, to become the World Champion **Los Angeles** Dodgers.

The end result of the 1959 season for me was a broken bone in my wrist. Once we were out of contention we continued to play games, but more emphasis was placed on the games we played after the ball games, and the drinking that went on. Late in the season I was running off the field in a hurry after a game, with my mind on my golf date that afternoon with Mickey. I wasn't looking where I was going and I collided with a fan, fell and broke my wrist. That ended the season and started a miserable off-season. In actuality, that fall may have been the turning point in my Yankee career.

During the late fall of 1959 as I nursed my wrist, alcohol became a bigger problem in my life. My knee was still not 100% and the injury to my wrist had me worried about my ability to still throw as fast. But the cast on my wrist didn't impede my ability to lift a glass. My drinking was obviously an issue at home with Beverly because she was pushing me to read Alcoholics' Anonymous materials and attend meetings. In order to show conformity I attended several meetings but to no

immediate avail. I continued to act like a juvenile. Then came
Christmas Eve.

Despite my stingy ERA, my durability as a reliever, my All-
Star selections and my World Series success, George Weiss,
saw fit to ruin Christmas Eve in 1959, by choosing that day to
deliver my proposed contract for the 1960 season, with a $4,000
cut in salary. Merry Christmas Ryne, love, George Weiss.

George Weiss (1894-1972)
*Baseball Executive, General Manager, President 1932-66
Yankees, Mets*

*Weiss was very successful as a baseball executive, gaining
admittance to the Baseball Hall of Fame in 1971, in recognition
of his many accomplishments, starting with a semi-pro team in
Connecticut while he attended Yale. Yet for all his success on
the field, his players hated him. He was cold and earned a reputation as being a penny-pincher. Weiss had no second thoughts
about sending a player a contract with a cut in salary, as he did
to me in 1959. After all, he tried to cut Mickey Mantle's salary
after Mantle won the Triple Crown in 1956. The players who
almost all worked second jobs during the winters to maintain
their homes and families, had little regard for the wealthy
Weiss, earning him his nickname, Lonesome George.*

The proposed cut to my salary wasn't personal, although
I felt it was at the time. It had to do with the fact that the
Yankees finished third and Weiss' reasoning was if the Yankees
didn't win nobody got a raise. Everybody got cut. It wasn't
just the Yankees who operated that way at that time. The
owners had the clout and they were using it. Hall of Famer
Ralph Kiner gets a big kick out of relating his salary dispute
with Branch Rickey. Kiner led the National League in home
runs, but his Pittsburgh Pirates finished in last place. When
Kiner complained to Rickey about receiving a proposed
contract that included a substantial pay cut, Rickey responded
by telling Kiner, "Take it or leave it. We finished in last place
with you, we can finish in last place without you!" My first
instinct was to rip up the contract Weiss had sent me and walk
away from the Yankees, but instead I called Weiss to discuss it.
Sure enough, he brought up the fact that my ERA went up in

the second half of the season, but beyond that he wouldn't talk with me. The options he left me with were to sign the contract he sent me, or not.

After receiving the contract with the proposed pay cut, I went out of control again. I did nothing but drink and curse my fate, from Christmas Eve until the day I reported to spring training. It was becoming clear to anyone who was actually watching my behavior that my conduct was not a number of isolated incidents, nor just a chain of incidents. It was the progression of the alcoholism.

When I reported to St. Petersburg, for spring training, Weiss' position hadn't softened. He said I could sign the contract or quit if I wanted to. He was an arrogant guy and he was really pushing me. In fact, because I was not signed, the Yankees wouldn't let me into spring training camp. I had to live on my own and I worked out on my own. But this was baseball in 1960, you were still property of the team no matter what, and I was about to find that out.

After I arrived in St. Petersburg, and joined up with my buddies, I drank like I never drank before. Looking back at it now, the spring of 1960, in my mind, was when my liquor consumption and erratic behavior had first escalated to very dangerous levels. I had been on a dangerous collision course for years, and by 1960 the turns were getting trickier and the surface slicker. But facing danger, instead of exercising caution like a reasonable person, I reacted with alcoholic machismo and slammed on the accelerator of life. One night at the hotel, blinded and rendered unreasonable by the alcohol, I started ranting and raving at high volume. Then I started attacking any person that came near me. The first one was the hotel manager who was trying to restore peace and quiet. I tossed him out of my room. When I ran out of people to attack, I started on the furniture. Piece by piece, I tossed it out of the room. When I finished with the furniture I left the hotel and took off for the beach. I hid out there with a woman I had met. Word of my indiscretions reached the Yankee front office and they decided to fine me. Only thing is they couldn't find me to fine me. But when they found me they fined me. (Sure sounds like Yogi.)

At that time, although the Yankees weren't very happy with me, I got along very well with all the writers. Maybe it was because we used to go out drinking together on occasion. I was basically saying good-bye to them, telling them I was going home, leaving the Yankees, when they said, "God, you can't do that." I said, "Well, that man (Weiss) has said that was my contract, take it or leave it. So I'm going home. I can make a better living at home than I can here at that price." Til Ferdenzi, a reporter for the New York Journal American, said, "How much do you want to make?" The Yankees had a gag order that prevented players from revealing their salary to anyone. So I sidestepped the restriction by giving the writers the following proposal: "I'll tell you what. I don't know what the right amount is, but you take the average figure that you guys, all the sportswriters, think I'd ought to make, and whatever it is I'll sign for it. I want to play, but I think Weiss is being absolutely unfair and unjust." Til was very well respected among the sportswriters and would eventually become the President of the Baseball Writers Association of America. He took my suggestion to heart and acted on it. After polling the writers, Til shared with me that the average amount was $17,500. It didn't take long for the number, and how it was arrived at, to circulate throughout the training camp. Just as quickly, Weiss had me ordered into his office. Roy Hamey (the Assistant GM) was the only one that would ever speak to me and he said, "This is the worst thing that any ballplayer's ever done to me. Here's your contract." All I looked at was the amount, which was the $17,500. the sportswriters suggested. Without any concern for Hamey or Weiss' displeasure, I signed the contract. Because of my misadventures at the hotel, and the approach I took to get a contract, I might just as well have been signing my trade papers, undated.

I wasn't the only one in a salary dispute with the Yanks in 1960, nor was I the last one to come to terms. With my deal done, the team still had not yet signed Mantle, Kubek, Andy Carey or Ken Hunt, and Weiss went public with the statement that the holdouts were "ungrateful and unreasonable." The Yanks were looking to cut Mickey's salary by $15,000, and Weiss took the offensive saying, "We're not going to get down on our knees and beg Mantle or any other player to take our money. We're not calling anybody. If they want to talk contract with us, they can come and do it. We're through making overtures." He added Kubek could "shovel snow in Milwaukee the rest of the winter before the club would contact him."

My exploits when drunk were well documented and the fact that Mickey and others drank to excess at times was known to anyone close to the team. But I don't think the general public ever really had full knowledge of the extent to which alcohol was consumed at the major league level back then. I have looked at the team picture of the 1960 Yankees and by my count thirteen of the twenty-five men on the roster were drinking. Whether or not they knew it, they were using enough alcohol so that it had to affect their play, and them physically. By my understanding of the term, they were into "alcohol abuse." Those thirteen are just the ones I knew about, and a number of those guys are gone now. There were others that had very serious problems and died, and I'm starting to think they may have been closet drinkers. You don't know. But you can't point a finger at the Yankees. It was not a one-team problem. On some other teams it may have even been higher. That was throughout baseball.

There were days I played with a pretty bad hangover. But there were two or three guys playing with the same kind of hangover mostly every day, either on the same team or playing against you. So why would I feel guilty, or think I was different or odd? The prevailing feeling was, go out there and air it out and do a hell of a job. You're just that much of a better man if you could perform with a hangover. That was the thinking. Some guys may have actually snuck into the clubhouse during a game to catch a beer or two, but that was not part of my alcoholism. My upbringing was you never drank before work. You drank after work. That was reward for having worked hard, like when I was a fourteen year old kid getting a beer when the day was done. When your work is finished then you can have a couple of beers, or twenty. Like Ralph Houk said, he would reward us with a case of beer, after the game. That was one per man, which was good for starters in the minor leagues, but hardly enough to prime the pump for me in 1960.

The 1960 season brought us Roger Maris and a return to first place and the World Series. After having spent seven or eight weeks of the off-season with my arm in a cast as a result of my fall at the end of the 1959 season, my pitches didn't have the same zip in 1960 that they did in the previous two seasons. I still struck out more than one batter an inning on average, (67 strikeouts in 49 innings) but all of my pitching numbers dropped in 1960, except the one that a pitcher wants to decrease, my ERA, which ballooned to 4.96, more than double what it was in 1959. I appeared in more games in 1960 (42) than I did in 1959 (41), but I pitched 27 fewer innings and walked more batters. By the end of the year I had regained some arm strength and I was throwing the ball much better. Around the middle of September, I was cut around the eye when hit by a ball in the bullpen, and had only pitched a third of an inning in eight days when Casey told me I was starting against the Washington Senators, in Washington, on September 27th. I responded by pitching four strong innings, striking out seven batters, including the first five batters of the game. Starting a game with five consecutive strikeouts was a feat accomplished by only three other pitchers in baseball's modern era, since 1900: Lefty Gomez of the Yanks, in 1937; Walter Johnson of the Senators in 1912; and Dazzy Vance of the old Brooklyn Dodgers in 1926. All three are members of the Hall of Fame - pretty fancy company.

Besides the boost given us by Roger Maris, one main reason the Yankees won the pennant was Whitey Ford. He overcame early season shoulder problems and finished strong. In one four game series with Baltimore late in the season, Whitey won the first game, and then came back on short rest and beat them again. He was simply amazing. Another reason was the mid-season acquisition of Luis Arroyo from Jersey City in the International League. Bobby Shantz and I had been the workhorses of the Yankee bullpen until Arroyo showed up on the scene in July. In his one-half season he compiled a 5-1 record with nine saves, preparing the way for his real emergence in 1961, and my departure from the Yankees.

We came into the 1960 Series as a big favorite over the upstart Pirates, and firmly believed we would be World Champions again. But that was a very strange series, including the dramatic ending, Bill Mazeroski's Series ending home run in the bottom of the ninth inning of Game Seven off Ralph Terry, a moment that is now part of baseball immortality. At times, it seemed like we could score at will, and then there were innings when we just couldn't get the hit we needed when we were up, or the out we needed when we were in the field. The Pirates, on the other hand, made all their runs count. After six games, we had outscored Pittsburgh, 46-17, but only had three victories, and the 1960 World Championship hung in the balance to be decided in a do-or-die Game Seven at Pittsburgh.

It was a very curious Series from the aspect of how it was managed. In retrospect, some of my teammates and I now surmise that Casey Stengel knew the Yankees were going to let him go after the Series, no matter what, because of his age, and because Houk, who was waiting in the wings, was ready. Stengel, who didn't want to go, and always seemed to have a way to make a statement with a wink of an eye, managed the Series his way, as if to say "the hell with the Yankees."

The first curious thing he did was to start Art Ditmar in Game One. Art and Whitey had very similar pitching statistics in 1960, except that Art had won more games.

Here's their records:

	FORD	DITMAR
Age	31	31
Games	33	34
ERA	3.08	3.06
Won	12	15
Lost	9	9
Games Started	29	28
Complete Games	8	8
Innings Pitched	192.2	200.0
Hits	168	195
Home Runs	15	25
Strikeouts	85	65

What you can calculate from those numbers is that having pitched only seven and a third innings less than Ditmar, Ford gave up twenty-seven fewer hits, ten less home runs, and struck out twenty more batters. What those numbers won't tell you is that Whitey was a "money pitcher", the guy you wanted on the mound when the money was on the table, and he was the ace of the staff in the hearts and minds of his teammates. That is to take nothing away from Art Ditmar, but with the assistance of time and history, we can all look back and see that Whitey Ford was something special. His election to the Hall of Fame was not a fluke. To a man, except for Ditmar and Casey, the team felt that Whitey should have started Game One, which would have made him available for Games Four and Seven.

Stengel made other questionable moves, but the ones with the most impact were made in the memorable Game Seven. The Pirates were in a bunting situation in the eighth inning and Casey had Bobby Shantz on the mound, one of the finest fielding pitchers in baseball at the time. He removed Shantz and replaced him with the poor-fielding, slow-footed Jim Coates. The result of that substitution was that the Pirates used Coates' weak points to their advantage. Bob Skinner bunted as expected and moved the runners up, then Roberto Clemente's at bat resulted in a ground ball up the first base line. Coates was slow off the mound while Clemente was fast out of the batter's box, hustling down the line safely to first. That kept the inning alive and Clemente eventually scored. Most people associate our loss that year with Terry giving up the ninth inning home run to Mazeroski, but the Pirates would have never been in that situation if Coates hadn't given up a three run home run to Hal Smith in the eighth inning. After Coates' lack of foot speed cost him the opportunity to get Clemente, his lack of pitching speed made the stands reachable for Smith, while I was ready and champing at the bit in the bullpen. I always regret that they didn't have me in the game because I thought I was a better pitcher at that point than Coates was. Hal was a dead high fastball hitter and he got three swings at high fastballs from Coates, allowing him to time the third one and hit it out. Despite whatever troubles I had earlier in the year, I was pitching well in the Series. I had only given up one run in four innings of work. I knew I could blow three fastballs past Hal Smith, and they wouldn't have been up in the zone where he wanted them, but Casey chose to stay with Jim Coates. His decision may have been influenced by his pitching coach, Ed Lopat, who was a big Coates fan, having coached him in the minor leagues. Whoever made the decision, it wasn't a good one. Not everyone remembers that the Yankees were winning

Game Seven, 7-4, going into the bottom of the eighth inning, and after Pittsburgh scored five times to take the lead, the Yankees came back with 2 runs in the top of the ninth to knot the score at 9-9. Bill Mazeroski led off the bottom of the ninth for Pittsburgh. After Ralph Terry had thrown the first pitch for a ball, Casey went out to the mound to talk things over with him. Whatever words of wisdom Casey imparted are probably just as well forgotten. Before Casey had even returned to the dugout, Mazeroski had reached Terry's next pitch and sent it just over the high ivy-covered wall in leftfield. I was in the visiting bullpen, down the leftfield line at the time, standing next to Whitey Ford. It was sick, I'll tell you that. Whitey said, "Let's go" as soon as he saw the ball hit, and so we ran, heading for the clubhouse. I think I beat Mazeroski to home plate. It was a wild Game Seven and a wild Series. I'll never forget the scene in the clubhouse. Mickey Mantle sat at his locker and openly cried. Losing the Series to the Pirates was not what the Yankees expected of themselves and not something we could easily accept. To my knowledge, it was the first time a World Series ended with a game ending home run, which has now come to be known as a walk-off home run. Game Seven remains as the only game in World Series history without a single strikeout. The competitor in me tells me I would have changed that if I had the chance.

This picture was taken during the 1960 Series in Pittsburgh, but unfortunely it was not Game Seven. I still regret not being given the chance to face Hal Smith in the eighth inning. (Photo source: Personal collection of Ryne Duren.)

Fifteen

PLAYING ON THE SIDE OF THE ANGELS

By the time the 1961 season rolled around there had been plenty of rumors that I was about to become Yankee history. Luis Arroyo's strong performance in 1960 gave the Yanks some leeway. Ralph Houk had taken over as Manager and Beverly's first reaction was that Ralph would trade me, rather than be put in a position of having to constantly deal with my conduct. I removed all doubt by my raucous behavior, starting in spring training.

I started to think maybe it would be a relief to get out of New York, to be away from the Yankees, away from the rumors and everything. I suppose that you would be a little bit crazy not to want to play for the Yankees, but it would get me away from George Weiss and his cutthroat ways and the pressure of playing for the Yankees.

One of the first speeches Ralph gave to the players in spring training included his views on drinking and behavior. Some of the old Ralph Houk from Denver was apparent in that speech, where he said it would be perfectly understandable for a player to drink a beer after a game, or to have a drink at dinner, but the new major league manager Ralph also made an appearance, as he laid down the law about curfews and a prohibition against any player being seen in public drinking hard liquor. It should come as no surprise that the first player to put the new rules to the test was yours truly. Ralph called me into his office in St. Petersburg to tell me he thought my behavior was detrimental to the team and he was going to fine me $250. Starting with the choke sign I gave to the umpire in 1958, the $250 fine was starting to be like my own personal form of annual tithing to the Yankees and Major League Baseball. Ralph told me about it and didn't tell any of the reporters covering the team. When it eventually became known to the press, it quickly took on the look of a cover-up by Houk. That added some unnecessary excitement and grief to Ralph's first major league spring training.

By April 13th, Houk had announced that Bill Stafford would be the short reliever for the Yanks for the season. I had officially lost my position as the "closer." That started the trade rumor mills going and the press had me traded to Baltimore, but that didn't happen.

Besides being a pain to management, I think my drinking had started to alienate me from my teammates. There was an incident on our flight from Minneapolis to Los Angeles that season, where I pinched a stewardess and she responded by throwing wine in my face. That created an uproar, which resulted in the Yankees deciding not to have alcoholic beverages available for the players on commercial flights. A lot of the guys were pretty upset with me about that, so maybe it was time for me to move on.

I got the news of my departure from the Yankees from Ralph himself, on the telephone, while I was dripping wet out of the shower. The Yanks were in Los Angeles, with Kansas City being the next stop on the road trip. The team had given me permission to fly home to San Antonio, to visit with Beverly for a few days because she was seven months pregnant. Ralph called and told me that the Yanks and Angels had cut a deal that would bring Bob Cerv and Tex Clevenger to the Yankees and the Angels wanted me. I accepted it as part of the game, and looked forward to a fresh start in a new town.

The Angels were an expansion team playing their very first season. I went from playing for the most celebrated sports franchise in the World, playing my home games in a sports cathedral, to a brand new team, who played their games in a former minor league park, called Wrigley Field, not the Wrigley Field of my childhood dreams.

Wrigley Field, Los Angeles
1925-1966

Wrigley Field in Los Angeles was opened in 1925, and served as the home to the Pacific Coast League's Los Angeles Angels from 1925 to 1957, and to the Hollywood Stars from 1926 to 1935, plus 1938. It was designed to look like Wrigley Field in Chicago and was named for William Wrigley, who owned both the Chicago Cubs and the PCL Angels. The stadium was only used as a major league park for the 1961 season, and during that year a record 248 home runs were hit there. It was demolished in 1966. Starting in 1962, and through the 1965 season, the Angels shared Dodger Stadium with the Dodgers. At that time it was called Chavez Ravine. In 1966 the Angels moved into Anaheim Stadium, which is now called Edison International Field.

The Angels were owned by one of baseball's greatest owners, Gene Autry, and were managed by Bill Rigney. Rigney had been an infielder with the New York Giants in the late forties and early fifties, and then became the Giants' manager, first in New York and then in San Francisco. In a move paralleling how the expansion Mets would hire former Yankee skipper Casey Stengel, the Angels hired Rigney as their first manager. Rigney was a fun guy who had been around baseball a long time, and was a bit of a hot dog who played under Leo Durocher.

The team was formed by drafting players from each of the other existing teams – players that those teams left "unprotected." So the feeling among the players on an expansion team, at first, is that they were abandoned by their original teams and were now playing with guys they didn't know. It takes a little time to get to know your teammates and for the team to forge an identity. It can be unsettling. Imagine being told at work one day that you now work for a new company three thousand miles away, your twenty-four fellow workers come from eight other companies around the country, and you will all be working together under a new boss none of you know. Between guys at the end of their career and others who were untested rookies, we managed to win 70 games (a record for an expansion team) and we finished ahead of the Kansas City Athletics and the expansion Washington Senators, who both won only 61 games. Consider that one year later, the New York Mets played their first season and won only 40 games.

I was named to the 1961 American League All-Star team along with fellow Angel pitcher, Ken McBride. Honestly, I think I was picked because of my history with the Yankees as a relief ace, rather than for my half a season with the Angels. And I guess they were short on pitchers, so McBride, our number one starter went with me, although he didn't have a winning record that season either. I'm not too sure about this, but I think there was a requirement that each club had to be represented with players on the All-Star team, and maybe that's how come we made it. To be honest though, I still had a good fastball. I was still striking out more than one batter an inning, on average, and every so often I showed glimpses of my 1958 and 1959 form. In fact, twice that season I got my name in the record books for my pitching. In a game against the White Sox, on May 16, 1961, thanks to my catcher, Del Rice, letting a third strike get by him, allowing the batter to reach first base, I tied a major league record by striking out four batters in one inning. Then, against the Red Sox at Fenway Park in Boston, on June 9, 1961, I set an American League record by striking out seven consecutive batters. I struck out Frank Malzone to end the first inning and then struck out the side in the second and third innings. Carl Yastrzemski broke the streak by grounding out to start the fourth inning.

J.C. Martin
J.C. enjoyed a fourteen-year career in the majors, with the White Sox, Mets and Cubs. He first faced me in 1959, his first full season.

"I remember facing Ryne Duren for the first time. It was 1961 at Old Wrigley Field in Anaheim. I was playing for the Chicago White Sox and Ryne was playing for the Angels. It was at the end of his career, having been traded to the Angels from the Yankees. One of the veterans on our team told me Ryne was

washed up and had lost a lot off his fastball, which was his best pitch, and I could look for something good to hit. I went to the plate with that thought. The first pitch passed me with a sound like the cover was ripping off the ball. I asked the umpire to check the ball, and to my amazement he checked it and said it was fine. I saw two more pitches and returned to the bench having struck out, as did three other guys that same inning."

Chuck Schilling
Chuck was the starting second baseman for the Boston Red Sox in the early sixties. As a rookie, in 1961, Chuck played in 158 games. After baseball, Chuck had a distinguished career as a teacher. He was a fine ballplayer, and was, and is, a fine gentleman.

"*Like any New York baseball fan, I had heard and read all the stories about Ryne and watched him many times on TV pitching for the Yankees. He threw hard, didn't always know where the pitch was going, and batters certainly didn't lean over the plate or dig in against Ryne. By the time I was in my first year with the Red Sox in 1961, Ryne was pitching for the expansion LA Angels. I had the 'privilege' of batting against him a few times. Of course, by that time he had lost a little 'smoke' off his fast ball, but he was still intimidating, and I got to see first-hand what everybody was talking about. I was the victim for the sixth of the seven consecutive strikeouts Ryne recorded against the Red Sox in 1961.*"

I also had a hitting highlight that season, probably the only one of my career. The Yankees came to Los Angeles in June, after they traded me out there, and Rigney had me start against them on a hunch. I was anxious about it, and in anticipation of the game I envisioned how I would pitch the whole game to my former teammates.

Bobby Richardson: "*When Ryne was traded we didn't think it was a laughing matter. We now had to bat against him eventually, and we knew about his drinking.*"

In baseball they say you always pitch three games: the one you want to pitch, the one you pitch and the one you wished you pitched. On this day all three came together for the first six innings. I had pitched my game and held the vaunted 1961 Yanks to only one run so far. Unfortunately, we hadn't scored at all so they were beating me 1-0 in the bottom of the sixth inning with two out, when it was my turn to bat. We had the bases loaded and Rigney let me hit. If there had been one out he would have pinch hit for me. In fact, Earl Averill, Jr., was already swinging a bat in the on-deck circle for me but had not yet been announced. But when we made the second out of the inning, Rigney decided to let me hit, since I was pitching so well. He was also aware of my desire to beat the Yankees, and he allowed himself and me the luxury of following his hunch. My reward was I got to face "Bullet" Bob Turley. Turley got two quick strikes on me. I swung at the first one, and the second one I took because I thought it was outside. Then Turley makes a motion that tells me, for sure, he's going to throw another fastball. And he did - high out of the strike zone, not real high, just high. My bat was choked up and I whacked at that pitch - drove it right back past him. He couldn't get down quick enough, and the ball got by him, just missed Kubek and rolled into centerfield. We were ahead 2-1 and those fans would not sit down. It was my first hit in three years! Albie Pearson followed me with a home run and we went on to win, 5-3. Rigney always said it was the greatest call he ever made. I think of all my incidents in the major leagues I truly remember the details of that particular game and moment more than anything else. Ralph Houk always said that Turley was never the same after that. Joe King of the World-Telegram called it "the greatest game in a 'greatest' town in the brief history of the Angels, for an uproarious crowd of 14,674."

I was a notoriously bad hitter. By the time my career ended, I had spent all or part of nine seasons in the big leagues. Over that period, I managed to get only 7 hits (six singles and one double) in 114 at bats, striking out 66 times. During my time with the Yankees, which spanned a little over three seasons, I got one hit, in my rookie year, and I never scored a run as a Yankee! I walked nine times in my career, and don't ask me how, but I managed to score eight runs and bat in five. Most of that offense came in 1963 when I batted a career high .143, with three hits and one walk and scored four times. After getting the hit off of Turley, my lifetime batting average soared from .034 to .050 (3 hits in 60 at bats). By the time I retired my career batting average was .061.

Don Ferrarese: *"Ryne was a great pitcher but a terrible batter. In 1958, while I was pitching for the Cleveland Indians, Ryne came up to bat against me in the top of the ninth inning. We were winning 3-2, the bases were loaded and the count went to 3 balls and 2 strikes. I was pretty tired from having pitched the whole game, but I just could not risk walking him. I threw a slow to medium speed fastball right down the middle of the plate and Ryne watched it for strike three to end the game. Later that night I teased him about how come he let that lollipop of a pitch go. Ryne told me, 'Casey Stengel had the take sign on. He was afraid I was going to swing at a bad pitch.' When the manager gives you a take sign with two out, the bases loaded and a 3-2 count, you know you're a bad hitter."*

Beverly was due to deliver our second child and the Angels gave me some time off, allowing me to be there when our second son, Craig Duren, was born just before the 1961 All-Star Game. I remember I was there for the birth and I remember I was drunk when I first saw Craig in the maternity ward. That stands out in my mind, because the nurses at the hospital made a big deal about my condition. Craig was born prematurely, by Caesarian section, and he and Beverly had to stay in the hospital a few days until the baby was strong enough to go home and Beverly recovered from surgery. I left them in San Antonio and rejoined the team.

About a week or so later, McBride and I traveled to San Francisco for the All-Star game. I was sitting in a bar having a few drinks when Whitey Ford ran in. He told me Hal Hudson had called the hotel looking for me and I needed to call home. Hal was an old friend from San Antonio, who also came up through the Browns minor league system. He had a cup of coffee in the big leagues, or at least made Spring Training, so he knew Whitey. When I called, I learned my infant son had died. He was only ten or twelve days old. At the time I thought the cause of death was related to a breathing problem caused by his premature birth. I think now that it was Sudden Death

Syndrome, where he just couldn't breathe anymore, but you didn't hear that condition referred to by that name back then.

I left San Francisco and flew back to San Antonio and although I was chosen for the 1961 All-Star team I actually wasn't there for the game. But that was the last thing on my mind. It was pretty devastating losing an infant child, but I handled it like I handled everything then – I drank heavily. I immediately blamed myself for Craig's death. To my way of thinking, my drinking had produced an unhealthy child. Look how far I had fallen, from the proud stock of one of Cazenovia's fine pioneer families, to being incapable of siring a healthy child. And even as I cursed alcohol for having taken Craig from me, I sought solace in it, from the pain of his loss. The heavy drinking led to some heavy fighting with Beverly.

The loss of Craig, the drinking, the fighting with Beverly, the cross-country trade, all of it got to be too much. I was really feeling beat and tired. Before the season was over, I was placed in Inglewood Hospital in California. Officially, they diagnosed me with walking pneumonia. I thought it was just exhaustion from all that happened, taking its toll on my body whose resistance had been lowered by the constant beating I gave it with alcohol and nightlife. It was during that hospital stay I noticed one big difference between the Yankees and the Angels. One day I looked up from my hospital bed and there at the foot of the bed was Gene and Ina Autry, who came to visit me. Leonard Firestone, of the Firestone Tire family, one of the major investors in the Angels, was also among the several Angels personnel who came to visit me. Hell, I was in the hospital in New York for a week or better, when I had my knee operated on, and George Weiss was the only one who stopped in on me and he came to see me once. And I think that's because he heard somebody cut me and he wanted to make sure the cut was substantial.

Being so close to Hollywood, we were a natural attraction for movie and television stars. Maybe it was because Mr. Autry was in the entertainment business before owning the Angels, but it seemed like there were always actors and actresses at the ballpark and stopping in to the clubhouse. The players were all giddy about the Hollywood crowd, and the funny thing is they were asking us for autographs. I knew that playing in

Los Angeles, for a brand new team, would be fun and a lot less tense than playing for Mr. Weiss and the Yankees, but I had no idea just how much partying went on in California. Legend has it that I came back to my room one night after partying in Palm Springs all night and called the front desk of the hotel requesting a 7:15 a.m. wake-up call. The clerk sheepishly told me it was too late for that. It was already 7:17 a.m.

Drinking and pool parties were big in California, and that can be a dangerous combination. One time in 1962, I was having a great time poolside, at Ernie's House of Serfas, consuming drink after drink, when I sustained one of my blackout episodes. I have no memory whatsoever of entering the pool, but I have a vivid recollection of waking up with my face against the pool floor. I believe it was my hitting bottom that woke me up in time to save my life. I would not come to realize the prophetic nature of that metaphoric event for several years. That night I squished my way into the bar and ordered another drink.

Steve Duren: *"In 1962, Dad didn't make the All-Star team, so he had some time to spend with me during the break. I remember the Angels, the Boston Red Sox and the Los Angeles Rams chartered this big boat to go fishing for tuna out in the Pacific. As my birthday present, Dad took me along, and I was the only kid that got to go on this two-day trip. We headed out in the afternoon and around dark the guys started drinking in earnest and then they started playing cards. As the night wore on, they got louder and more raucous. Sometime after midnight they spilled out of the cabin and discovered the live anchovy bait. They proceeded to chase each other around the deck with the bait between their teeth, and then started throwing the bait at each other. In retrospect, it was like watching one of those movies like Animal House, but these were the guys that America adored and wanted their sons to emulate. By morning a lot of the guys were not only hung over, but were seasick and gracing the decks with last night's libations and, I suspect, some of our tuna bait sushi to boot."*

Rigney set a record for the number of pitchers he used in 1962, and he just about wore me out. Although the Yanks used me, almost exclusively, as a relief pitcher, Rigney used me, and the rest of the staff, whenever he could. I saved a lot of games, but I started games too. On Memorial Day, Teddy Bowsfield was scheduled to pitch the second game of a doubleheader against Boston. I had been out on the town the night before with my roommate, Art Fowler. Besides sharing a room, we shared a habit of drinking way too much. Between games, I was in the clubhouse, enjoying this really great spread the clubhouse guy had put out. I'm in there really packing away everything in sight, and in walks Rigney. Bowsfield couldn't make it because his arm was killing him. Rigney looked around and announced, "I've gotta have a pitcher. Bowsy can't make it. Who's the volunteer?" Then he looked right at me and said, "I just got one." So here I am, loaded with food, a liverwurst sandwich and then some, being asked to start against the Red Sox. Rigney countered my hesitancy with a bellowing "You can do it." My pre-game preparation consisted of going into the bathroom and forcing myself to throw up everything I just ate. Then I went out there and I shut them out for four innings, and we had a decent lead. At that point, four innings was a long outing for me. So, I went to Rigney and told him, "You better get somebody else out there." I'll be darned if Art Fowler didn't go out there for five innings and shut them down. The Red Sox got a total of two hits off us. Here's a manager who didn't have a pitcher at game time and his team ended up winning a two hit shutout.

Fowler and I teamed up more off the field than on it. Art and I were roommates and that spelled disaster, because we were both partying and drinking a lot more than anybody should. It was pretty well known by all the guys and by Rigney. I clearly remember one day we played a doubleheader and the second game went into extra innings, making for a very long day. Rigney yelled out, "Just hold 'em 'til midnight boys, because we got a couple of guys who can really get going about then." He was referring to Fowler and me, complimenting us on our relief work, but also digging us about our nightlife. We were having fun, drinking and carousing, but that's because we were acting like teenagers, not responsible adults. We would waste our free time playing juvenile games and drinking. The fun ended one night when after several hours of partying, Art started swinging a knife at me. He accused me of moving in on a girl he was trying to pick up. That was an example of what alcohol will do to your mind. We were roomies and friends, trusted each other with everything, but blinded by alcohol he was willing to cut me up over a girl he had just met and neither of us would ever see again.

Ted 'Bowsie' Bowsfield

Ted was my teammate with the Angels in 1961 and '62. He was a left-handed pitcher who spent a total of seven years in the majors. He was with Boston and Cleveland before Los Angeles, and finished with the Athletics

"Ryne Duren was a wonderful teammate, and could he throw a baseball."

Jerry Casale

Jerry was also my teammate with the Angels, being there most of the 1961 season. One thing we shared in common is that we spent too much time in the minor leagues. One thing different about us was that Jerry could hit. Jerry hit three home runs in his rookie year. Today he owns Pino's Restaurant in New York City. The food is terrific.

"When I was on the Angels with Ryne, he had a bar set up in his room in every city on the road, and I wondered how the heck he ever could pitch the next day, but he did, and he did it well."

Lee Thomas: "It was fun being Ryne's teammate because you never knew what to expect next."

One other story about Rigney. In 1962, we shared the Dodgers' Electra, a private plane, which they really had fixed up quite nicely. There were berths you could actually lay down and go to sleep in, and up front there was a compartment with four seats facing each other where you could play cards. There would be a hearts game on one side, where I was playing and Rigney and the coaches were playing bridge on the other side. It was Sunday night and we were leaving one town heading to another and there wasn't any booze on the plane. So, Rigney's sitting there looking around the plane and he said, "Anybody got anything to drink, any booze around or anything?" Then he

looked my way and repeated, "Anybody got anything to drink?"
Now my eyes hit his and he hollered to the clubhouse man
"Bring me bag number 30." which was my bag. Sure enough, I
had a fifth of whiskey in there. He knew he could count on old
Rhino to have stock. I never got paid for it. I know that.

Sixteen

GOING NATIONAL

When I reported to the Angels' Spring Training camp in Palm Springs, California, in 1963, I had been sober for about six weeks. I had renewed an annual New Year's resolution to stop drinking and had been successful in sticking to it for the rest of the off-season. While I was at home in San Antonio, with Beverly watching me closely, I was fine. Reporting to camp and seeing my teammates was the first real test of my determination. My first night in camp, I sat down at the bar at the Riviera Hotel with Bud Furillo, a sportswriter with the Los Angeles Herald Examiner, and I surprised him when I ordered a soda. After I told Bud I had been "off the sauce" since the first of the year, he responded by betting me twenty dollars I would break down before the Fourth of July. I accepted the challenge, thinking a lot more than twenty dollars was already at stake if I lost. I was trying, desperately, to hold on to my career, my marriage and my life.

After two weeks of workouts we were in Scottsdale for the opening game of spring training against Boston, I believe, and I was named as the starting pitcher. I was in the clubhouse getting my arm stretched and getting rubbed down a little bit, and Rigney came in. He said, "Ryne, I feel terrible about this, but we just sold you." I said, "Well, yeah, I'm sure, that's how come I'm starting today." That's when he told me, "No, you're not going to start. Grba's gonna start. We just sold you to

Philadelphia." And he wasn't kidding. I had been sold to the Philadelphia Phillies for $20,000. Say Goodbye to Hollywood, hello National League.

Eli Grba (1934 – Present)
Right-handed Pitcher 1959-63 Yankees, Angels
Eli Grba and I were teammates on the Yankees during the 1959 and 1960 seasons. When the Angels were created by means of the expansion draft in 1961, Grba was the first player selected by the Angels. Although Grba got that spring training start instead of me with the Angels in 1963, he didn't stay with the team much longer. He appeared in only 12 games for the Angels in 1963, and that was the end of his short career. Both of us came from the Yanks to the Angels, both of us wore glasses, both of us were right-handed pitchers and both of us tended to have control problems (Grba walked more batters in his career [284] than he struck out [255].) That caused sufficient confusion about our identities, but then we became linked together for history, when Topps Baseball Cards mistakenly put my picture on the front of Grba's 1963 card, creating a collectors' item. Last time I checked, it was selling for over $230.

Leaving the Angels was a very difficult thing to do. Unlike the feeling of relief I sensed upon leaving the Yankees, this trade left me feeling empty and sad. Being part of the Angels was the most fun I had ever had as a ballplayer. I was proud of what we had accomplished as an expansion franchise, and more importantly, I was very comfortable with the Autrys and the rest of the Angels family. Now, I was facing new umpires, new hitters, new teammates and a new city. I immediately began to experience anxiety about what was going to happen, and I was fearful that it would sabotage my uneducated, but well-meaning, attempt to stop drinking.

The manager of the Phillies was Gene Mauch, my old buddy who had spoiled my no-hitter bid. Mauch kept you in the game. I liked that, and I liked Gene. When he talked to you he challenged you a little. He would say things like, "Be thinking down here. I can't think of everything. I've gotta say yes or no, but come and tell me what you think." And he was the only manager that I know who did that. We finished in fourth place in 1963, with a record of 87-75. The team showed steady improvement under Mauch during the 1962 and 1963 seasons, and would battle for the National League pennant in 1964, before their now famous collapse during the last two weeks of the season.

I think one of my best baseball stories came about with the Phillies. Mauch had some good young arms on that club, Chris Short (21), Ray Culp (25) and Art Mahaffey (25), and on the other hand, at 34 I wasn't the oldest guy. He had Cal McLish who was 37 and Johnny Klippstein who was 35. He also had Jack Hamilton on the pitching staff. Jack and I were similar in a lot of ways: he also threw hard, and a little bit on the wild side. Mauch wasn't starting me and he certainly wasn't using me as much as Rigney did in California. I had made a real effort to lay off the booze in 1963 and I didn't want a bad season to become a good excuse to start drinking. While our team was taking batting practice out on the field, I went into Mauch's office one day, wanting to not die down in the bullpen. I said:

"Gene, you've been in the game a long time, so I need to ask you a question. How important on a good ball club, from a defensive standpoint, is good pitching? What part of the game?"

"I suppose it would be anywhere from 60 to 85%, depending on your staff."

"I've heard that from other people. Now, can you tell me then, why it is ever since I've been in this game I come to the park everyday and we have maybe up to three hours of batting practice every day - at least an hour and a half, and I have never been on a ball club yet, anywhere, that ever had any pitching practice, although we consider it the most important part of the game?"

"What do you mean, Ryne?"

"Well, I'm talking about pitching practice. We have batting practice so the hitters can get their timing, do we ever have pitching practice so the pitchers can see if they can offset the hitters' timing and work on their stuff?"

"Well, it's a great idea, Ryne, maybe, but who the hell would hit at you?"

"I don't know, but let's just go ask them."

When the Phillies surrendered the field to the visiting team for batting practice, Gene addressed the team, "Guys we're gonna have a meeting here, a quick meeting. Duren came up with an idea, and well, here, Ryne, you tell them what you said." So I went through it with them and I finished by challenging them with, "Now Gene tells me that none of you chicken-livered so and sos would want to hit at us. You don't care about us pitchers. We can die down in the bullpen" or something like that. I put it on them pretty heavy. Roy Sievers jumped up, I'll always give him credit for that, and he said "I'll hit at you, you four-eyed SOB, I'm not afraid of you." Roy was a rookie with the St. Louis Browns when I was drafted by them in 1949, and he knew me a long time. So the challenge was on, and that led to a lot of fun in the clubhouse, pitchers bragging to hitters and vice-versa. It was announced that the next day we would have a mock game (or maybe it was a Mauch game), Jack Hamilton against Ryne Duren. Mauch was behind the cage calling where the runners are, and the balls and strikes. It was fun. I beat Hamilton 1-0 in a five-inning game. I went on from there to go 7-2. I think if it wasn't for that chance to show myself, my career might have ended that year. I got my first start of the year on June 28th, and got a win, striking out eight Reds in six innings.

Despite my decent showing on the mound, I managed to find my way back to alcohol. I thought all I needed was willpower. I was ignorant as to the hold alcohol had established on my mind and body, and unaware of what it would take to finally break free of that. At dinner one night with my teammate, Don Hoak, and his wife, I followed their drink order with one of my own, without consciously thinking I was ending my sobriety effort. I had made it to the Fourth of July, but my personal bid for independence, from alcohol, was over. I had won my bet with Bud Furillo, but I was about to lose so much more.

Frank Torre
Frank was a left-handed first baseman, who hit .309 in the 1958 season, helping the Milwaukee Braves get to the World Series. Later on, in 1963, we were on the Phillies together.

"I was Ryne's teammate on the Phillies in 1963. He was a wonderful person as long as he was sober. He was starting to

have a real problem with drinking later in the season. He got very mean when he got drunk. Being a bachelor, I lived alone and Ryne knew I always had liquor at my apartment. One night, after hours, I wouldn't let him in to get a drink and he broke the door down to get in. It cost me $200 to get it fixed. The next day he was like a big kid telling me he was sorry."

I was spared being part of the famous 1964 Phillie collapse because in May 1964 I was traded to the Cincinnati Reds. Even though I was successful in 1963 with the Phillies, I had been throwing more and more off-speed pitches. I thought that the National League strike zone favored a finesse pitcher, and that I could use the slow stuff to set up my fastball. But Mauch and the Phillies bought me as a fastball, "power" pitcher and that's what they wanted to see. When I didn't meet expectations they shipped me over to Cincinnati where I was reunited with my old friend Fred Hutchinson as the manager.

When I got to Cincinnati, it was a different Fred Hutchinson from the one I knew in Seattle. Freddy was dying of cancer right in front us and that was a hard thing to watch. I think I learned a hell of a lesson from him about dignity, and not complaining about the situation that God has dealt you. If I didn't get the lesson straight from Freddy, God repeated it for me with Beverly as the teacher. Freddy would tell us, "This is what I like to do and this is what I do and so I'm going to continue to come out to the ballpark as long as I can." We would ask, "Are you uncomfortable, Freddy?" "No, it's just that my butt is so thin now that it hurts me to sit." He had an extra pillow under him, but he went from 220 pounds, and I imagine that by the time he didn't come to the ballpark anymore, which was fairly late in the season, he was probably down to between 135-140 pounds. He was just such a great guy, who had so much dignity and courage. Freddy died just about a month after the 1964 season ended. Every year the Fred Hutchinson Cancer Research Center in Seattle presents The Hutch Award in Fred's honor and memory to a player who displays "honor, courage and dedication to baseball while overcoming adversity in their personal or professional lives." It is a very fitting memorial to a fine man.

I suffered a recurrence of the pain in my pitching elbow in 1964, and saw limited use. I had good control, still striking out about a batter an inning, but I pitched less than 44 innings for the Reds. What I did a lot of was partying and drinking, both with the team and on my own. Cincinnati was a rowdy team and I allowed that to be a trigger for me, rationalizing that if all the other guys were drinking and carrying on then that was the way for me to behave. I remember some pool parties that turned into near riots, and one flight in particular where we were so out of hand that Delta Airlines refused to carry us from then on. The biggest fiasco was the Reds' management's decision to use our day off before a series with the Mets as a promotional event by having all of us visit the World's Fair, which was in Flushing that year, right near Shea Stadium. They wanted us to leave Philadelphia at seven in the morning after a Sunday night game. We were so ticked off at the loss of our day off, and the thought of having to get up and on a bus so early that as a team we decided to stay up and drink all night. The drinking continued on the bus and at the World's Fair. I don't remember much about the World's Fair, but whoever visited the Fair that day saw a one-day exhibition of world-class drunken behavior. Another night during a card game in my hotel room, in Pittsburgh, I dumped a pitcher of beer on Deron Johnson, Joe Nuxhall and Marty Keogh, causing them to chase me around the room and to then hold me outside the window upside-down by my ankles. We were sixteen stories high, no matter how you interpret that. One careless slip and they could have written my obituary that night, and it would have been a fitting end, considering my conduct to date.

That was the type of behavior that was driving Beverly away from me. Steve was now fifteen years old, older than I was when I started drinking. I was too immersed in the alcohol in 1964 to remember how much I looked up to my father and how much I patterned my behavior after what seemed important to him. What kind of role model I must have been for Steve. In actuality, Beverly had two teenagers on her hands – only she had no control over me, especially when I was out drinking and carrying on with the "guys." Beverly so hated how I acted in that setting that in 1964 she stopped coming to the ballpark. It was also about this time that I experienced one of the most upsetting episodes of my life as Steve's father. I was trying to watch him run in a junior high track meet and the coach came over to where I was and told me, "It's so upsetting to your son for you to be here. Would you please get out of the stadium so I can let Steve know that you're not here?" I wanted to be accepted by everyone, especially my peers, but my very presence was unacceptable to my son, and I believe that was because he was afraid of how I might behave, causing him embarrassment, because I was so unpredictable.

Jim Maloney
Jim made it to the major leagues, with the Cincinnati Reds, at the age of 19, in 1960. He was also a hard thrower, timed at 99.5 mph in 1965. During his career he won 134 games, with a winning percentage of .615. He threw three no-hitters, losing one in the 11th inning, and five one-hitters. In 1963, he topped me by striking out eight consecutive batters. Jim stills lives in Fresno and has done some terrific work helping people with recovering from alcoholism.

"I first met Ryne in 1964 when we were teammates in Cincinnati. I had remembered him as a star relief pitcher for the Yankees when I was a teenager in Fresno. One of the first times I went out with Ryne after a game, he got drunk and ended up in a fight in Philadelphia. I realized then Ryne was having problems off the field dealing with alcohol. I remember telling myself I was never going to be like that. As it turned out, after I retired from baseball in 1972 I had major problems with alcohol myself. I wasn't prepared for life after baseball."

The Reds had won the National League pennant in 1961 and still had some decent talent on that club, including very good pitchers like Jim Maloney, Jim O'Toole and Bob Purkey. They certainly had a couple of intense competitors in Frank Robinson and Pete Rose. Robinson was the team's offensive leader. He batted .306 with 96 runs batted in and 29 home runs. Rose was still very young and not yet accomplished, but you could already sense his intensity. From the standpoint of competing and desire, he came to the ballpark to beat you and to win. We kind of pooh-poohed his hustle but that remained through his career, and took him much further than one would have thought he would have gone based on just natural ability.

Like Philadelphia, Cincinnati came close to winning the pennant in 1964 before losing to the St. Louis Cardinals. We didn't collapse as drastically as the Phillies did at the end of that season, but we did blow the opportunity to win the pennant, which we thought we had in our hands. Toward the end of the season we won ten games in a row. I'll never forget coming home to Cincinnati in first place as a result of that streak. It was a Sunday night and approximately 10,000 people greeted us at the airport. The reason it sticks out in my mind is that when we could have used the hometown support was on Tuesday in a critical game against Pittsburgh. Unfortunately, less people were at the ballpark than were at the airport. We lost a 1-0 heartbreaker to the Pirates in 16 innings.

I was with three teams in the spring of 1965, because, truthfully, nobody could put up with my shenanigans. For a guy who so wholeheartedly wanted to be accepted, I was unacceptable to just about everyone, including my wife. I started out the spring of 1965 with the Reds in Tampa, Florida, but after a couple of alcohol-related incidents, including knocking down Pete Rose's hotel door and being arrested by the Tampa Police for drunken driving, the Reds gave me my outright release. In other words, they couldn't trade me to anyone for any value and they just wanted to be rid of me as soon as possible. That left me on my own to try and hook up with another team. Even I figured that my ability wouldn't get me a job, so I turned to an old friend, and called Gene Mauch who was still managing the Phillies. Gene told me to give him some time to work something out and he did, bringing me to the Phillies at the end of spring training. He told me all he needed from me was to throw the fastball the way I did in 1963 and he would be happy. The only problem was that the fastball I threw for Gene in 1963 was the result of my not drinking for several months that year. I was now living kind of fast and loose, but my arm was anything but that. Two years of the progression of alcoholism left me a much different person and player than I was in 1963. That was compounded by the fact that between my release by the Reds and being picked up by the Phils all I did was drink, angry that I had been released and apprehensive about whether or not I would be picked up. It was quickly obvious to Gene that I would be of no use to the Phillies, and I was released after pitching 11 innings in 6 appearances, giving up 10 hits and striking out only 6 batters. I looked around for a team to pick me up and was very lucky to get an offer from George Selkirk, General Manager of the Washington Senators, and on June 8, 1965 I signed a one-year contract for $15,000.

When I was with the Yankees a popular saying was "Washington, first in war, first in peace, and last in the American League." That saying had been around since it was first made popular by Charley Dryden, sports editor of the San Francisco Chronicle. The Washington Senators' penchant for losing was even memorialized in a novel: *The Year the Yankees Lost the Pennant*, which was later turned into the hit musical, *Damn Yankees*, in which a fan sells his soul to the devil in return for becoming a Washington Senator and winning the pennant. That history of losing was written about the original Washington Senators franchise that left Washington and moved to Minnesota to become the Twins. A new Washington Senators team came into existence at the same time the Angels were born, in 1961. The move to Minneapolis did wonders for the old Senators. Behind the pitching of Jim "Mudcat" Grant, Jim Kaat, Jim Perry and Camilo Pascual and the hitting of Harmon Killebrew, Earl Battey and Tony Oliva, the Twins won the pennant in 1965. Meanwhile, the new Senators took on the role of perennial loser, and we finished eighth in a ten-team league in 1965.

Well, the team finished eighth. I didn't finish the season at all. The only thing I finished in 1965 was my career. My pitching, if you will pardon my use of the term, was horrendous. I appeared in a total of sixteen games, pitching 23 innings and walking as many batters (18) as I struck out. I was at the end. Alcohol had taken its toll. From the time I got to the Senators I knew that I just didn't have it anymore, but I refused to quit the game because I had no other life. No family life to speak of, no other trade, no formal education. I was scared that without a baseball in my hand I was really nothing, and that my life would be over. The team trainer tried to resurrect my arm with medications. I would get shots in my arm from the trainer, but they didn't help. Neither did I, because I was adding additional shots, the kind the bartender poured, and they only helped to the extent they dulled my senses, but they certainly didn't help me pitch any better.

My manager that year was another baseball legend, Gil Hodges. I just thought he was fantastic, a fantastic guy and a fantastic manager, but because of who I was at that time, I really didn't get much of a chance to know him. I dealt with Gil on the basis of the less I had to see him or be close to him the better I felt, because I was ashamed of who I was and I didn't want to get any discipline. That is truly one of the great losses of my life, having lost the chance to enjoy a relationship with one of the great guys of the game. Chalk up one more thing I lost to the alcohol.

I put poor Gil through hell in 1965. One time he came into a hotel room where the maid thought I was dead. I was lying on the floor and she had called the hotel manager who called Gil. So he came to the room and woke me up. He got me off the floor and said "What are you doing down here?" and in that drunken bravado way of mine at the time, I said, "Well, I figured if I was here on the floor I couldn't fall anymore."

Shortly after that I subjected Gil, the Senators and myself to a very embarrassing goodbye to my professional baseball career. I was in the bullpen, nursing a bad hangover and a cold by taking Excedrins all afternoon. The bullpen phone is what woke me from my sleep. I warmed up, but I was wild even by my standards. I had nothing on the ball. I hit two batters and walked one and then gave up a long double to Mantle. I faced a total of four batters without retiring one. Mercifully, Gil took me out of the game. I remember staying in the clubhouse until the game finished, downing several beers in an effort not to face the fact that my career was over. I also remember after the game was over I headed to the Windsor Park Hotel, where I switched from beer to vodka martinis. I remember feeling the booze was the only thing I had control over anymore, or so I thought. I had nothing left but my drink: no marriage, no fastball, and no career. I don't really remember leaving the hotel and climbing the nearest bridge, threatening to jump and end it all, but that is what everyone tells me happened. I do remember a police car pulling up and Gil Hodges getting out to talk me down from the bridge. Gil told me I was too good a person to kill myself and I needed to get help. That was the end of my baseball career, and my first attempt at killing myself. Not counting all the craziness that happened while I was a teenager, alcohol had already put me in three life-threatening situations: the bottom of the pool in Los Angeles, dangling from a hotel terrace in Cincinnati, and the top of a bridge in Washington. Unbeknownst to me, the worst was yet to come.

Seventeen

GAME OVER

I may have been on the top of a bridge in 1965 according to witnesses, but looking back at my life I was actually approaching the bottom. I was washed up as far as baseball was concerned. The Senators released me on August 20, 1965. The guys that didn't know me also didn't owe me any favors and my talent was no longer strong enough to get me a job on my own. The guys who were my friends knew me too well, and couldn't risk their careers and futures in the game on a known drunk.

I was really panicky and knew I was faced with a serious problem. It wasn't that baseball was over. I knew that. Two years before, in '63, I was still making pretty good headlines pitching for Philadelphia, beating some quality teams. I was still a decent pitcher at that time and, not coincidentally, that was the last time I made a serious attempt at curbing my drinking that met with any success at all. But the two years between '63 and '65 were a precipitous decline for me. The baseball player portion of my life was gone.

I was much more concerned at that time with the fact I couldn't find a job, and I couldn't stay sober. That's what was going on. Nobody wanted me. I had no formal education and no trade. I was totally unprepared for a career after baseball. Worse yet, I knew the drinking and my reputation were keeping me from getting any kind of a job, even as an unskilled laborer. Every moment I was sober, every lucid interval I had, was consumed with the thought that I was unwanted, unacceptable and unemployed.

The only time I didn't feel the pressure of the situation was when I was drinking. The alcohol brought me false comfort. That is the point in an alcoholic's life when the downward spiral starts to tighten and the descent is accelerated. I was no longer drinking to be social or to be accepted or cool. I was now drinking to be numb, to purposely deaden my body and mind's natural reaction to the terrible situation I was in. Once I consumed a sufficient amount of alcohol I didn't feel nervous or anxious and I wasn't worried about money, or where my next meal would come from. But being drunk also prevented me from working to solve the situation, so the trip down the pit of despair quickened progressively.

In November of 1965, while at home in San Antonio, I drank enough alcohol to numb me into a subconscious state, while I had been smoking lying in bed. The result was a blaze that almost brought down my house, and did bring down my marriage. The fire eventually went out on both the house and the marriage. Beverly had it. She took Steve and made good on her oft-repeated promise to leave me. Alcohol had finally cost me Beverly, and Steve.

Steve Duren: *"It was the fall of 1965 and after a brief period of sobriety, Dad was back to his drinking ways. It was the middle of the night and I was dreaming about a fire, but when I woke up I looked out of my bedroom window across the backyard and saw real flames rising out of a window in the other wing of the house. About that time, I heard Mom scream and I hurriedly put on some jeans and jumped out of the bedroom window. I ran around to the front of the house and saw Mom with a garden hose making a futile attempt to put out the flames while Dad lay sprawled out on the lawn on his back, looking on in an alcoholic stupor. To my knowledge, that was the last night we spent together as a 'family' under the same roof, and I remembered thinking, with relief, that this was the end of the line for Dad in our lives. Mom filed for divorce soon after and Dad would eventually move to Wisconsin. I remembered thinking that I might never see him again (and at that time, I didn't care)."*

Add "no home" and "no family" now to my already sad list of "no job", "no education", "no baseball", and "no career" and it was starting to equal "no future – no hope." All of that placed an unbearable burden of guilt on me, to compound the anxiety, doubt and fears that were already constantly swirling inside my body, gnawing at my very existence. I became the San Antonio town drunk. I was like Otis Campbell, the eternal town drunk, from the Andy Griffith Show, only I wasn't funny, at all. I basically lived out of my car and drank, and too often I mixed the two, leading to situations where I was behind the wheel with the car moving and I was drunk. It led to at least one accident, and to a second suicide attempt. The San Antonio police found me sitting in my car with a six-pack of beer, parked across the railroad tracks. Luckily for me, although I didn't think so at the time, the police came by before the next train and they got me off the tracks.

Beverly made sure I could not get to her or to Steve, by obtaining a "peace bond" which is the equivalent of an order of protection. She also made sure I could not get to any money we might have had in the bank, whatever little was left. She got to the bank before I did and closed out our accounts. I moved into a smelly, small, skid row flophouse. It was all I could afford. I struggled with finding the way in a life I didn't know how to live, and was unsuccessful in trying to end, at least twice already. Over a four-year period, starting in 1961, I had made several attempts at kicking the alcohol habit during the off-seasons, at Starlight Village, a drying-out clinic in Comfort, Texas, run by Dr. Roundtree. My success at Starlight Village, if any, was short-lived. The only good to come of it was my relationship with a doctor who himself was a patient there, trying to kick his addiction to Demerol. Somehow, I found that doctor's number and gave him a call. After we spoke for a while, he sensed the depth of my despair and agreed to have me committed at the Texas State Mental Hospital in San Antonio. To those in the American public who didn't know my life had been on a steady decline for years, the sudden change in five months, from a $20,000 a year major league pitcher to third assistant pot scrubber in a mental institution, was dramatic and shocking.

Upon my admittance to the mental hospital, a psychiatrist who was an old Army colonel evaluated me. He took a look at my history and classified me as "anxiety reactionary," which is the classification you received if you weren't a chronic patient at the Hospital, with a history of alcoholism. He didn't know I was already tissue addicted. Because of my classification, I never got out of the receiving ward, although I did go to the alcohol ward for meetings and so forth. All in all, I was pretty sane without the booze and yet it belied how sick I really was, as I found out later.

But what an experience it was to be thrown into that ward. Hard as it may be to imagine, life inside that hospital was more horrible than life at a skid row motel. If you saw *One Flew Over the Cuckoo's Nest*, you have an idea of what I experienced. That movie was set in 1963 and was representative of the conditions that existed in mental institutions about the time I was there. The movie added a comic twist for purposes of entertainment, but there was nothing comic about really being there. Everybody sat in that one area and the nurses and doctors were up there observing you all the time. They treated everyone as if they were insane and medicated everyone, even though our conditions varied greatly. For the most part, all the nurses and doctors did in that ward was observe and make notes.

There were some very sick people coming in to that Hospital. It didn't take long for us as patients to figure out who the alcoholics were and who were the patients with psychiatric problems like dementia or schizophrenia. The guys with the "drinking problems" sobered up after a while, and without the alcohol in our systems we were acting pretty sane. The patients with other conditions continued to act out their psychosis, and some of them did that in some very disturbing, threatening ways. In a matter of a relatively short period of time, the ward was split, with the alcoholics on one side and the other mental patients on the other. God, there were some experiences in there I'll never forget. The patients who were talking to themselves, or carrying on a conversation in two totally different voices were the least offensive. You wouldn't believe how sick these people were and what I saw – catatonic states, and feces, and urine, the screaming and the hollering, it was something else I'm telling you! It was just a nightmarish existence.

Steve Duren: "I remember visiting Dad in the state hospital when he was a patient. This was his second time to go in for a thirty-day treatment program. The first time was when he was still playing ball and it was a fancy retreat type place up in the hill country north of San Antonio, lots of professional people, doctors, catholic priests, etc. This time, it was the dregs of society with the smell of urine and feces and psychotic people screaming into the night. Here was my father ... the idol of baseball fans across the country who six years ago was the star reliever for the greatest team in baseball, reduced to a destitute patient in a mental hospital. The funny thing was that even though I was embarrassed and humiliated by my Dad's present condition, I noticed that he seemed to be truly grappling with who he was and what had brought him to this state. His humility and openness gave me hope that he might actually be capable of change."

They were giving me a drug called Serax. It was one of several new anti-anxiety tranquilizers that were coming out then. It was the drug most widely prescribed to alcoholics to fight depression and the other symptoms of acute alcohol withdrawal. What it did was nullify my response to anything. I didn't feel up and I didn't feel down, I just kind of was there. And to a person who obviously had a lot of ups and downs in his life, I didn't like the feeling of not being able to feel good or bad, or anything. I realized my lack of any feeling, and I began to refuse the medication, which was eventually stopped.

Serax
Generic Name: oxazepam
Serax is used in the treatment of anxiety disorders, including anxiety associated with depression. It is most often prescribed for anxiety, tension, agitation, and irritability in older people and to relieve symptoms of acute alcohol withdrawal. It belongs to a class of drugs known as benzodiazepines. It can be habit-forming or addicting. The most common side effect is drowsiness. Other side effects can include: Clumsiness or un- steadiness; dizziness or lightheadedness; slurred speech; blood disorders, change in sex drive, excitement, fainting, headache, hives, liver problems, loss or lack of muscle control, nausea,

skin rashes or eruptions, sluggishness or unresponsiveness,
slurred speech, swelling due to fluid retention, tremors, and
vertigo.

I was not given any shock treatment, I guess because I didn't
appear dangerous to myself or to the staff or other patients.
Once I sobered up, and without any alcohol within sight or
reaching distance, I was in markedly better mental and physical
condition than most of the other patients. In fact, after a while,
I was allowed to attend meetings and educational sessions
at the alcoholics' ward, in exchange for performing chores.
Some of the chores consisted of innocuous stuff like bringing
basketballs and other recreational equipment around to other
wards, but they also had me assist them in bringing some of the
other patients for their shock therapy. That was not a pleasant
job. Most of the patients needed to first be sedated and then the
medical staff had to make sure the patients didn't swallow their
tongues during the shock therapy. Many of them instinctively
reacted by defecating or urinating right on the gurney during the
treatment.

During my visits to the alcoholics' ward and lectures, I
met an old fellow over there by the name of Jack S. Jack
was a good old guy, steeped in the traditions of Alcoholics'
Anonymous. He spoke and lectured on it. After the patients
had attended his lectures for a period of time he gave them an
exam. I achieved a score of 100, and Jack claimed I was the
smartest guy that ever went through his lecture series. It really
didn't mean a thing, other than that I understood his theory of
alcoholism. The real test was life outside the walls of Texas
State Mental Hospital, life that I was released to again after an
82-day stay there. Despite my perfect mark on Jack's exam, I
eventually failed the real test after a short period of time.

After the stay in the mental hospital, I surrendered one of
the life insurance policies I had previously purchased. That
netted me $500 which I used as my seed money for a little gas
station in San Antonio. Based on my having gone through the
Mental Hospital experience, and being seemingly responsible
enough to start my own small business, Beverly said she would
try to work with me, if I thought her presence would be helpful.
The gas station was a very time-demanding thing and after

about four months I threw in the towel, or I should say the oil rag, on that one. Then I sold cars for a couple of months. All in all, I had been sober for about eleven months when I was asked to appear in Houston at an Old Timers' Game. I don't know if it was the anticipation of being in uniform again, or the overwhelming fear of that whole other life again, or just what, but I could feel all the old familiar ingredients starting to mix up inside of me again. First "doubt" raised it's voice about whether I should go to Houston, then "anxiety" spoke up about being in those surroundings again, and "fear" chimed in about facing the guys as a tee-totaller. The next thing I knew I was sitting in the local bar ordering a beer, just like I had never missed a beat. Old Jack's test could have just as well been a coaster that day for all I cared. I was back in the high life again. I headed out for Houston with a six-pack of beer in the car and I made sure I also had enough with me so I could drink on the return trip. That old addict's mind was working again. As long as nobody was in the car with me, and nobody saw me drinking, I could rationalize that I didn't drink - so much for the 82 days in the hospital. It's as if it only served as a period to dry out the sponge that had become my system, and now I could fill it all up again. One visit back to baseball and my mind equated it with drinking again.

Eighteen

ALCOHOLICS ANONYMOUS

In the fall of 1959, while I was still with the Yankees, but after the season was over, I went to my first Alcoholics Anonymous (AA) meetings. That was an attempt to bring some measure of peace to my household, and to give the appearance of making an effort to deal with my drinking. Beverly was increasingly upset by the extent of my drinking and by who I became when I drank. She knew I drank as an adolescent; we all did back in Cazenovia. It was an ignorant rite of passage to try to drink "adult" drinks. It made us feel like men. I think it is fair to say that Beverly expected that I would mature psychologically as I aged physically, and that I would deal with alcohol on a more mature basis. But I didn't. If anything, the drinking and my activities based on the drinking, got worse. The amount of the drinking increased during my stay with the Yankees. In hindsight, I believe that my success at the major league level in 1958 and 1959, despite the extent to which my teammates and I were drinking, fooled me into believing it was okay to drink that way, and that it was not having an adverse effect on me.

The direct conversations between Beverly and I about my drinking usually led to arguments, which usually led to more drinking. So, Beverly, to her credit, tried to find a better way to reach me. She obtained a book and some other materials about AA and placed them in the house during the fall of 1959, in a place where she was sure I would find them. When I discovered them I realized Beverly must have felt there was a very serious problem if she was trying to get me to read those materials. My first overt reaction was to tell her I didn't need the literature and I wasn't going to read it. But behind her back I picked up the book and read a few stories. What I found a little scary was I could see myself revealed in the stories told by those alcoholics. The descriptions of the emotions the various drinkers experienced were familiar to me and that made me uneasy.

One morning, in a hungover state resulting from a drinking binge, I was depressed and remorseful, which is a cycle all addicts go through. We eventually give in to our desire, then binge on our addiction, seemingly enjoying it and deriving comfort from it. Then, realizing how the addiction controlled us again, we are depressed, and that expresses itself as anger or sadness. In that remorseful state, I was talking with Beverly, once again seeking answers to my addiction. She suggested that I call the local chapter of AA, talk to some members and find out more about it. I called and a few local AA members came to the house and took me to my first meeting in San Antonio.

My very first experience at an AA meeting was an embarrassing one. Despite having read the materials, I really didn't know what to fully expect at the meeting. One thing I was hoping for was that it would be "anonymous" as advertised in the title. I was apprehensive about how the image-conscious Yankees would deal with the fact that their star reliever was attending AA meetings. As I entered my first meeting I noticed that an old drinking buddy of mine from my days in the Texas League was at the meeting. I hadn't seen him for quite some time and I was hoping that he wouldn't recognize me until after the meeting. However, as soon as I walked into the meeting and he saw me he revealed my identity to the group by saying, "Here you are, Duren. We've been waiting for you."

I continued to attend meetings for a while, but I began to feel I was going for the wrong reasons. I was going to show that I was conforming to my expected behavior, and in response to pressure from Beverly. I did enjoy the social aspect of the meetings, but I was aware I was not attending those meetings for the purpose intended by AA or by Beverly, because, being honest, I had no real intentions to stop drinking. I did when I was remorseful that morning. I did when I first went to the meetings, but the desire to quit waned, and once I got back out among my old teammates at spring training, the need to fit in and belong was a hell of a lot stronger than any desire I had to quit drinking.

Drinking was one thing, but admitting I was an alcoholic was quite another. So, although my Yankee teammates and Yankee management knew I drank, I had no intention of giving them the opportunity to label me a self-confessed alcoholic by being "caught" at an AA meeting. At least that was the rationalization I used to not attend any AA meetings in New York while I was with the Yankees. Prior to the fall of 1961 I was not attending any AA meetings, anywhere, on a regular basis, but between the '61 and '62 seasons I did attend several AA meetings, and I resumed attending in 1963 in Palm Springs, while I was in spring training with the Angels. That off-season between 1962 and 1963 I made a serious and successful, albeit temporary, attempt to stop drinking, and I attended the AA meetings in an effort to pick up any possible momentum I had created by my several "dry" spells during the winter. I wasn't happy about getting traded from the Angels and after the trade I didn't attend any more AA meetings during spring training, telling myself I would start again when I got to Philadelphia. In fact, I was able to make it through July of 1963 without any drinking or adverse behavior caused by my drinking. I kept trying to sober up, but life, the baseball life, my need to belong and that whole programming about being a drinking man first, was too overwhelming. When I was out to dinner with Don Hoak and I ordered that drink, it was as if somebody had thrown a switch. Immediately, I was back in trouble again. I was the sickest of the sick. I needed to stay alive long enough until treatment programs got good enough to help someone as sick as me. Going to the AA meetings fulfilled that need. After I had truly hit bottom and became serious about my recovery, after 1968, more than nine years after Beverly first introduced AA into my vocabulary and consciousness, AA's principles and approach became more meaningful to me.

I think AA serves a purpose and has a role in the fight against alcohol abuse. There is a period of time when an addict is trying to recover from the addiction that he or she needs an enormous amount of emotional support and encouragement. The recovery can only be accomplished if the addict is resolved to do it, but the addict cannot do it alone. The feeling of being alone is one strongly associated with the addiction itself. For the recovery period to be successful the addict needs to feel that he or she has the support and encouragement of the important people in his or her life. I think that in that sense, the AA meetings serve as a bridge to normalcy, and need to be seen that way by the recovering addict, rather than as a place where he or she is condemned to be.

If your only social outlet is going to AA all the time, I think then alcohol probably still has control of your life. My feeling about it is that most people, after they are sober for two to five years, can venture out and be part of the "real world", and the drinking by others around them doesn't bother them enough to draw them back. However, most of us who have recovered, or are on top of the program, don't like to be around drunkenness. We abhor it in a sense and I think that was one of the self-loathing things that we were doing when we were drinking, and that was also part of our denial. We would deny that we were as bad as we were, simply because you couldn't tolerate that. Maybe the blackout is nature's way of keeping the addict from knowing the worst – how low can you go? Many times I'd said to guys, "Where did we go last night?" or "Did I get in any trouble?" Blackouts were amazing. You couldn't predict them and you couldn't predict nor remember your behavior.

Once you understand the principles of AA, you can have your own meetings without any formality. Meeting a friend for breakfast or lunch can serve the same purpose as an AA meeting, as long as there is honest give and take, without any pretensions. The baseball world, (and my life at that time, I can't blame it all on baseball), and the business world, for that matter, are all pretty pretentious. There is a lot of one-upsmanship, and name-dropping and all of that kind of stuff – to influence someone, to gain an upper hand or a favor or to enhance the bottom line. Well, in the world of recovery that stuff is a luxury. There's no doubt about that. What the recovering alcoholic is limited to, in order to recover, is truth, straight and simple. That is what he or she needs from their support group, formal (AA meetings) or informal.

I believe that AA is extremely useful and can be helpful for an alcoholic trying to get back to normalcy. In fact, I will go so far as to say any recovery program is actually based on the twelve-step approach of AA, as was the Hazelden model I followed. You have to admit that there's a problem; you have to admit that you can't do anything about it by yourself, and you have to subscribe to some type of program for help. Those are the first three steps. Then you have to apply some type of format for the program – the rest of the steps are that. So, the twelve steps are designed for recovery and you might well be working an AA philosophy and never make a formal AA meeting. So, the AA meeting and the AA philosophy aren't both the same thing.

As a society, we have become a little numb to the terms "alcoholic" and "alcohol abuser", but as soon as you mention AA it gets everyone's attention. I'm reminded about the fellow who tells his friend, "I just came from a funeral."

"Is that right, who died?"

"My uncle. He died from alcoholism."

"Well, did he ever try AA?"

"Hell, he wasn't that bad."

That's kind of the way we look at it.

Bill Wilson (Bill W.)
1895-1971

Bill Wilson was the co-founder of Alcoholics Anonymous. He was a World War I veteran (Second Lieutenant) who became very successful on Wall Street and was then left penniless after the market crash of 1929. Like many other alcoholics, Wilson couldn't trace the exact start of his alcoholism. It could have been when he first started drinking during the war, or when he drank to celebrate his success on Wall Street, or ease the depression caused by the market crash. Wilson was hospitalized on four separate occasions for his drinking, despite his repeated promises to his wife, Lois, that he would stop. It was during his last hospital stay, at Manhattan's Towns Hospital, in 1934, that Wilson claimed to have seen a very bright light, a flash that he interpreted as a "spiritual awakening." Though his first attempts at reforming other alcoholics were not successful, he came upon the basic formula for Alcoholics Anonymous, the company and support of other alcoholics, while on a business trip in Ohio. Seeking company to avoid the temptation to drink again, Wilson called local churches in Akron until he located Dr. Bob Smith, an alcoholic. Smith, originally reluctant to talk to Wilson, agreed to meet for a short time. The two spoke for hours, and feeling relief in the company of each other agreed to meet the next day. From their meetings, and from Wilson's earlier experiences with the Oxford Group, an evangelical society utilizing religion to fight alcoholism, Alcoholics Anonymous was formed. In the spirit of anonymity, which is a cornerstone of the organization, Wilson would start early meetings of the group by saying, "My name is Bill W. and I am an alcoholic." At the time of Wilson's death in 1971, there were known to be over 75,000 chapters of Alcoholics Anonymous meeting around the world. Wilson's wife, Lois Burnham Wilson, founded Al-anon in 1951 for families of alcoholics.

Nineteen

TRYING TO END THE PAIN

Alcoholics, in our mind, always start out with the idea that we know what we did wrong last night and we're not going to do that again when we're out drinking tonight. I'm not going to drink the whiskey, I'm just going to drink the beer, or I'll tell you what, I'm going to stay away from whiskey and I'll just drink brandy, or maybe I'll eat a little bit before I drink, lay a good foundation and that will stop me from getting drunk. We always rationalize that we can handle it or that we're going to be able to control it. But it always comes back to the same sad truth: we can't control it.

Facing that realization, that feeling of being out of control, leads to a deep despair. When you start each day, knowing down deep that by the end of the day you will have given in to the alcohol again, you just don't want to face another day. From the bottom of that "pit of despair" there is no sign of brightness whatsoever, no sign of hope, no lifeline to cling to. And it's not just that you are in a cavernous pit, it's a pit inhabited by every fear you can imagine, accompanied by every feeling that gives you that empty sense in your gut. The fears and feelings occupy you, permeate you, and dominate you. Their effect is heightened by your sense of being alone. You sense that no one else knows how trapped you are, and what's worse is if they do know, they certainly don't care.

And you must remember that because of the constant use of alcohol your maturity has been suspended. Therefore, you are facing all of these horrendous feelings through the mind of an adolescent. Remember how, as a teenager, whatever problem you had seemed to be of epic proportions. Things that you could, and do, handle in stride as an adult, were seen as "the end of the world" as a teenager, and you would seek refuge by locking yourself in your room and screaming in anguish. The despondency of that pit of despair I have described is that when you seek refuge instead of being locked in the sanctuary of your room you are in a fathomless unknown area, with none of the pleasant surroundings there to comfort you, no recognizable method to reach out to others to share your fears and feelings. The lights won't work, and every time you turn on the radio or television everyone is talking about your problem and how terrible it is, without offering solutions.

Finally, following the cycle every alcoholic follows drives you to the point of insanity. Feeling no escape from the fears and feelings, you seek numbness, which is provided by the alcohol. After having consumed the alcohol and achieved a temporary respite from the anguish, you eventually return to full consciousness and there staring you right in the face are all of the horrors that you originally sought refuge from, and now you are two feet deeper in the pit, where new, darker, previously unimaginable horrors are revealed to you.   You not only resign yourself to death, you seek it out as a permanent relief from the agony, despair and pain. It's a terrible, terrible place to be. Unless you've been there I would say that it is very difficult to imagine.

It has often been said that whatever doesn't kill you builds character. What I can say about that is there is an enormous strength that comes from having survived that "pit of despair." Once you have survived that, you know you are equal to all of life's challenges after that, as long as you stay sober. Your mettle has already been tested. With that comes the strength. No matter what you've gone through in life and how difficult, something positive can be taken from it, but you have to live through it and resolve it before it can become positive. Sure, all of that stuff is a positive thing for me today, but I'd hate to have to go through it again. I don't believe I would survive it, and I sure have no desire to try.

Twenty

BACK FROM THE BRINK - DePAUL

I crawled into DePaul Hospital because I couldn't succeed at killing myself. I came perilously close, but, ultimately, having a drink was more important. My ex-boss at International Harvester, who loved me, and who probably had a drinking problem himself, came by to check in on me after my accident with the company car and after my last failed suicide attempt. As I related earlier, he was the one who drove me to DePaul Hospital, because it was obvious, even to us as drinkers, that my condition had gotten beyond control.

I'll remember my first day at DePaul as long as I live. DePaul Hospital was different than any other place I had ever gone for help or treatment. In fact, you could say I had never really been in treatment before, compared to what I experienced at DePaul. Their staff was very organized in their approach and their treatment of addicts. They followed the Hazelden treatment program. Hazelden was founded in 1949 and was one of the first facilities in the United States dedicated solely to the treatment of chemical dependency. They are known worldwide for having developed the Minnesota Model, which used the 12 Steps of AA as its basis. The Minnesota Model differs from other programs in that it is a multi-disciplinary approach -- using physical, emotional, spiritual and social assessments -- to treat chemical dependency.

DePaul is where I met Father Dave Kelly, and he made the one statement that was the key for my getting well: "Gentlemen, we have a simple problem: we're drug addicts, just as surely as if we're hooked on heroin." I can hear him and see him saying it, still. I was a drug addict and didn't realize it until Father Kelly said it. I had been calling myself alcoholic for years, but I didn't fully understand it. I went to Alcoholics' Anonymous. I must be an alcoholic. I'd get up and say "My name is Ryne, and I'm an alcoholic." I never said I'm a drug addict and I never knew that alcohol was a drug. Maybe I heard it in passing, but I never heard anybody emphasize it like Father Kelly did and then explain why we were drug addicts. He is the person that led me to understand that alcohol is a drug and I was addicted to it, just as anybody would have become addicted to it had they bought into the drinking profile like I had, rather than allowing me to continue to believe there was something wrong with me as a person because I couldn't drink. The words "alcoholism" and "alcoholic" were so stigmatized that saying them and concentrating on my status as an alcoholic were not helpful to me. Based on what Father Kelly told me I no longer had to say I was alcoholic. When I got into really seeing myself as a drug addict and seeing alcohol as a drug, I could see the whole thing much more clearly. When you see alcohol as a drug and the drug effect that it has, you understand it better, you just simply do. It also allows you to see that the progression of the addiction and the results of using alcohol are no different than if it were any other drug. Once I could conceptually classify alcohol as a drug, I more readily understood the damage it caused me and why I should avoid it, because as a young person I had made a decision not to get involved with drugs. I knew drugs robbed you of your masculinity, but I saw drinking alcohol as macho. I knew drugs kept you from being strong, but I considered the men who could drink the most and still do a day's work as the strongest of the strong. When I swore off drugs I was thinking of things like tranquilizers, and uppers. I even made a decision not to take aspirin because I had heard they could be addicting. But until Father Kelly made his statement, I never considered alcohol a drug.

The physical part of the detoxification at DePaul was not the difficult part for me. Usually the first seventy-two hours of a detox period are critical. That is the stage where the majority of addicts suffer the most from withdrawal symptoms. The most common reactions of the addicted body to not getting the substance it craves are convulsions, which can be life threatening, and incredible nausea, which is less dangerous but painful and unpleasant nonetheless. I believe that Librium is still the best withdrawal drug and has been quite useful in saving lives that would have otherwise been lost during detox periods. Librium is the drug they administered to me at DePaul and it helped me tremendously in lessening the physical symptoms of withdrawal. It was the mental part of dealing with the alcohol and everything that went with it that I found most difficult.

Librium
Generic Name: chlordiazepoxide
Librium is used in the treatment of anxiety disorders, and is also prescribed for short-term relief of the symptoms of withdrawal in acute alcoholism. Like Serax, it belongs to a class of drugs known as benzodiazepines. Librium is habit-forming and you can become dependent on it. Although Librium is used to diminish the effects of alcohol withdrawal, you can experience withdrawal symptoms if you stop taking Librium abruptly. The most common side effect is drowsiness. Other side effects can include: Confusion, constipation, fainting, liver problems, lack of muscle coordination, nausea, skin rash, swelling due to fluid retention, and change in sex drive.

At DePaul I was dealing with a host of deep emotions, mostly anger, hostility and defiance, and if I had to pick the overriding feeling it was anger. I was angry at life, because I couldn't live in it. I couldn't get along in life. I knew I harbored hostility because I wanted to strike out at people, and on occasion I did. I think the defiance was a manifestation of the fact that I was still mentally a teenager rebelling against authority and the establishment. Rebellion and defiance are odd kinds of emotions. The people observing those emotions see them as rebellion and defiance. To the teenager they are independence and expression. Some teenagers rebelled with tattoos, some by running away from home, some with rock music. Today some teenagers rebel with body piercing. For me it was always about the alcohol and some crazy conduct I did in its wake: playing trombone on the neighbors' roof at midnight, throwing furniture and people out of hotel rooms, driving at crazy speeds, or getting into fights just for the fun of it. All of those things I continued to do were really adolescent acts. Usually, as you mature out of adolescence, you clean up your acts and move on and everyone can deal with it. But when your adolescence lasts twenty or thirty years your whole life becomes kind of vague and complicated because of the chaos you've created. Everything that lies in your wake becomes a mess.

The staff at DePaul helped me to see that alcohol had become everything to me, like it does to all addicts. It became a panacea. I also learned that alcoholism was a progressive illness. As I read about the illness and learned about the different parts of the progression, I felt practically all of it applied to me. I learned that when I had used alcohol to make things easier when I asked a girl out for the first time, it really made things tougher because it trapped me in the adolescence and I never did learn to deal with the social fears without the alcohol. I was doing things, like asking for the date and going on the date, but the alcohol was doing it for me.

DePaul is where I learned that the prefrontal lobes of your brain are the very first things affected by alcohol and that's where the fine-tuning of your social senses occurs. The alcohol precludes your brain from being able to grasp and sense a situation. It disables your social senses and your conscience, so you act in ways that are not socially acceptable because you are unable to discern what is appropriate. The alcohol places you in a mental state equivalent to the little kid that just blurts out what's on his mind at the time, whether it is tactful or not. As portrayed by Jim Carrey in *Liar Liar*, good social sense does not always allow you to just say what's on your mind without avoiding hurt feelings and possible social disaster.

At DePaul, part of the treatment was group therapy and it was very effective. I believe the reason it worked is that it was really a crash course in adolescence. I was interacting with a lot of other people who told me how they felt, and who gave me feedback on how I felt and what I said. A non-alcoholic teenager grasps the concepts of "who I am" and "where I belong and fit in", over a three or four year period in their late teens and a lot of that is accomplished by the teen figuring it out from the feedback of his peers, and calculating by himself or herself how he or she measures up against the people in the group. The alcoholic going through group therapy compresses that learning into a much shorter period, probably a month for every year of alcoholism.

But, just because you stay away from alcohol doesn't mean that you are going to get that done. It means only that all your senses are available to you now. Without the group therapy, you won't be working on that and other people don't know and understand what you're going through at that time. You're 40 years old and you're still 16 in your senses, and you don't know where you belong or where you fit in. Some guys were able to go to AA and finally get that. They got up in front of people and said, "My name is Ryne, I'm an alcoholic" and then started talking about how they felt and sensed things, but many people would go to AA for a year before they'd even venture that. So, group therapy in itself is a short cut through that, especially if you have professional people working with the meaningful other people in your life telling them where you are and what's going on. It bridges the gap for those people who are important in your life but who aren't part of the group therapy per se. During my stay at DePaul was the first time, in any of the treatment that I was subjected to, the AA philosophy was present, and it was enhanced by the professional staff who knew something about it and how to use it to help us.

Although reaching out to the addict's family and circle of friends and work acquaintances was part of the treatment program followed by the hospital, my family wasn't involved with my rehabilitation at DePaul. They didn't want to get involved. Nobody. They said "Oh, we've been this route with him for years." They were very negative about any chance I might have at rehabilitation. And truth be told, if they were going to be negative, it was best that they were out of the way at that particular time. My treatment at DePaul was successful, despite the absence of my family, when measured by several standards: I survived the physical detoxification without serious problems; I was sober from being abstinent from alcohol for thirty days; I came to realize who I was and that just because I suffered from alcoholism I wasn't a bad person, surely not one that should be purposely drowned, or thrown off a bridge, or run over by a train. Most significantly, I had learned what Father Kelly taught me about alcohol and about being an addict.

When my stay at DePaul was completed, work remained to be done. The group therapy was to be continued on an outpatient basis, and I had to address my re-introduction into society. Also, because of the lack of participation by my family at DePaul, I would have to go back to them with two goals: one was to show them who I really was now and how I had gotten on top of my addiction, and the second was to get their support. Both goals were important and the competitor in me wanted to attain them. Although I would come to realize that I would have to survive with or without their support, just as I would have to survive without alcohol, I was still a little insecure upon leaving DePaul and would have loved the support of my family. It took me two or three years in order to develop enough strength to go back to them. I wouldn't go near my family without a fellow alcoholic or somebody else with me. I didn't dare go around the family for fear that I would hear from them how I embarrassed the family and they would question "what the hell was wrong" with me. I knew if I went back to them and said alcohol was a drug, they'd say, "Oh, we've heard all this hogwash before. Who needs this? We really don't need you to come back here and preach to us about our drinking. Look at yourself." That would have driven me to anger, which would have probably driven me back to drink. Until I could summon the strength to go to my parents and siblings, I visited with my Aunt Marion and Uncle Rudy and looked to them for family support. They knew about alcoholism because Rudy had lost his brother to it and Marian had lost three brothers to it.

I spent thirty days as a patient at DePaul Hospital, before the doctors felt I was strong enough to continue my treatment as an outpatient. Thirty days of treatment, delivered in the thorough and organized manner as DePaul did, can be a sufficient starter period to get an addict on the right course, provided the treatment continues on an outpatient basis, and further provided the addict's surroundings during the outpatient treatment are not working at cross-purposes with the treatment.

When I was just about finished at DePaul, the Head of Rehabilitation and my outpatient director, decided that a good place for me to work during my outpatient treatment would be at a boys' school. They arranged an interview for me with Fred Burrow who was the Superintendent at Norris Foundation School, which was about 20 miles southwest of Milwaukee. When Burrow interviewed me he knew I was coming from treatment at DePaul Hospital. Everything was on the table. I remember telling him, "They tell me you can tolerate the truth about my past, but if I drink I'm gone. I know that. But the other thing is I want to be able to come in to you at any time and speak my mind to you." That second part was still a touch of the adolescent in me, letting the authority figure know I had a voice and I would use it. That was the introduction to the next phase of my life, and a very, very important phase it would be.

Twenty-One

THE NORRIS FOUNDATION

The Norris Foundation School for Boys was an old establishment dedicated to educating and reforming boys with various problems, from having committed petty crimes to abusing alcohol and other drugs. Today, children in those situations would be called "PINS", Persons In Need of Supervision. Back then we had a less politically correct name, Juvenile Delinquents.

Anywhere from seventy to eighty boys attended Norris, and they were housed there as well. So, when I assumed the position of Relief Leader, it was truly a full-time job, which required me to sleep on campus also. They had a spare dormitory that was only used for guests or in case of an overflow in student population, and that became my home while at Norris. Actually the room and board they provided was a big help, because the pay was only $275 a month, but I was very happy to be making that with my less than exemplary track record.

As the Relief Leader, I was really a combination of Den Mother, Father, Coach, Counselor, and Dormitory Monitor for these delinquent boys. I don't know if it was because of my age, almost 40 by then, my status as a former player, or my German stoicism, but people saw strength in me. I didn't feel it myself at first, but they saw it. As a result, they assigned some pretty tough kids to me, confident that I could deal with them. The Foundation's sense of me was better than my own. The kids loved me and I felt very comfortable in my work there. It may have been the sobriety which I was starting to sense for the first time as an adult, but I experienced a sense of belonging finally. I was being accepted as a person, something I had longed for. I was at Norris for four years and I lived on campus the whole time. Eventually I became the Supervisor of Counselors and Director of Projects and Activities at Norris.

The Norris Foundation was exactly what a recovering alcoholic needed, a controlled environment with supportive people around who knew and understood what my needs were. During my first two years there, I stayed in group therapy as follow-up treatment, which was a mandatory part of the DePaul program.

Working at Norris gave me an opportunity to work on several different areas of my life that now needed to be developed to compensate for all the years I had put my development as a person on hold, for the sake of my development as a baseball player. I found it to be very helpful for me that at the Foundation we were dealing with juvenile delinquents and the problems and issues inherent in the adolescent process. I was thirty-nine when I first started working at Norris, but when we had staff meetings to discuss how to handle the teenagers, the emotions they were feeling and the developmental stages they were going through, I could very easily see how everything we discussed applied to me.

I also had to learn some fiscal responsibility as part of my maturation process. Whatever money I had made as a ballplayer was gone. Most of the money I drank before it ever made it home to Beverly. She couldn't work because she had to raise Steven, and there was a good period of time when they ate oatmeal two or three times a day, because I was spending the money on liquids made from other grains, like beer, rye and whiskey. After my stay at the Texas Mental Hospital, with my bank accounts such as they were, frozen by Beverly, I cashed in whatever life insurance policies I had in an effort to set up the garage and car sales businesses. By now, it was all gone: Beverly, the bank accounts, the life insurance policies, and the businesses. When I entered DePaul I had to sign a statement that I would be personally responsible for the bill. I didn't know how I was going to pay for it, but they were willing to wait for the money and I couldn't afford to wait for the help. When I started work at Norris Foundation I made a concentrated effort to pay off my debts, a little bit each month, starting with what I owed DePaul, especially since I felt like I owed them my life.

One of the most important areas of my personality I had to work on was learning to deal with women and intimacy. Prior to this time in my life all of my sexual and intimate relationships with women, including Beverly, were alcohol involved. Drinking and sex were synonymous, from the first time I knew what sex was. I grew up with that kind of thinking. I became well enough aware of who I was, and courageous enough, to start dating while I was at Norris Foundation, but I think it was at least six months before I went out with anyone. As I remember, that scared me enough that I went back in my celibate cell again for a while.

Many people ask me if the suicide attempts, the near brushes with death, were enough to scare me into sobriety. As I have written earlier, the answer is no, and that is because I hadn't been properly treated and the only way I knew how to stop was to die. The only thing that can really stop an alcoholic is hospitalization, to get stopped, and then a support system after that to help stay stopped and that has to be pretty protective and intense. The depression during my alcoholism was terrible, and the depression continued after I got sober. During the first year, and for even a little longer, I'd have some deep depression from time to time. Periods of unexplained depression are not uncommon to teenagers. For some, despite good grades, good health, good friends and good homes and family, they feel moody, irritable or anxiety-ridden from time to time. It is part of the turbulence of the teenage years and the process of figuring out one's place in life, and dealing with all of the changing relationships and responsibilities. I was no different as I matured through mental puberty as a forty year old. In fact, I had the additional burden of dealing with all that I had and had let slip through my hands, or through my lips, to be literal.

As the periods of depression became less frequent, I was able to start asking other people for forgiveness. Then came a very difficult period, in spite of the fact that I hadn't had a drink in a while, because I had to seek forgiveness from myself. Forgiveness for not being in the Hall of Fame, for being an ex-ballplayer and a drunken nobody and all of those things. I think the toughest person to forgive is yourself. The first thing that makes that difficult is you know more about yourself and your wishes and desires than anyone else, and you know more about yourself than you really know, you know what I mean? That sounds like another Yogi-ism. Seriously, only you know what your goals and aspirations were, and since you know more about yourself than anyone else, just about the time you think that you've forgiven yourself for everything you've done and every goal you've missed, your subconscious reminds you of something else. So, it's an ongoing process.

About twenty months into my recovery, while I'm working at Norris, I was driving to DePaul for outpatient group therapy and I realized I was finally able to think about almost anything and it didn't seem to bother me. I wasn't getting anxious about it, no matter what I thought about. That was a milestone. I'm not sure now just what the thoughts were then, about dying, or about things that I could have been, or how I really abused the sacred oath of marriage. Or I could have been thinking about my family, and how they just about starved when I was burning money on alcohol. But all these things and more were coming to my mind and it didn't seem to bother me to the point of making me anxious or overcome with emotion. Then I played a game with my mind, saying, "Okay, bring up anything." All of a sudden I realized that I wasn't running scared of my own thoughts anymore.

The others in my group therapy were always talking about a spiritual awakening that was the key to their recovery, and how that was different things for different people. I couldn't wait to share with the group the awakening I experienced while driving that night. I was excited about my newfound ability to think any thought without being anxious. When I got to DePaul I said, "I have something to share with the group. On the way in tonight it just seemed like I wasn't running scared of my own mind or my own thoughts anymore. I tried to think of the worst things that bothered me and it didn't seem like I was scared anymore. It was kind of a funny feeling, but a nice feeling." The group leader said, "Welcome to the adult world. You're finally out of adolescence." He felt I had resolved who I was in life. I think that enters into the statement I made that the hardest person to forgive is yourself. Although I don't think my forgiveness of myself was complete at that time, I was far enough along in the process to have resolved some of the things I was truly conscious of. I had a good understanding about this drug addiction I was in and I didn't blame myself for having become hooked on it. I was almost more grateful for the fact that I finally found out what was wrong with me than the fact that I wasn't drunk. Understanding the addiction made it clear to me that I wasn't different or weird or odd, and prior to that "alcoholic" might mean all those things.

One other area I needed to work on was my relationship with my son, Steve. Beverly and I were apart legally, with the divorce having been finalized, and we were apart physically. She and Steve were in Texas and I was in Wisconsin. As I started to sort out my life, and progress with my maturity, I wanted to spend some time with my son, and get to know him and seek his forgiveness for my behavior and how it impacted him. I arranged with my uncle who was in the construction industry for Steve to get a summer job in the Milwaukee area. So Steve came up in the summer of 1969 and he brought along a friend, who I put to work at Norris Foundation. That arrangement worked out for two straight summers. And another year Steve came up and he had a job at Wisconsin Dells working in the tourist industry. So it worked out that while I was at Norris, Steve spent the summers with me. During those times we rehashed all of the history between Beverly and me, and between Steve and me. It wasn't any formalized thing, but we could talk about anything without any anxiety or anger on my part, and so we did.

Steve Duren: "After Dad moved to Wisconsin, I pretty much wrote him off and focused on the normal things a seventeen year old does: finishing high school, girls, social life, and track. I managed to get some track scholarship offers, and since we didn't have much money, it made it possible for me to go to a good college. (Mom and her sister, my Aunt Pat, helped out as much as they could.) I'm not sure when I first heard that Dad

*was back in treatment again, but at some point he contacted me
and told me that he had finally gotten the message and would
never drink again. I had heard this many times before and
so I was pretty skeptical at first. At some point, I think it was
Christmas holidays, he came down to SMU to visit and stayed
with me for a few days, and I started to think that maybe he
might really have gotten on top of it this time. I can remember
that he really wanted to get back together with Mom, but she
was finally self-sufficient and happy with her own life, and
didn't want to get burned again. I felt like she knew that they
might slip back into their old negative dynamic and it could be
disastrous for Dad's recovery and Mom's new life. That next
summer (1969), Dad lined me up with a job with my Uncle
Rudy's construction company in Milwaukee, which was where
Dad was living and working as a counselor at the Norris home
for juvenile delinquents. So here I was, an eighteen-year old
kid trying to figure out the meaning of life, rooming with my
forty-year old father who was grappling with the same issues
I was – basic beliefs with regard to religion, philosophy, and
the ultimate meaning of life. Dad was totally open to my ideas
in a non-judgmental way, with no preaching or dogma. I felt
an openness and humility in him that I never thought would be
possible in our relationship. It was like having a new college
roommate that happened to be my father."*

By the time I completed my group therapy at DePaul I
had been "dry" for a little over two years. It was the longest
period of time I had gone without an alcoholic drink since
I first indulged as a teenager. Since my drinking and my
behavior had received a lot of press attention based on my
status as a ballplayer, my sobriety, even in its infancy stage of
two years, was equally newsworthy. Ex-ballplayers make for
interesting subjects in the human interest or "where are they
now" sections of sports magazines and newspapers. A local
boy who became a New York Yankee, an All-Star, and a World
Series champ, while being an alcoholic, made good reading,
especially since it appeared I was sobering up and working with
kids. Understandably, sportswriters and newscasters wanted to
know some details and before I knew it, major league teams

were calling me to make appearances at Old Timers' Games and promotions.

I was extremely hesitant to step foot back into the baseball world. I am not blaming baseball for making me an alcoholic, but I would be less than truthful if I said that the baseball lifestyle was not an "enabler." Many excellent athletes and gentlemen were able to compete and complete wonderful careers in baseball without falling victim to addiction. But for many others, including me, the months away from home, the hours of spare time, the beer in the clubhouse, the camaraderie of the guys, and the pressures of the game, all piled together to form a very slippery slope. I so cherished my newfound sobriety that I absolutely feared stepping back on even the periphery of that slope. For over a year after my entry into DePaul, I avoided any involvement whatsoever with baseball. In 1969 the Autry family reached out to me personally, aware of my situation, and invited me to attend a promotional event in Los Angeles, featuring a game between the Angels and the Dodgers. I agonized over that decision, and only accepted because of my sincere regard for the Autrys. They were like family to me. The Angels flew me out to Los Angeles and throughout the flight I wondered what it would feel like, inside, to step back into a clubhouse, into a dugout and onto a field, with all my senses working. Who would I run into? What would they say? Could I finally appreciate and handle it all without falling back? My mind was playing the same game I played on my ride to DePaul that night, and I still felt okay with everything. As it turned out I was very happy I attended the event. Everyone was very supportive of my recovery and I will always remember Casey Stengel coming up to me that night, giving me one of his patented winks and saying, "You doing all that work back there with them kids. I think that's just wonderful. You're not drinking anymore. I think that's a great thing you've done." That was a moment to cherish.

In 1970, while still working at Norris, I felt confident enough about my recovery, and strong enough about the problem drinking that existed in the major leagues, to contact Bowie Kuhn, who was the Commissioner of Baseball at that time. That September I met with Mr. Kuhn at Milwaukee County Stadium and discussed my desire to help. In October of 1970 I received a letter from him stating he was "confident that we presently have available in baseball the broad ranging medical competence to deal with that [alcohol abuse] and any other type situation that might arise." Obviously, the "big boys" weren't quite ready to take their heads out of the sand, so I kept on working with my teenagers at Norris.

I enjoyed my work with the children at Norris so much my friends at DePaul suggested that I look into counseling as a career. Father Marotti had thoughts of opening a long-term after-care program for alcoholics in Milwaukee, and they wanted me to be prepared to be part of it. With their encouragement, during my fourth year at Norris, in 1972, I started attending some classes in childcare at the University of Wisconsin at Milwaukee during the day, while the boys at Norris were in class. As some of the writers started to report on my sobriety I received requests to speak to groups at recovery wards and AA clubs. Based on my baseball background I became quite popular on the AA speaking circuit. AA has a party on the anniversary of the founding of each club, and I was speaking at one of those parties in Madison, Wisconsin, where Bill Hale, the Executive Director of the Community Hospital at Stoughton, was in attendance. After my presentation he came up and said, "I really would like to visit with you." He was already thinking about having a rehabilitation department in his hospital, but he couldn't find the person he wanted to direct it. A short time after that program, Bill came over to Norris Foundation to meet with me and we spent some time discussing his plans. As I remember, it was the spring of 1972 and we continued our discussion at a ballgame at Milwaukee's County Stadium. It was there that Bill told me, "We want to open a treatment program and we want you to manage it, and to run it." He told me about some of the community opposition I would run up against, but that didn't discourage me. So there, in the middle of a ballgame, he convinced me to come over to Stoughton to meet some of his staff and take a shot at starting and running a treatment program.

Twenty-Two

STOUGHTON HOSPITAL

When I first visited the Stoughton Community Hospital I met Norm Gerber, who was the President of the Hospital's Board of Trustees, and Dr. David Nelson, the individual Bill Hale had in mind to be the lead medical person for the rehabilitation clinic he envisioned. Dr. Nelson had attended medical school at the University of Minnesota, which had been active in alcohol abuse rehabilitation, and Bill figured he would avail himself of Dr. Nelson's background. I also was introduced to several members of the Hospital's Board of Directors. They questioned me about my knowledge of alcohol use and abuse, and about my background. By then I had become very well versed about all the different aspects of alcoholism. I had not only studied them, I lived them, and survived them. Dr. Nelson and I really hit it off from the first time we met, and that was instrumental in my agreeing to take on the task of helping to develop the alcohol rehabilitation center at Stoughton and to run it.

The Hospital had purchased a nearby house for possible expansion and that became the headquarters for the rehabilitation center, and also my temporary living quarters. Eventually as the center grew my room was needed and I relocated to an apartment downtown. The center started by treating the several people who were patients of the Hospital in the medical wards, and people who were referred to Bill Hale by his contacts at AA. After a little while we relocated to a wing of a brand new nursing home in a town fourteen miles from Stoughton. But that created a problem because the insurance companies would not pay for treatment outside the hospital, so we had to bring the program back inside the hospital. By 1975, our growth figured in the expansion of the hospital, and we took over the whole third floor. We had fourteen beds allocated to us, a dayroom for everybody, a reading area with couches, and a closed room, which was the therapy room.

The program was called SHARE: Stoughton Community Hospital Alcohol Rehabilitation Education program. SHARE was a substantial, comprehensive program, built on two basic approaches that I think set it apart from other programs: first, reaching out and educating the meaningful other people in an addict's life, which is missing in some other programs; and second, not focusing so narrowly on alcohol and alcoholism, but attempting to address the addict's needs to learn to deal with life without the crutch of the substance. Many people who went through the program probably developed better social skills than they would have, had they not had an alcohol problem.

As the Director, I was responsible to the Hospital Administrator, but I was given wide latitude in designing and implementing the program at Stoughton. I believe that Dr. Nelson, Bill Hale and Norm Gerber were counting on my use of the knowledge I had acquired during my own addiction and recovery. As far as alcoholism and treatment were concerned, I knew sagebrush from timber, as my old running mate, Don Hoak, would say. I had lived enough of the alcoholic's life and experienced enough of it. All of those times I was sober for six months or ten months at a time, were the results of very serious attempts to get well. During each one of those attempts, I studied about alcoholism; I'd go to meetings and attend conferences. But it wasn't until DePaul that everything clicked for me.

Naturally, I gravitated to the use of Hazelden's Minnesota Model when I designed SHARE, with the added elements of addressing the addict's significant others and teaching life skills. To give the Hazelden program its due, when it originated it did not have satellite offices and most people who attended the Hazelden clinic were sent there from their hometowns.

That made it very difficult to incorporate the other significant people in the addict's life into the program. What Hazelden did, and did well, was deal with the individual, but not with the ignorance and the needs of the family around that particular person. We had an advantage at Stoughton since we were a community hospital and a community program. I would use that to our benefit by bringing into the treatment the addict's family and friends, most of whom were located right there in the community.

In designing the program I was very particular about the people who would be working there. I handpicked everybody over a period of time with certain criteria. I wanted them to be from the town or nearby communities; I wanted people from the town to know who they were. During my tenure there the program and the staff grew. By the time I left, our staff was probably eighteen to twenty people. In addition to our staff, we presented the addict and the meaningful others in his or her life with sixteen different lectures by professional people over a four-week period. We brought in psychiatrists, a psychologist, a sex therapist and other specialists, including local clergymen who were excellent speakers. We also addressed the addict's physical needs, and provided recreation and physical therapy for the inpatients.

Early on in the establishment and development of the SHARE Program there was great resistance from the medical staff and the community. The medical staff saw us, and especially me, as non-certified, unqualified, laymen. They questioned our ability, our motive, our very existence as part of the Stoughton Community Hospital. The community itself was not originally supportive of our program, based on the NIMBY mentality (Not In My Back Yard). They didn't have the medical background to question our lack of one, but they saw us as a bunch of ex-alcoholics setting up shop and bringing in a new bunch of alcoholics to hang around the Hospital every few weeks. They just didn't want that happening in their community hospital.

I can honestly say that during the period of time we were trying to establish the program, the pressure from the community and the disdain from the doctors made me consider seeking solace in alcohol. Just the idea of being able to get

away from it all entered my mind. But I was successful in
avoiding that. In sports they often say sometimes it's better to
be lucky than good. I can't say if I was smart or just lucky, but
I know I was very happy I had great counsel. I sought out and
established my own personal Board of Directors - people that I
liked and I trusted: Dr. Nelson was one of them; another was the
chief executive officer of one of our area's largest corporations
who was in the program; and I added a couple of the men from
town who were AA guys. So, when I felt pressure I used my
Board. I sought counsel from them and confided in them.
Many times they put things in perspective, allowing me to back
off that angry feeling toward that unidentified whatever. Those
were tough times, but I had been through tougher, and at least
now I had the satisfaction of knowing that I was helping to
rebuild and save lives.

One thing that had always helped me gain popularity was my
ability to pitch, and now that I was comfortable with who I was,
I had no problem with having people accept me for my athletic
ability, if it would translate into also accepting the rehabilitation
clinic. I had been out of baseball almost eight years already by
1973, yet I was in great shape from having worked out with the
kids at the Norris Foundation, throwing a lot of batting practice.
When I came over to Stoughton, the administrators asked me to
work out with the local Home Talent League team, and I did,
although I really didn't want to. I still had a fear of getting
back too close to the game. I'd had it with baseball and I was
afraid that if I got too close to it again, I would get drawn into
another alcoholic misadventure. But Doc Nelson and Bill Hale
felt that to get the program better integrated in that community
I needed to participate like a member of the community. After
I refused their advances twice, they sent a few members of the
team to pay me a visit, and they pled their case as to how much
better the program would be accepted in the community if I
would come and be a part of the team. Finally, I relented and
agreed to throw batting practice for them. I'd show them some
pointers about baseball, and in the meantime I'd throw a half
hour of batting practice. Then they started to challenge me a
little: "C'mon throw it harder." So, I'd pop that ball through
there and they couldn't hit it, and then I'd throw them a good
slider.

The funny part is when I was coaching baseball down at the Norris Foundation. I was showing the kids how to throw the curveball. During my playing days, I never had a chance to practice the curveball after Paul Richards had me damage my elbow that one spring, because the clubs wouldn't let me. They were in love with the fastball and that's what they wanted to see. (That was one of the things that led me believe that people only liked me as long as I could throw a ball over a hundred miles an hour, and didn't like me for who I was.) Well, after a while at Norris, I came up with a good curveball. I threw some curves that caused me to just shake my head. Is this me throwing this good a curve? The guys would say, "Ryne, that's a real good curveball, but you didn't have a curveball, did you?" And I'd say "Guys, that isn't a good curveball. You ought to see how some of those guys in the majors can break it off." But I was pretty amazed at it, and so were the members of the Stoughton team, who couldn't hit it in batting practice.

The next thing you know, they're after me to pitch in a game: "You know, if you'd pitch for us maybe we could raise a little money and raise a little excitement and awareness about the club. How about pitching just an exhibition for us?" I don't recall if I agreed to pitch in the exhibition game altruistically, just to help the club and the program, or if a little bit of my competitive spirit raised its head enough to make me inquisitive as to how much I still had left, but I agreed to pitch in an exhibition game between Stoughton and the All-Stars of the league, a night game at Sun Prairie. I pitched five innings and struck out 14 guys. I gave up one hit and I didn't walk anybody. Needless to say, that whet their appetite, and admittedly possibly mine. They hadn't seen anybody pitch like this, for them anyway. The next day they're back in my office saying, "You know if you pitch for us we can win the pennant. We can really win if you pitch for us." I said, "No, I don't think so." Then they threw the program at me again, and reminded me of how much more it would be accepted if I was seen as part of the community, and I agreed. So, in April 1973, my name appeared on the roster of the Stoughton Home Talent League team, in the Eastern Section League. Twenty-five years after pitching the Cazenovia Reds to the Sauk County Home Talent League Championship, I was right back where I started. How telling, that with my maturation process arrested by my drinking, upon my recovery I would take up right where I left off.

In my first outing I pitched five innings. I didn't give up a hit or a walk, and struck out eleven of the sixteen batters I faced. My arm was a little sore in the elbow again, and that was the spot that was bothering me when I retired from the majors. In my next outing, I pitched six innings, struck out fourteen batters and also didn't give up a hit or a walk. I felt like I had the greatest presence on the mound then. If I wanted the ball here it was here, if I wanted it there it was there, and I had a good slider. I could throw the curve if I wanted to and I also had a good sinker. I really had great command, for the first time in my life. I don't think I was throwing as fast as I did when I was with the Yankees, (take into account I was about 44 years old at the time), but I don't think I ever pitched better. I had been sober, really sober, about five years at that time. I realized it was the first time I really pitched with all of my senses working, unimpeded by alcohol. I performed well and it felt great.

After that game my elbow got very, very sore, and I had it examined by the orthopedist. I asked, "What's going on here, Doc?" He said, "The cartilage is all gone in your elbow. You can continue to pitch, once every ten days to two weeks, if you don't want to play golf, but if you want to play golf, then you're going to have to give up the pitching." So, that was it for the pitching; but I think the good Lord gave me the chance to experience those games so I could see first hand how much of an effect alcohol had on my central nervous system, causing me to not be able to totally utilize my natural ability while I was drinking.

Despite the early resistance from the medical staff and community, a lot of great things happened at Stoughton. Bill Hale, Doc Nelson and I stayed close. We decided we should integrate the program throughout all the different departments of the Hospital. Bill Hale and Doc Nelson started out by rotating the duties of all the nurses in the hospital, requiring each nurse to come through our program and spend two or three weeks, participating in the groups, removing the mystique and therefore the stigma. But through those early years, Doc Nelson was the only doctor having anything to do with us. Slowly, very slowly, the other doctors would show some interest. A doctor may say, "C'mon in while I get dressed. I need to talk with you." He'd talk to me about a patient of his. And then pretty soon another one would. Then maybe unofficially they were asking me questions about drugs that were addictive. "What do you think about Valium? Do you think it's addictive?" What helped validate our program, and me as the administrator, were the opinions of the outside professionals, the psychiatrists, the psychologists, the therapists, who would speak to the Hospital Board or the medical staff at meetings. They would tell the medical staff that I indeed knew what I was doing, or the medical staff would be asking our outside specialists questions, and they were getting the same answers they were getting from me. So pretty soon I no longer was the ex-alcoholic, ex-ballplayer but I was truly validated as a bona fide counselor. When it came time for me to leave Stoughton, one of the physicians on staff came up to me and told me, "I just want you to know that when you came here I thought this was the worst thing that ever happened to this Hospital." He was a straight shooter. He said, "I wanted your ass out of town. Now, after you've been here for a while and we all learned from you, now this is the greatest thing that ever happened to this Hospital and I think you're one of the greatest guys I ever met in my life." It took a while, and a lot of hard work, to defeat the resistance that was there when we started.

One of the things that helped us become more acceptable to the community was our outreach to local businesses. I would visit many of the small companies located in the area at the request of their President or Personnel Manager after we successfully treated one of them or one of their employees. They would have me talk to their management staff and maybe even the rank and file about the clinic and the work we did there. Those talks always continued to produce more referrals to the clinic. The work we were doing then is now called an Employee Assistance Program. We were truly a little ahead of our time.

What distinguished Stoughton as an alcohol rehabilitation clinic was the extent to which we incorporated the addict's family and the meaningful others in the addict's life. By doing so, we were able to have a success rate of approximately

500%, if you measure the alcohol abusers or pre-alcoholics we were able to rehabilitate by the number of patients we saw, because we were also able to rehabilitate family members who were just as addicted as the patient, but who didn't see it, or didn't admit it. I didn't look at the individual who came in as the case of alcoholism. I looked at the individual that came in to the program only as a license to treat this case of alcoholism which included the ignorance about alcohol in that whole group of people from which the addict came – those the addict worked with, those the addict lived with, those the addict spent recreation time with – and the extent to which they valued alcohol. Our intake interviews revealed the average alcoholic touched fifty other lives. That's what the book, *Games Alcoholics Play*, (by Claude M. Steiner / Mass Market Paperback / Ballantine) also said. We tried to see how many of those meaningful other people we could get into our educational and awareness program using the individual that was there as a license to ask these other people to be involved.

My memory is that within that group of fifty people, on average, there were five other alcoholics. So, if we got all of the meaningful others in an addict's world to come to the program for a period, and educated them, on average four or five or six of those people may stay sober. And in that group of people, because they had placed alcohol on a pedestal, the percentage who had problems with alcohol would probably have been higher than the general population at large. Education changed these people, and I knew that it did because these people changed their drinking habits. Maybe some of them had to get help beyond that, but at least we planted the seed and on many occasions got a number of those people to make a change in their life.

While I truly believe that my work was beneficial to the Hospital and that the Hospital was beneficial to the community, I also derived some benefit from my time at Stoughton. It was there that I first met Diane Jackson, during one of my introductory visits while I was still at Norris and was being courted by Bill Hale to come to Stoughton. She was a nurse, serving as the In-Service Director. At that time her first husband was still alive. Diane was a very well organized, very capable and effective speaker. She would travel and deliver presentations on behalf of the Hospital. I specifically remember a program she presented at a convention in Colorado Springs on the physical effects of alcoholism, and I believe it was the best talk I ever heard on that topic. Diane was also traveling to other established clinics, including Lutheran Hospital in Chicago, and Hazelden, making observations and reporting back to Bill Hale so he could incorporate her suggestions into his new program. In 1974, after Diane's first husband died, we became very attached to one another and got married. Diane has been a blessing to me. It is the first long term, male-female relationship I ever really had as a mature man. I not only was able to enjoy Diane's love and friendship, but the love of her children, Mark and Brian and Cynthia, and her grandchildren, who all readily welcomed me into their family, and became part of my family.

The second benefit derived from my work at Stoughton, I believe, is that my work counseling others helped me stay away from going back to alcohol. Really, after my fifth year of sobriety, about 1973, I really didn't have any desire to drink anymore. The periods of depression were gone. The anxiety of not knowing who I was and where I fit in was gone. I didn't need to drink alcohol to be able to talk to a woman. I no longer thought I needed a drink in my hand to be accepted by others.

Stoughton also brought me recognition, more than I could have possibly imagined would have come out of that program. I started speaking at the University of Wisconsin Medical School. I was a regular speaker at the Social Work School at the University of Wisconsin, and then I was on the Wisconsin State Board on Alcohol, the County Mental Health Board and several different committees, including the Governor's Board, to which I was appointed by Gov. Lee Dreyfus. I was starting to be in demand around the country, presenting programs on rehabilitating alcoholics. Different hospitals around the country that wanted to start a program would bring me in to talk to their hospital board or the community at large. I remember going to Rochester, New York. They were going to open a program and did shortly after I was up there. Some of the hospitals I presented speeches at tried to hire me away from Stoughton, but I was happy there and really didn't care to leave.

Then a producer contacted me about making a movie based on my life story. CBS put up $50,000 to develop it and they flew me out to Hollywood to review a script and consult on the casting. At the last minute the project was scrapped and a movie with a similar storyline, The Boy Who Drank Too Much, was released. The original idea for the movie on my life was generated by several magazine pieces about my recovery and my work at Stoughton. I also appeared on The Today Show, Good Morning America, a CBS talk show in the evening, and the Tom Snyder Show on NBC. It just seemed like all the time there was more and more. Over a period of time in 1976 and 1977 I co-wrote my first book, The Comeback, with Robert Drury. Although I was very proud of that book and my eight years of sobriety to that point, I felt the need for this book for two reasons: firstly, a lot has happened since 1976 as far as the work I have been able to accomplish in alcohol education, especially with young people, and secondly, I feel that with the passage of time and a maturing of my sobriety, I have a much clearer insight and understanding of what really happened to me, both before and after May 2, 1968.

Twenty-Three

WHAT PRICE ALCOHOL?

One of the questions I am most often asked is what my addiction to alcohol cost me. With the advantage of hindsight afforded by time, I look back at my life and truly feel that my years of addiction to alcohol carried a very high personal price tag. It is impossible to accurately list all that I lost, because some of it would be conjecture. I can only dream what I would have achieved, on and off the ball field, if I were never addicted to alcohol, and I can only imagine what my personal relationships would have developed into if I had been mature earlier in life.

I think, from a baseball point of view, my addiction cost me a Hall of Fame career. I have that feeling based on several observations. First of all, I realize that it is only a guess because making it to the Hall of Fame is somewhat political and based on numbers that are important to the people voting at the time. Except for the magic of 500 home runs for a hitter, or 300 victories for a pitcher, induction is obviously not achieved by an objective standard. If it was, there would be so much less written and discussed about who is in and who is not, and some of the great people in the game who I had the blessing to play with and for, like Roger Maris and Gil Hodges would be in the Hall already. (Although maybe there is now renewed hope for both of them, and others, based on the new Veterans'

Committee voting rules.) Secondly, the length of my career was shortened, on both ends, by my alcoholism. As I related earlier, my career ended, for all intents and purposes, with my hungover appearance against the Yankees leading to the bridge incident. And although no one came out and told it to me at the time, it has became obvious to me in retrospect, that my prolonged stay in the minor leagues was the result of my drinking habits. The excess drinking manifested itself in two ways: it retarded my maturation, which kept me involved in adolescent pranks and foolish behavior, and it retarded my development as a pitcher, robbing me of control and consistency. I had the power and strength to throw a ball in excess of one hundred miles an hour, allowing me to keep minor league teams from getting any hits, but in the same game I would walk a dozen batters or hit one or two, and in the next game be a different pitcher.

Beyond my career being shortened as a result of my addiction, I truly believe that my performance as a pitcher suffered because of the progressive nature of the addiction and the damage to my central nervous system. I think that alcohol's effect on the central nervous system, as I came to understand it, kept me from having hand-eye coordination, the single most important asset to a baseball player. At no time during my professional career, including the minor leagues, was I playing with all of my senses working. Almost every time I drank, and that was quite often, I would overdrink. Once I started to drink I had the need to drink everything in sight. It would take 10 to 14 days for my central nervous system to get back to normal and totally recover from each such event. Consequently I never did achieve total control over my control in my major league career.

Ralph Houk: *"Ryne was an outstanding pitcher. I really thought he'd even go better than he did in the big leagues. I thought he'd really last, but maybe with all that stuff that happened ... There's no telling how far Duren would have gone had it not been for the alcoholism. He would have been, without question, one of the top relief pitchers in baseball. That's what you were looking for, even then. Somebody to come in and just throw the ball hard, and get it over. A short man today, you know how important they are. If you've got a guy* *who can come in and pitch two good innings, or even one, who could do like Ryne could have done, that's what you're looking for. In my opinion, without a doubt, he had the ability of a Mariano Rivera or a John Wetteland."*

Although I achieved notoriety pitching for the Yankees in 1958, I understand now that some of that was due to the novelty of being a 29 year old rookie, playing for a World Champ, and the speed with which I could pitch. But all in all, I believe that I was a better pitcher in Philadelphia in 1963, the season I was able to withhold from drinking, at least until July, although I still didn't have great control. How much control I might have had and what success that control might have meant to me while I was still young enough and strong enough to throw a ball 100 miles an hour, was brought home to me by how well I was able to pitch for Stoughton in 1973, at age 44, having been out of baseball for seven years. That performance led me to believe that a young Ryne Duren, pitching without any booze in his system, would have had that great command during the major league years, and coupled with my ability to throw hard, nobody ever would have touched the ball. If I had allowed myself the freedom to pitch with all of my senses working, I truly believe that today I would be a member of the Baseball Hall of Fame.

I also rely on the opinions of many of my former teammates and contemporaries as to what my abilities were. They have been very gracious in supplying quotes for inclusion in this book, but I was also curious as to what they were saying about me then. So I researched sources ranging from my sister's scrapbooks to the Library at the National Baseball Hall of Fame in Cooperstown, and I was enlightened and yet a little saddened at the same time: enlightened in that I read for the first time some very flattering quotes and statistics, yet saddened to know that it was even more talent than I remembered that I had squandered.

Dan Daniel, May 23, 1958: "There is no doubt that Duren throws harder than any other pitcher in all baseball. AL umpires are authorities for the statement that no hurler in that circuit, and that includes Herb Score, matches his speed. For veteran observers, Duren has revived memories of young Walter Johnson."

Ben Steinberg, Columnist, 1958: *"Managers, coaches and veteran American League hitters, including Ted Williams, claim that Duren's blinding fastball is better than Bob Feller's in his prime. New York writers have been waxing eloquent over the 29-year-old hurler, already rating him alongside 'Fireman' Johnny Murphy and Joe Page as the best Yankee relief pitchers of all time."*

Dan Daniel, Sporting News, July 23, 1958: *"Inevitably, you come back to Rinold Duren, the bespectacled guy who looks like a college professor, and who can throw a baseball harder than anybody else in the major leagues."*

Reedsburg Times Press, July 3, 1958: *"Sal Maglie speaks of Ryne Duren in superlatives: 'The fastest I've ever seen' the Barber says of the Yankees' new speed king. 'He's faster than Herb Score, and maybe he's faster than Bob Feller was. All I know is what I see and when he's pumping out there on the mound, that ball explodes. It gets right on top of the batter, then it takes off. It moves.'"*

Stan Isaacs, Newsday, 1959: *"It is possible all his pitches will not be true, though they will be as fast as ever if Ryne wants to let the hard ones go. He was throwing on the sidelines at Miller Huggins Field the other day and the ball sounded like a bumble bee as it displaced air on its way to the plate. 'Fastest man on cleats,' said rookie catcher John Blanchard."*

Curley Grieve, San Francisco Examiner, March 15, 1963: *"Rhyne has one of the strongest arms in baseball. 'I never saw anybody faster last year,' said American League Umpire Hank Soar, who was here for the Giant-Cleveland conflict. Leon Wagner, former Giant and now the slugging star for the Angels, expressed a generally indorsed view when he said: 'I'm glad he's out of our league – if he had to go. When he hits you in the side, the ball doesn't come out.'"*

However, the possible loss of the Hall of Fame is minimal in comparison to what I know my addiction cost me. Other than the damage I did to my own life and career by my drinking addiction, I think the lives of my first wife, Beverly, and my son, Steve, were most affected, as I've related. But I know my addiction also had a deep, deep impact on my mother. God, how my mother cried when she learned about my addiction. She didn't fully understand alcoholism, even though her brothers and brothers-in-law and a number of people from our town had died or were dying from it. Nobody from that little town of Cazenovia saw it for what it truly was. But after I came over to Stoughton to run the treatment program, as I said before, the program caught on and I started to achieve some press. It started with articles in different papers, then interviews, and then the television spots. Somewhere in discussing my situation I said, "I'm an alcoholic." My mother read that statement in the Madison papers and just broke down and cried. She said to me, "Why would you say such a thing?" and I said, "Mother, because it's true." She had a very difficult time with that. Seeing her sons drink was just part of who we were, but admitting that I had an addiction was almost too much for her to bear.

But as time passed my Mother and Dad learned what my behavior was. They came to understand that what they saw as terribly embarrassing was a terrible disease that I had come to conquer. They became very proud of the fact I was recovering from my drinking problem. They enlisted me to help one of my brothers get sober and then I also tried to help one of my other brothers. Dad heard me speak a couple of times, and one night as we rode home together he told me he was so proud of me and the fact that I was on top of the problem and he was very grateful that I tried to help the family. Then, as we were riding just the two of us, he said kind of sheepishly, "I was wrong about alcohol, wasn't I?" He realized that he had seen it as a man's thing to really be able to drink, and now I saw it as a drug, and if you didn't understand it and treat it as that, problems were sure to happen. Mother and Dad and I had lengthy discussions about alcohol, at our old kitchen table in Cazenovia, back in the middle 1970s, when I'd visit. There we were, some thirty-five years later, sitting at the same table where

I sat as a kid and listened to my Dad talk about Big George, and where I first relished those stolen sips of beer. Now we were engaging in what was possibly the most informed, rational discussion about alcohol to ever occur in Cazenovia. So, my parents both went to their grave really understanding what this thing was that had been killing people all along, and proud of my recovery. Causing my mother so much grief and pain, and hearing her cry, was one of the most exacting prices I had to pay for my addiction. Equally costly were the loss of Beverly and the years of Steve's youth that I missed. Knowing that my Mom and Dad came to fully understand my addiction and were able to feel pride in my meaningful accomplishments after baseball has made me feel much better. While I will never get back all the time, memories, and special moments I lost with Beverly and Steve, I felt very fortunate that I got to spend Beverly's last week in her presence. And I am very happy to say that my relationship with Steve is terrific. He is a very bright, industrious person, who is happily married, to Bette, and has blessed me with a beautiful granddaughter, Sabre. Rarely a day goes by now that we don't talk at least once.

Twenty-Four

PREVENTION, INTERVENTION, TREATMENT AND AFTERCARE

PREVENTION

As school children we all learned the proverb, "An ounce of prevention is worth a pound of cure." I would have to say that as I lived my life, I learned that saying to be true in almost every circumstance I can remember. But the question we must address is whether or not preventive medicine works with respect to alcohol or other drug addiction.

I think preventive medicine is effective, but to a certain extent you have to accept that on faith. It is clear to see if an addict is recovering or not as the result of treatment or an intervention, but it is speculative to credit prevention with a person not becoming an addict. They may have been able to avoid addiction without it. The best we can do is to measure the percentage of a certain population who have addiction problems when not exposed to a program of prevention as opposed to the percentage of the same population who have problems after following such a program. One experience I was involved in was working with the Atlanta Braves organization in the early 1980s. Before the institution of our program, on a self-reporting basis, approximately 70% of the players involved said they had problems with alcohol, or were alcohol abusers, by my interpretation, not theirs. After our educational process, only 8% of the players reported having a problem. I can't insure that the drop of 62% was solely related to the education we provided, but I do take some pride in the drop, and coincidentally, or maybe not, it was right after this educational program was completed that the Atlanta Braves went on to become one of the winningest teams in Major League Baseball.

When I talk about preventing addiction to alcohol and other drugs, the preventive "medicine" I am talking about isn't dispensed by pill or liquid. It is education. If you educate people early in their life (pre-teens) so that they can use that information, and the good habits they form, through their critical developmental years, you have a good chance of being successful. If you try to educate them when they're in the throes of the problem without hospitalization and without the proper setting, the education almost reinforces the denial rather than help the addict. They adopt the mental attitude that nobody else knows what its like to be an alcoholic and everything anyone is telling them is only words. Some very intelligent people died from alcoholism, resisting the help that was not only available to them, but offered to them. From my own personal experience I can share with you that during one of my stays in a treatment center I met a renowned surgeon, one of the nicest human beings I ever met. He was in treatment with me. He let me read some of his books on plastic surgery and reconstructive surgery. He was an extremely bright man, but he got caught up in an addiction to alcohol and he could not get out of it. He died on his second or third trip to that same rehabilitation center. I don't know how many other situations like that I've seen.

Alcoholism, I think, is based on myth and ambiguities and a lack of knowledge. The drinking man's profile or image that I adopted in little Cazenovia, Wisconsin in my childhood in the 1930s is still being foisted upon our children today, 2002, in every size hamlet, community, and city in America. Only today it is worse because of the power and reach of the communications industry. For every group that gains some attention or recognition for having large companies remove cartoon like characters from their advertisements for alcohol or cigarettes, dozens of similar advertising campaigns continue to exist, overtly or subliminally telling our children that its macho to drink and drink plenty. Alcohol is still displayed on a pedestal to our teenagers as the legal substance that will define them as real men if they can drink it, and plenty of it. Sadly, I've heard young women, in high school and college, state that to them feminism justifies that they too can now get as drunk as just the guys used to get. I find it hard to believe that all of the women, who fought for equality in our society, starting with the right to vote, and removal of the glass ceilings in corporate America, had getting equally drunk as one of their goals.

Beyond the myth of the drinking man as hero, lies the problem caused by the ambiguity with which we dispense alcohol. Some of the brewing and distilling companies take great pride in the fact their advertisements contain the educational phrase "Drink Responsibly" or "Friends Don't Let Drunk Friends Drive." Well, what is drinking responsibly? Is it the same for an eighteen-year-old 98-pound girl as it is for a 280 pound 35 year old lumberjack? Experience tells those of us who are older that the answer is no, but the very people who need the knowledge lack the experience. Similarly, the campaign to have a "designated driver" is admirable. A very large percentage of automobile accidents are the result of a drunk driver. However, it is ambiguous because it also sends the message that it is acceptable to drink to excess as long as you are not driving a vehicle. There are many other activities that are life threatening to a drunken person besides driving, like walking down a flight of stairs, or crossing a street, not to mention the damage to the brain's frontal lobes and central nervous system just from drinking with no other activity, and the pain and loss which will ensue from an addiction to alcohol whether the addict drives or not.

A third factor which I believe contributes to problem drinking is the lack of knowledge we possess as a society about alcohol as a drug, combined with the lack of awareness we have as to what constitutes social drinking, what constitutes moderate drinking and when is it an addiction. There's no question in my mind, and I believe in the mind of the medical sector, that alcohol is a drug. Although with the end of Prohibition prescriptions were no longer required to obtain alcohol, we didn't, as a society, insist on properly educating the public about alcohol consumption. Every other drug that is sold "over the counter", without a prescription, still contains advised dosages and warnings about what is considered an overdose, possible side effects, and warnings about not taking that substance if you are taking certain other substances. No such warning exists on alcoholic beverages. The only requirement to buy alcoholic beverages in this country is to have a sufficient amount of money and to be of the age required by your respective state, which is usually somewhere between 18 and 21, despite the fact that most research reveals the brain isn't fully developed, and adolescence doesn't normally end, until about age 24 or 25. If you don't know from experience, a bottle of aspirin tells you clearly on its label to take two tablets every six hours, not to exceed eight tablets a day, and not to take any aspirins at all if you are suffering from certain conditions, or are taking certain other medications. Nothing, except experience, tells you how much alcohol to drink before you experience drowsiness or nausea, and not to drink it all if you are taking certain other substances. Without the experience and without the education, there may not be a second experience.

Based on my positive experience with the Atlanta Braves organization, I believed that preventive education should have been adopted as mandatory in hospitals. From what the doctors and my research were telling me, at any given time as many as 60% of the people in any hospital are there because of alcohol or drug addiction or abuse, or the condition they are in the hospital for has been worsened because of intake of alcohol or other drugs. If that's the case, then why aren't we treating it right there, and treating it preventively? Those were the numbers back then and I don't think that they've changed significantly.

The Betty Ford Center in Rancho Mirage, California is known worldwide for its work in helping people recover from addiction to alcohol and other drugs, and I had the pleasure of speaking there and working with their counselors. Bob Newton was an All-American football player at Nebraska in 1970 and played in the National Football League from 1971 through 1981. He is currently a Chemical Dependency Counselor at The Betty Ford Center, involved in the Professional Recovery and Relapse Program, and also runs a program known as HalfTime, out of the State of Washington, which he presents at conferences, youth groups, business meetings, and community forums, using his personal experience "to help as many individuals as possible broaden their view of alcohol and drugs." I asked Bob to provide us with a little of his insight into prevention, education, and interventions. This is what he had to say about prevention:

> *Prevention and education are extremely important for young people beginning in elementary school all the way through middle and high school. It is hoped that parents will begin instructing their young children at a very early age not to drink or use other drugs to cope in our society or to bow to peer pressure. I think it is important that parents participate in education and prevention methods because our young people are bombarded with so many messages through advertisement and media to drink, smoke, or are under peer pressure to use other drugs.*

> *Children that come from a family where there is a historic predisposition of addiction are at extreme high risk. It is very dangerous for young people to begin drinking at age 12 or 13 because they are still developing psychologically and physiologically and using mood-altering chemicals will inhibit this development. Young people start using alcohol or marijuana at age 12 or 13 and then start experiencing severe difficulty in high school. This is a major reason kids drop out of high school or become involved in the legal system.*

INTERVENTION

If I was good at anything in particular during my years at Stoughton, I was good at interventions. I think I was an outstanding worker in alcoholism, because I was forceful and I was knowledgeable about human behavior and denial. When an alcoholic seeks help it is very important to seize the moment. A delay in action provides the alcoholic with an opportunity to change his mind and to avoid dealing with his addiction.

When an addict or his family or meaningful others would come to me and ask for help I would go behind the scenes and fully program his intervention, so when we started it we could address all of his possible excuses. For instance, in preparing the intervention for a doctor who suffered from alcoholism, I first talked to his wife and his partner, I talked with his kids. I had his wife pack his clothes. I reserved a bed at Hazelden for him, and I purchased his airline ticket. Every time he tried to block the progress of the intervention, we'd have an answer:

"Well, I can't go yet because I've got all these appointments."

"Your partner's already taken care of all that. All your appointments are covered."

"Well, maybe so, but I gotta have time to pack and everything."

"Your wife's already got everything packed for you."

"Well, but I want to talk with the kids and tell the kids about it."

"The kids all know that you're going and they're inside waiting to talk to you."

"Well, I couldn't possibly get a reservation tonight."

"We've already got it."

"Yeah, but what about the ticket?"

"Here's the ticket."

"Well, I don't have anybody up there. How am I going to get to the center?"

"I've already called them. They know exactly what you look like and they're going to meet the plane."

Every intervention is different, and one of the things that make it so is the variation in the people who are important in the particular addict's life. When you start to interview the addict's family you find out who all the "players" in this particular case are, and in recovery each type of "player" has a name: there are the Enablers, the Rescuers, the Persecutors and the Victims.

Enablers *are those people who are most responsible for supplying the addict with the means or the excuse to drink. This includes people who supply the money necessary to obtain the alcohol (employer, spouse) and those who supply the feelings that make the drinking desirable (drinking pal, mistress). The Enablers are not the real cause of the addiction, although the addict thinks they are.*

Rescuers are those people who save the addict from acute physical, emotional or monetary danger. They drive him home, put him to bed, pay his bills, bail him out of jail, provide alibis for spouses and employers, care for him while sick as a result of drinking, and forgive him for all he has done while drunk.

Persecutors are those people who do not understand the nature of the addiction, who attack the addict as being weak and blame the addiction on the addict, rather than seeing the addiction as a disease and the addict as afflicted.

Victims are those people who are the targets of the addict's loss of control and self-anger, hatred and anxiety. The problem from the addict's point of view is that once they victimize someone, they subsequently suffer such guilt that they resort to alcohol again to relieve the guilt.

From your experience as a counselor you can figure out what role all the meaningful people in the addict's life play and who is going to be positive at an intervention and who is going to be negative in it. In order to insure the best result, you try to present all of these people to the addict in the best order and manner possible. You need to be able to discern who will be strong and who will be too weak to be effective. You must be prepared to do whatever will work, and in order to be properly prepared you must do your homework. For example, if there is someone you think will deliver a powerful message, but can't deliver it in person to the addict, then you have him or her write a letter with his or her feelings in it and you read it to the addict during the intervention.

Coordinating everyone's schedule, to insure that all the meaningful people in the addict's life can be present at an arranged location, with the addict there, is one of the toughest parts of staging the intervention. Once you start an intervention, it's **NOW**; it isn't tomorrow. That's why you must strive to have all the loose ends covered; because once the addict eludes an intervention, it's very difficult to get them back into it.

You hold an intervention at the work place, or at home, or wherever you feel the best spot is. The intervention itself is having each of the "players" tell the alcoholic about his or her drinking and how it affects them, and what it is they would like the alcoholic to do. If, as a counselor, you have properly laid all the groundwork, you may be able to move the alcoholic directly from the intervention into treatment, which is the best immediate follow-up to an intervention. If you've prepared properly for a successful intervention, you've already had a place reserved for the addict in a treatment center.

It really is a tough job, but it can be accomplished. Sometimes the difficulty in getting the intervention accomplished is getting the family members to be able to face the alcoholic, even in writing. But a good counselor knows if the person doesn't get into treatment at that time, it's hard to set that stage again. If the addict gets out of a tough intervention, without heading to treatment, you know you're playing with a person's life. If you fail, the addict may never get well. People who you feel may make a strong impression may not want to get involved. Do you eliminate a person from the intervention because you feel they are weak? You have to really use great judgment for the intervention to go forward and be successful.

One of the other things that make every intervention different is which type of statement will be most effective to the particular alcoholic on the day of the intervention. It won't always be the same type of statement that is effective. Like a football coach who must prepare his team with the best offensive strategy for an opponent's particular defense, but also have a Plan B, a good counselor must prepare the participants in an intervention to address those areas which he believes will be most convincing to the alcoholic, but also be prepared to reach out to all of his emotions.

You don't always know exactly where the intervention will go. There is no script, especially for the addict. For example, the alcoholic may say, "Well I do a good job as a father and

I'm a good provider", and the kids respond, "Yeah, but Dad you're never here and when you are here we really can't communicate with you." The wife will say, "You're a mauler", or "You're never around for intimacy, you're always drunk" or "You embarrass me at this place or that place." He defends by saying "Oh, yeah, but you do this and you do that" and you go round and round and he's fighting the family at that point and it appears you haven't gotten anywhere. But, you have a statement from his boss and you read it to him. The boss says the alcoholic has missed work and he knows that the situation is only going to get worse. He insists on treatment or a different job, but if the alcoholic goes to treatment it will all be paid for. Insurance will pay for treatment and the time away from work will be covered. The boss' statement ends with the fact that either the alcoholic goes to treatment or loses his job. Faced with the loss of employment, which to this alcoholic means loss of money and no future supply of alcohol, the statement from the boss, coming after the discussion with the family works. In another situation, maybe the boss could have said that first and it doesn't necessarily move the alcoholic, but then the little girl in the family, who Daddy adores, says "Daddy" and she makes her statement to him and that does it. It's hard to say where the Achilles heel of each alcoholic is, but if the counselor has prepared properly, the thing that means most to the alcoholic will present itself from within the group of people at the intervention. The addict's link with credibility and respectability lies somewhere within the information in that intervention.

Bob Newton: *"We, at the Betty Ford Center, feel that every intervention is a success even though the patient may not immediately enter into treatment. The reason for this belief is that information has been presented to the addicted person and verbalized, usually from the employer or from loved ones and friends that they have a problem with alcohol and other drugs. There is a high percentage of interventions, probably 80%, where the patient will go into treatment. It is also helpful for the family of the addicted athlete or person, because many times they will seek help as a result of interventions on their loved* *ones. The family and the loved ones need help also because alcoholism and chemical dependency is a family disease."*

What the counselor needs to keep in mind, I believe, is that an addict at this stage isn't really seeking to be cured. He or she thinks they can still drink and handle life and take care of all the essentials. What is most important in that addict's life is his or her next "fix" and what he or she has to do to get it. This is the hardest thing for people to understand – the most intimately personal feeling that an addict, a drug addict, can have is their next fix, even more important than life itself. When I had that rock in my hand, in Lake Michigan, and the water was over my head and I went to kill myself, I was cold, and I said to myself, "Stupid, go get a couple of Brandy Manhattans and warm up first." The alcohol was more important than life itself, don't you see?

The intervention itself isn't going to cure the addict. What the intervention will do is present the addict with a dose of reality. It will present the important people in the addict's life, all at once, telling the addict that he is not "handling it." If that reality hits the addict, then maybe he or she realizes they have to put their fix on the back burner and kind of conform for a while and then later when they get all this taken care of, then they can drink again. They are always motivated to their next drink, and in the meantime they're just going to conform. That's the way it goes. I know very well when I'm doing an intervention that the addict is just going to conform to get the heat off them. That's all I did as an addict for nine years – try to figure out how I could drink and not have a problem. I would tell myself I'll stay sober and conform and I'll get Beverly off my back by staying sober for a while, but when this winter is over I'll be in spring training with the boys and the hell with not drinking. This is the thing that addicts understand but most sober people don't.

After the intervention we've only gotten through to the addict enough for him to say, "How can I make everybody in this room happy now, to the point where they won't bother me and I can go have a drink?" It then takes treatment and a period of time, when conformity develops into a habit; the alcoholic builds a backlog of credibility to the point where it's a vested interest in a new way of life that he doesn't want to jeopardize. One day he'll say, "Maybe I don't need to get high again, living without this fix is a possibility." Pretty soon that thought pattern takes hold and all of this now becomes a drive to keep that new way of life; it becomes as strong as the original drive to drink.

Even after treatment the original intervention has an effect. It varies with different people, but the commitment to all of the people who were involved in the intervention, and your honesty with all the people around you, becomes part of the protective mechanism against that next drink. That's why years ago when we just had people dry out for themselves, and we didn't treat the family or we didn't treat the meaningful others in an education program for them, the recovery rate at that time was 10-15%. By the time we were running the rehabilitation treatment center in Stoughton Hospital, we were achieving a sobriety success rate of between 60-70%. But from a preventive standpoint, we were much more effective, because the addict was usually part of a group of people who abused alcohol or who placed alcohol on a pedestal, living and drinking ignorantly, and we involved those others in the addict's intervention. That's why earlier on in this book I stated that reaching and educating those others, by involving them in the intervention and treatment, increased the program's success rate to 500-600% rather than the 10-15% that we were doing quite a few years ago. So, education is the difference to the group involved with the addict before they cross that threshold into true addiction.

TREATMENT

Most of the celebrated cases of treatment the public has become aware of involve sending the alcoholic to a center for a "28 day treatment." Based on my personal experience, both as an alcoholic and as a counselor, twenty-eight days of treatment doesn't do anything for you, other than simply start to get the alcoholic's tissue addiction and physical needs out of the way and it really only gives the counselors or the treatment program a chance to get a good look at the case. But if they haven't done anything with that social world that the alcoholic belongs to outside the treatment center, to have that as an educated place where other people understand the addiction and the addict, and use that twenty-eight day period to set up ongoing programs and counseling, and also educate these other people so that they can be positive forces in the recovery rather than negative ones, then it doesn't accomplish any lasting result.

I was hospitalized seven times in some type of treatment center and none of them, until the last one, accomplished any lasting result, because I went right back to that group of people that I had lived with before, who were ignorant about alcohol. Now, I'm not blaming my addiction on the other people, although I probably did back then. What I am saying is that as human beings we are social and have social needs. We need each other. Those needs would have me back drinking if the group around me was going to reject me if I didn't drink.

After I was into my recovery for a while I attended a reunion of one of my former teams. Soon after I got there my old teammates were getting on my case "Rinold, c'mon and have a few drinks with us like the good old days. Never mind that sobriety or that abstinence stuff" or however they said it. I went right to the bottom line and said, "Hey, guys, I found out I'm alcoholic and I'm just not going to drink anymore." They laughed at me, "They said you're no more alcoholic than we are." And a couple of them were. If I had not had proper treatment, or was not as far along in my recovery as I was, I might have fallen back at that time. On the other hand, if those fellows had been part of a group of people that was included in my recovery process and educated about alcohol, that scene would not have happened. But without education, that way of life, and that style of life is more important to them than whether or not they buy into what I'm telling them.

Bob Newton: *"Many professional athletes in our society are in constant pressure to succeed and are being evaluated publicly either on a daily or weekly basis during their season. Many times their self-esteem is directly connected to their performance on the athletic field. They are usually constantly in the limelight and have little privacy. Some of the stressors are: the challenges of the constant need to travel; facing injuries that can cause insecurity about their careers, difficulty in adjusting to sudden wealth. Sometimes the athlete's success prevents them from surrendering to the disease of alcoholism/*

chemical dependency. It is difficult for a professional athlete to grasp that they cannot have one beer. But an abstinence based recovery treatment program has been determined to be the best program. It is also important to get the addicted athlete's family into treatment to help the spouse and the children, because they have been affected by the athlete's use of alcohol or other drugs.

"An athlete thinking that they will be miraculously healed in 28 days is a dangerous thinking process for relapse. An athlete's therapeutic process needs to be evaluated on a weekly basis. The severity of the athlete's addiction and what stage of addiction the athlete is presently experiencing will determine the clinically driven number of days of treatment. There are many levels of treatment that can be helpful to an athlete, including: partial hospitalization, intensive in-patient treatment, intensive out-patient treatment. It will be extremely necessary that the athlete follow a continuing care plan, which will include: group sessions, individual sessions, and the attendance of 12 Step meetings. I believe there are many misperceptions in our society that an athlete can go into treatment for 28 days and be magically cured from the negative consequences of alcohol and other drugs. That is a severe misconception because the patient needs to follow the continuing care plan to protect sobriety and grow in recovery."

Not only does a quick "28 day program" not produce a lasting result, I think in some instances it accomplished more harm than good, especially for professional athletes who are addicted. If we tell them they are "cured" after a 28-day program, without educating the meaningful others in their lives and without appropriate after-care, we are fooling them and releasing them into dangerous territory, with an apparent blessing that others can now treat them as if they have no problem. I think the rule of thumb for how long the addicted athlete should be away from the game is one month for every year since he or she started using the substance. For instance, if a person starting using mind-altering or mood-altering substances when he was 13 or 14 years old, and now he's 25 years old and he's got a serious problem with it, he's got 11 or 12 months to turn that around. That doesn't mean just not using the substance, but getting counseling, and learning to deal with all of the adolescent issues including where he fits in. The addict needs to come to understand himself, probably get in touch with his feelings about authority and dealing with authority, becoming his own person, and so forth. All of those things have to be covered and they're best covered in group therapy along with some individual therapy. Additionally, once the player does return to participating with the team, the treatment can continue, even more effectively with the help of those around him. I think that you have to have on that team, or in that clubhouse, for him, eight or ten people who have agreed that they will sit in a couple of therapy sessions with him and will talk some of these things through with him, where he asks them for permission, or he asks them to please help him through this period of time, with all the knowledge and understanding of his addiction and what his needs are. It isn't that heavy a thing. It would be a pretty easy thing, so long as they were not negative. It's an easy thing for me to see. But most teams tend to put the team first, and the player's personal concerns last, and with that being the priority, having to deal with a player's recovery properly would be considered a distraction to a team concerned with just winning the championship.

Another problem with the 28-day programs is that the public now says, "Well, this guy just went through treatment so he must be alright now." And when he has another fall, as he will, if not treated properly, the public starts to see him as a loser and a bum, although he has never really gotten the right treatment. I'm not absolving athletes who misbehave from accountability for their actions, but I am saying that we can not realistically expect a person who has not been properly treated to recover or act like they are recovered, and giving an addict 28 days of treatment and releasing him to the world as having finished a recovery program is misleading. I'll tell you where it went wrong, truthfully, and here's how it happened. Each ball club aligned itself with a treatment center and in return the treatment centers wanted exclusive agreements. They told the ballclubs that if they were going to be the "exclusive treatment center" then they would have to get guys like me and Don Newcombe, who had been talking to the players trying to help, out of the

clubhouses. I don't think that was so bad. I wasn't the alpha
and the omega. Nor was Newcombe. But at least we got the
door open to the possibility there was a serious problem there.
After the treatment centers got the exclusives they started
advertising: "Exclusive Treatment Center for the New York
Yankees", for instance, or for whatever club. Now when the
club sent somebody into treatment and the treatment center said
we need that person for six months, the ballclub resisted and
insisted that the player be back within a month. The treatment
center said, to itself, "Well, we are the exclusive treatment
center for a professional team and that's a very important thing
for us to be able to advertise. So, okay, we'll have the athlete
back on the team in less than a month." That's the essence of
it. Now, the poor guy goes in there and he comes back and he
hasn't had the proper treatment. He needed six months. That's
the way I read it, and I think that's true. The 28 day treatment
policy was a compromise and in our great American system you
may have compromise in the Congress, and you never quite get
the exact legislation you want, but there is no compromising
with drug addiction. You either get the program or you don't.
You either get what the illness needs to get on top of it or you
don't.

AFTERCARE

There are some people who were addicted that go back to
having an occasional drink, social drinking, without a problem,
but I don't think the ones that are tissue addicted can ever do
that. My particular philosophy is why would a person go back
to using it? I didn't want to be messed up with drugs in the first
place. That was my conviction as a young person. Why would
I ever take a drug and risk being hooked on it? Even aspirins.
As a young man I heard you get hooked on aspirin if you start
depending upon them to deal with your pain, and that it wasn't
very manly if you have to take something for pain. So, drugs
had no appeal to me. But I had no reservations about drinking
alcohol and then getting hooked on it, obviously, because I
didn't know it was a drug. But today I can accept life as it is
and I don't have to have a fix to get through. I have the tools
today to deal with life without having to take something.

I think after an addict has been in recovery for five or six
years he gets totally reprogrammed and alcohol just doesn't

have any appeal. But once in a while, there's no doubt that things might become a little too much to handle, and the numbing effect of alcohol sounds like a solution. I have come up with a few ways that are effective in helping me resist that: If my mind is racing at night as I go to bed, I may lay there and start building something in my mind. I'm a halfway decent carpenter, electrician, plumber and mechanic, so I start either rebuilding an engine or building a car or house and try to start putting the details in. That's one way of doing it; another way is to turn on a radio with the timer on it. I never remember it going off. Usually the music or my attention to the details of building will be enough to change my train of thought. But, if I've got something that's really eating at me, I usually can find someone to talk to about it. It doesn't have to be a counselor or anybody with specific training. It may be a stranger for that matter. But the act of talking it out, without resorting to alcohol, gets me by the event.

Twenty-Five

WINNING BEYOND WINNING

Looking back at my life it would be easy for me to blame whatever problems I had – with alcohol, with my conduct, with my wife – on my life as a ballplayer. But that would not be accurate or fair. I got my lumps as a ballplayer. Baseball was a very tough grind and I truly think that along the way I was abused by the game and by the way certain of its executives chose to deal with players. But, on the other hand, I have memories and friendships that very few other people can claim. I was center stage with one of the greatest franchises in sports history, during their glory days. My list of friends and acquaintances reads like a roll call of Baby Boomers' sports idols.

My experience as a ballplayer qualifies me for membership in a very close fraternity of former professional ballplayers. The game was never easy for any of us. To be at the top you had to work at it, and you had to go through an awful lot of the trials and tribulations of the game, there's no doubt about that. When I meet another former ballplayer, even if we didn't know each other during our playing days, I know that guy had to sweat out the axe in spring training at some point in his life, just like me. We know the common experiences we shared, and we immediately bond.

Baseball has also provided me with a pension and a little retirement money generated by card shows and autograph signing sessions. So, all in all, the game has been good to me, and if given the chance I would not change my choice to be a ballplayer.

What I would change about my life would be to have made myself more aware of alcohol as a drug, so that I could have avoided addiction. Also, I would have pursued my formal education with more attention. Looking back on it after all these years, my Mom was right to stress education. Knowledge is indeed power, and a college diploma that certifies the fact that you studied enough topics successfully to graduate opens doors for you. I definitely would have spent more time preparing for my life after competitive baseball was over.

The lowest period of my life was the time between the end of my baseball career, in 1965, and the start of my sobriety, in 1968. The anxiety over the loss of my baseball career was the result of several factors. One was the loss of my baseball identity. In searching for my acceptance in life by being a baseball player, I lost track of the fact that that was what I did for a living, not who I was. Compounding that was the knowledge that I had no money saved to take me through any transitional or learning period and no wife or immediate family to share my burdens with. Cast over all of that was the simple fact that I had no talent or knowledge that would enable me to make a living after baseball, and when I turned to alcohol for an answer to all of these problems, that itself became an even bigger problem.

When I first heard about the work being done by Rusty Torres and the directors and volunteers at Winning Beyond Winning, Inc., educating children as to the benefits of sports beyond winning, and emphasizing the need for education first, I wanted to be involved. When I came to fully realize that their mission was to prepare young athletes for life after competitive sports, and to provide them with the education necessary to lead lives free from dependency on alcohol and other drugs, I threw my full support behind it. I firmly believe in the power of educating our young people, and the effectiveness that alcohol education will have in lowering the number of addicts in the future.

Winning Beyond Winning, Inc. is the organization that would have changed my life if it existed in Wisconsin in the

1940s. The former professional athletes involved in Winning Beyond Winning, Inc. are using their life experiences, their successes and their failures to help future generations be more educated, more aware, and more successful. Rusty and the athletes he has assembled, including Frank Tepedino, Felix Millan, Ralph Garr, Chuck Schilling, Fred Valentine, Judy Sladky, and others, know that kids are attracted by the fact that they were professional athletes, and once they have their attention they stand a good chance of having them listen. I immediately realized my life would have been different if Big George had visited my home when I was a teenager and told me what alcohol was doing to him, honestly, instead of glorifying it, or if one of the Chicago Cubs I adored told me face-to-face that staying sober and maintaining a household and providing for my family made me more of a man than draining a six pack of beer and being the last man standing.

Thanks to the bond that exists between former players, when one of us reaches out to the others to help us educate children about the dangers of alcohol and other drugs, no one turns us down. Over the past four and half years we have been joined in our efforts by great people, including Jim "Mudcat" Grant, Jim Maloney, Frank Quilici, Al Jackson, Mookie Wilson, Dave Lemanczyk, Ralph Branca, Bobby Thomson, Phil Linz, Bob Tufts, Fred Cambria, Bobby Nystrom, Bobby Murcer, Emerson Boozer, Arthur Mercante, Sr., Vito Antuofermo, Levern Tart, Gary Baldinger, Bobby Richardson, Tony Kubek, Joe Pignatano, Bud Harrelson, and Mrs. Joan Hodges.

When I speak to young people about drugs, and alcohol as a drug, I explain to them how the drug system works, why we have the Food and Drug Administration and why a doctor has to write a prescription for drugs. I discuss how drugs, whether they are sold over-the-counter or by prescription, are dispensed by allotted dosages. I explain how people with many years of education have studied and analyzed drugs and their effects on humans for years, resulting in our knowledge as to what drugs are effective for which illnesses, and how much of the drug a person should take and how often, depending on their age and body weight. Then I discuss alcohol and what its effects on the human body are, and the fact that nowhere on any alcoholic beverage bottle, can or package does it tell you how much to drink and how often, nor what the side effects could be, nor what the result would be of consuming too much. I'm trying to toss some logic at them so that they may see a little more clearly what the world refuses to show them clearly.

I also want the children to know that before anything else I wanted to be a good parent, I wanted to be a good person, I wanted to be a good brother, I wanted to be a good husband, I wanted to be able to learn and to hold down a decent job. I didn't know I was going to have great baseball ability. I didn't know anything about that. My aspirations, very early in life, were just to be a good person. I am that person today, but why did I go through hell on earth in order to get here and to figure all that out, and it was because I was misguided about alcohol as a drug. That's first and foremost in my mind. So, I present the information that I think could have saved me from suffering the shame and degradation that I experienced, hurting my family and maybe keeping myself out of the Hall of Fame, and all of the other things.

I am trying to convey to them the information that our society is not giving them, because I believe the economic bottom line in the alcohol industry has been given a higher priority than our well being. I believe that furnishing our youth with this information is a sensible thing to do, and that is all I am trying to do. I'm not trying to control the children, or what they do in their life. But with this information, I believe they can have a better life. I have completed my job when I have told them that and my desire is that they have a better life. Now, it's their responsibility what they do with it.

I think an important aspect of the Winning Beyond Winning programs is that we explain the benefits and advantages of positive behavior, not just the pitfalls of alcohol and drug use and abuse and lack of education and discipline. So this is as much offense as defense, if you will. We provide literacy programs, wellness programs, career counseling, nutrition guides, workshops, conferences and clinics. We also maintain an extensive reference library of books, magazines, digests, and videos, on issues of importance to children, young adults, parents and coaches involved in sports.

Winning Beyond Winning also reaches out to the parents in the community. That can be a difficult chore because parents do not want to hear that they're doing it wrong. So, we don't tell them they're doing it wrong. What we do is furnish them with the information they need to help their children. We can't assume that the parents necessarily know about alcohol as a drug and its effect, or some of the other topics we speak about. Why would they know it, if they've never been taught it? If they don't understand and know they can't tell their kids based on anything, other than based on hearsay and ambiguities. So, we are obligated wherever we can to bring the parents into it. Over the years, I would not go into a school district to talk with the young people if they didn't schedule a meeting at night, so that parents may attend. Now, one of the ways you can best get your points across to young athletes, is to make it mandatory that every kid going out for athletics has got to have his parents attend a session before the particular sport starts. Otherwise, you cannot play. You have, at that point, a tool to get the parents there. So now you have someone like myself come in and talk about alcohol as a drug. We destroy those myths that it's okay for the kids to have something, and after all they're going to drink and if they're going to drink I'd rather have them drinking at home than out someplace. We explain the faulty logic behind those statements and the thousand other excuses that exist. Those things are based on ignorance. You explain to the parents: here's what alcohol does, here's why we should have the age limit and maybe it even ought to be higher because the adolescent process starts along about eleven or twelve and it isn't over until twenty-five. It isn't over at twenty-one. Eighteen is hardly half way through the adolescent process. How do you know that? Well, we know because of behavior. Look at the alcohol and drunk driving statistics for kids and deaths. All of a sudden at age twenty-five it drops off sharply. What happens when a person drinks on the team? Well, I'll go through that with them. Does it enhance the athletic performance? Absolutely not. Destroy all of those myths. Along with the former ballplayers who speak to children, we provide drug and alcohol counselors, career counselors, educators, and other professionals.

I'm very grateful to be a part of Winning Beyond Winning's efforts in this area, and thank God for guys like Rusty Torres and Frank Tepedino and Tom Sabellico, the President of

Winning Beyond Winning, Inc., and Pat O'Brien and Ralph Caruso, and everybody else who's involved in it. It is an excellent program, and as more and more schools and youth groups become aware of it people are rallying behind it. The organization has provided programs to over 20,000 children since its inception.

The basic thinking behind Winning Beyond Winning is that many organizations exist to help people who have developed a problem, whether it is an addiction to alcohol or another drug, or who are bankrupt, or who find themselves without a marketable skill or trade later in life, but that we have an opportunity, as former professional athletes, to reach out to the next generations of athletes and help them prepare so that they don't develop these problems. Our belief is that if a person takes the steps necessary to obtain a solid education, can keep himself or herself financially sound and physically fit, can lead a life free from dependence on alcohol and other drugs, and can act in a proper way toward authority, including their parents, educators, and law enforcement, those people will continue to be productive members of society for many years, whether or not they ever become professional athletes. We do not take away a child's dream of becoming a professional athlete. In fact, we will help that dream come true, if we can, by helping to develop the talent he or she has; but we ask that the child and his or her parents keep that talent and that dream in perspective, and when he or she is not practicing his or her particular sport, they should have their mind on education, nutrition, and their future careers. We also explain the odds of becoming a professional athlete, and the average length of a professional athlete's career, making it clear that there is a need to be prepared for the period after competition. The motto of Winning Beyond Winning, originally penned by its founder, Rusty Torres, is *"Getting knocked down is part of every game, including life; being prepared for it, and getting back up is what winners and champions are made of."* We hope to prepare as many young athletes as possible for what lies ahead, so that as few as possible fall as far as I fell.

The work I have done after baseball, from Norris to Stoughton to Winning Beyond Winning, has given me a very fulfilling feeling. It kind of gave me the feeling of being on a par, in a sense, with the doctors in the Hospital. On many occasions they must get a great satisfaction out of being able to make a change that's so positive that it probably did save someone's life. And I think of their preparation for it, for having done that, and all I did as preparation for it was save my own life, or had my own life saved, I guess is a better way of saying it, and in the process learned enough to be able to help someone else. Although we kind of arrived at the same place I did it without the formal education that they had. I have already had people come up to me and tell me that because of a speech they heard from me, or because of their having gone through treatment at Stoughton; they feel that I saved their life. I feel very fortunate to be alive myself, but to be in a position where other people think of you as someone very special in this world for saving their life, is a hell of a feeling. At this stage of my life, if my work with Winning Beyond Winning can help to save one child from going through the hell I went through it will be more important to me than any save on any baseball field, and any plaque that anybody could ever give me.

Rosendo "Rusty" Torres
Outfielder 1971-1980 Yankees, Indians, Angels, White Sox, Royals
Vice-President, Co-Founder, Winning Beyond Winning, Inc.

"I never faced Ryne Duren as a batter, but I was a teenage Yankee fan growing up in Brooklyn when Ryne was dominating the league as a relief pitcher for the Yankees, and I remember how powerful and effective he was. It is truly an honor to now be associated with a man of his ability and character. What Ryne has accomplished by maintaining his sobriety for over 34 years is no small task. What is even greater is his knowledge of the addiction and how powerful and effective he is as a speaker. I have heard Ryne speak on many occasions and he grabs my attention every time. Having witnessed Ryne speak to thousands of children and parents over the past four years was like taking a graduate course in alcohol addiction prevention, treatment and recovery."

The Press Photo for the Ryne Duren Celebrity Golf Classic to raise funds for Winning Beyond Winning and related charitable causes. (Photo source: Personal collection of Ryne Duren.)

Epilogue

By Tom Sabellico

In the course of learning all I possibly could about Ryne Duren, I asked Ryne the following question: "If you had the ability, without being seen, to overhear some of your former teammates and friends talking about you, what is it that you would wish they would be saying about Ryne Duren?" His answer was, *"I hope they would say things such as, 'He really got it turned around. He's been able to help a lot of people.' or 'He's left his mark.' or something like that. I would hope that that's the case, because that's the way I feel about it. I'm lucky to be able to say that, I know, but I guess a lot of us have taken our bows because of our luck."*

After having spent hundreds of hours with Ryne, and reading every book section and magazine article ever written about him, and every newspaper clipping we could salvage from his sister's scrapbooks, and from the microfilm collections of several libraries, I know how much anxiety Ryne suffered because of his longing to feel accepted, and how much that contributed to his addiction. Knowing that, and knowing how Ryne wants to be remembered, I think that the following remarks furnished to me directly by Ryne's friends, contemporaries and former teammates constitute a living testimony to one of the greatest comebacks ever:

Yogi Berra: *"I know Ryne's struggled a bit with the drinking, but he's done a great job of getting his life back. He's* *a good speaker with a good message to kids ... It's great to see him make a real positive contribution."*

Tommy Lasorda
Tommy was a left-handed pitcher with the Brooklyn Dodgers, and with Kansas City. He is a member of Baseball's Hall of Fame on the strength of his successful twenty-year managerial career with the Dodgers. Tommy also managed the US Olympic Baseball Team that won the Gold Medal.
"Although Ryne could not resist temptation, he overcame his problem and is an outstanding citizen, a loving family man and a devoted patriot."

Barney Schultz
Barney was a right-handed knuckleball relief pitcher who had a seven-year career in the major leagues, with the Cardinals, Tigers, and Cubs, spanning 1955 to 1965.
"I have the utmost respect for Ryne and praise his friendship. The time he devotes working with charity organizations proves he has great consideration of others in need. All in all, Ryne has proven to be a true champion, going through a dreaded disease and mastering it, something very few have done. So that leads up to one basic point: Ryne Duren proved to be a Big Leaguer on the field and off the field."

Phil Rizzuto: *"Everybody gets into a little trouble. I was glad to see Ryne get back on his feet. There were some tense times caused by Ryne's drinking, but I think it is wonderful that somebody who was as big as he was and as tough as he was, could come back from the problems he had and take the time to work with others and tell them his story to try and help them. He is doing a great job."*

Bobby Richardson: *"What a change in Ryne once he was able to quit drinking. He has helped so many other athletes that might have had problems. He is really dedicated as a recovering alcoholic to reaching out. I know of few people that are having the impact Ryne Duren is having. My hat is off to my teammate, my friend, and a Christian gentleman."*

Jim Maloney: *"Over the years, Ryne has raised thousands of dollars to help various charities, especially charities that help those less fortunate and with drug and alcohol problems, and he has enlisted many former players, which has been helpful to them and to the charities. In 1990, five years into my own recovery, Ryne got me involved and it has been helpful to me. In my opinion, it was through his alcoholism, both during and after his baseball years, that Ryne Duren, today, is the true and real person God intended him to be."*

Jerry Casale: *"It's just great to see how Ryne straightened himself out. It's a miraculous change. God bless him!"*

Jim Landis
Jim was a good friend and an excellent defensive outfielder for eight years with the Chicago White Sox (1957 – 1964) and then divided three seasons among the Athletics, Indians, Tigers, Red Sox and Astros. Jim was a Gold Glove winner for five consecutive seasons, from 1960-1964, was in the top ten MVP vote getters in 1959, and only once made as many as six errors in a season.
"I am very glad to see that Ryne's life is in great shape."

Frank Torre: *"I am happy to report that Ryne and I have stayed in contact over the years and he has done an outstanding job telling his story to others. I am proud to call him a good friend."*

Fred Valentine
I spent some time in the Orioles' minor league system with Fred, who had a seven-year career with the Orioles and Washington Senators. Fred is still in the Capitol area, with Clark Construction Company, and lends his time to working with kids.
"It is great that Ryne is working to counsel others about alcohol. It will prolong his life and set an example for others."

Chuck Schilling: *"It wasn't until his playing days were over that Ryne Duren faced the most important 'save' situation of his life. He confronted the beast of alcoholism and won! The* *advisory work he's doing for hospitals, rehab centers, and youth groups is to be admired by all who know him. To me, this is his greatest victory."*

Jim Kaat: *"I really admire how Ryne has overcome his addiction and is using his life to influence people in a positive way."*

Russ Kemmerer: *"I have great admiration for Ryne and others who have overcome their problems through great determination and will power. Ryne has done everything he could to encourage young people not to use alcohol and drugs. Ryne experienced the thrill of playing on a championship Yankee team, but I believe he is a bigger champion to those who have listened to his story and have turned their misdirected lives into successful futures."*

I had a chance in the mid 1980s to spend an hour, one-on-one, with the late, great Ted Williams, at a Major League Baseball Alumni function. It was fascinating, and I believe you can detect my admiration for Ted in my face. (Photo source: Personal collection of Ryne Duren.)

Appendix I

Pitching

Many fans ask me about my experiences as a major league pitcher. I am most often asked my opinion as to who were the best hitters of my time, and the toughest batters I had to face. Because of my wildness I am also asked about throwing to hit a batter on purpose, and at least one person in every audience wants to know just how fast I threw the ball. Based on the many questions I receive, and the fans' love for "inside info" on the game, I have added this Appendix to include some of my thoughts on my pitching experience.

PITCHING PHILOSOPHY

It never really bothered me to see batters digging in. Actually, I loved to see the guys come up that wanted to swing hard. If any hard swinger, especially long ball hitters, wanted to come up and take a big cut, that was fine with me. Here it is, hit it. One classic confrontation of "power against power" that sticks out in my mind was a battle I had with Rocky Colavito, who had a big swing. I needed to get him out for the last out of a game in Detroit. We were ahead by one run and the bases were loaded. I had two strikes on him and he'd foul a pitch off; I'd throw him another one and he'd foul that off. Finally I'd throw him a pretty good slider, and he'd foul that off, and then another fastball and he'd foul that off. Well, I had to get him out, or risk losing the game or letting Detroit tie it up. After Rocky spoiled a good seven or eight pitches, with the count full, he finally swung through one for the strikeout. I'll never forget that at bat, or the feeling of that competition. It didn't matter how many people were in the stands at that time, or what anybody was saying or yelling. At that point, in my mind, there were two people in the world: Rocky trying to get on base and me trying to get him out.

The oft-cited "book on baseball", which I never read but felt like I lived, says if you're going to get beat, get beat with your best pitch. Well, my best pitch was a fastball, but it wasn't always the best pitch to throw in a situation. I thought your best pitch was the one that you're most apt to get that particular batter out with. If he's set up for a fastball, a high fastball, then that's your best pitch or maybe a slider low and away is your best pitch to him, but you sure lend yourself to be second-guessed if you don't throw your best pitch.

Jim Kaat was a pretty darn good pitcher and if you listen to him announce games now, you hear him talking about "pitching to the scoreboard" and that's something that young pitchers need to learn. You need to be smart and pitch a little differently depending on the score, the situation, the inning and the batter. One of the things that I think made me successful, (although it distorted my record a little bit – I look a little wilder, statistically, than I was, in base on balls) was I never let the really good hitter beat me and I wouldn't give in to a hitter. That was a philosophy I got from Jim Turner, the pitching coach: you didn't have to give in 'til you had to give in. (That sounds like Berra again.) Somebody would always help you out swinging at a bad pitch. They wanted to be a hero. I wouldn't throw a pitch down the middle to a guy just to get strike one or to keep from walking him. Sometimes there'd be a hitter up there that was hot that I couldn't get out. But I knew I could get the next guy out or he might swing at a bad ball, so I had no fear of walking a batter unintentionally intentionally, if you will.

THE TOUGHEST HITTERS

I was in awe of Ted Williams when I pitched against him, and if I've got the statistics right he hit .400 off me, two ground ball singles, 2 for 5. My approach in pitching to Williams was to throw him sinking fastballs. If you held Ted Williams to a single, I thought that was pretty good, because I believe Ted

could have pulled my good stuff out of the park. He was quick
with the bat. I saw Dick Farrell throw a couple of balls by him,
but I didn't want to challenge him up there. So I threw him the
sinking fastball and he did hit it on the ground to the right side,
and it did have eyes, but he hit it pretty good. I don't know
what happened the other times.

I think it was Ted's teammate, Pete Runnels, who was the
guy that probably hit me the hardest of anyone. Nellie Fox was
the toughest out because of his strike zone and his ability to
keep the bat on the ball. In my role as a relief pitcher, I hated to
face Fox for the fact that it usually took ten pitches to get him
out. He was so tough.

Nelson Fox (1927-1975)
Second baseman 1947-65 Athletics, White Sox, Astros
*"Nellie" was born in St. Thomas, Pennsylvania on
December 25, 1927. Nellie signed a contract to play professional baseball with Connie Mack and the Philadelphia
Athletics in 1944 when just a sophomore in high school. He
went on to have a great career as one of the outstanding second
basemen in baseball with the Chicago White Sox. Fox was an
All-Star for twelve straight seasons, won the Most Valuable
Player's award in 1959 and was among the top ten vote getters
for the MVP in six different seasons. Fox often led the league
in games played, plate appearances, at bats and hits. He had
amazing bat control. He averaged approximately 625 plate
appearances per season and struck out an average of only 15
times a year. He led the American League in hits four times
and in fewest strikeouts 11 times. He compiled 2,663 hits,
while striking out just 216 times in 9,232 at bats. The Veterans'
Committee elected Fox to the Baseball Hall of Fame in 1997.*

Harvey Kuenn also got the bat on the ball a lot. In a start
I made in Detroit in September of '58, I think the Tigers got
three hits off me and Harvey had all three of them. They
wouldn't reach the outfield grass if you put all three together.
One hit home plate and bounced high in the air. By the time it
came down in my glove he was across first. The second was
a swinging bunt, which rolled so perfectly down the third base
line that nobody could throw him out (I suppose it was Andy

Carey who just had to pick it up and hold it). And the other one was a ball hit on the fists out towards Bobby Richardson that had backspin. There was no play and Harvey was over at first base looking at me with that big wad of chewing tobacco in his cheek and laughing. I knew Harvey from Wisconsin. I'll never forget. He's over there laughing and I'm throwing the ball over to first base time after time, trying to hit him with it and Skowron kept catching the ball, telling me "Go on now, pitch." And I said, "Dammit, let it hit him!"

Harmon Killebrew, I think, hit the most home runs off me. He hit me three times, twice in one game.

I didn't mind pitching to Mickey Mantle. I could strike him out. Although he did hit a big home run off me out in LA. It was late in the game and it wasn't my best stuff. I would throw him the high fastball. High fastballs, when he was batting left-handed, would be by him.

If I had to rate the top three hitters during my time, I would certainly list Williams as one of them, of course, although he was at the end of his career. Al Kaline I thought was an outstanding hitter. And I think it is interesting that as much as I respected him as a hitter, he had mutual respect for me as a pitcher. Kaline said, "When you face Duren you know what he'll throw, but it's no help. The ball jumps up and in on a right-hand hitter." For me the tough hitters were contact guys like McDougald, Berra and Hector Lopez, and I'll tell you who was a damn tough out for a few years, especially in the role he was in, was John Blanchard. John could hit that ball, and he never got any "leg hits." I don't know, it's so hard to say, but Kaline always impressed me, there's no doubt about that, and of course, Harvey Kuenn did do, for straight away hitting.

PURPOSE PITCHES

It was written quite often that hitters feared hitting against me because of how fast I threw and how bad my eyesight was, making them afraid they would get hit. I was able to use that fear to my advantage, as most pitchers do, and maybe a little more. Casey has been quoted as saying that if I hit a guy they would be talking about him in the past tense. I think the purpose pitch definitely has a purpose, and that the inside pitch sets up the low and away pitch, although I never really had it down that fine. I felt that the outside part of the plate would belong to me anyway, because not too many guys really stayed there really firm when I pitched. So I had awfully good luck, especially if I threw my slider on the outside part of the plate.

But I think most pitchers will tell you they'd rather play with the top and the bottom of the bat than they would with the end and the handle. You can hit a soft line drive off the handle for a base hit and you can break a bat by hitting it on the end and it'll still fall in. But if your playing with the top it's a pop up and the bottom is a ground ball. So rather than try to make my stuff be in and out I tried to make it be up and down.

Once in a while I had to purposely throw at a batter. One time in Kansas City, Bob Cerv was with the Athletics then, and he went in to one of our infielders real hard at second base. The "code" of the game dictated that I had to hit him, to send him the message that he shouldn't have slid in so hard. Cerv knew it was coming. There were other times too, that I had to throw at a batter to deliver a "message", but I would just drop down to the side, and sidearm them behind their butt. They would just back into to it and that would be it. The instruction might come from the manager, but, the batter and the other players all kind of knew and understood when it was a time for retaliation. Nobody had to draw you a picture. In fact, on a couple of occasions, one of my teammates would say, "Stay away from his head now." They wanted me to hit the opposing batter, but not hurt anybody.

I had to overcome the fear of hitting batters. I lived in fear I'd kill somebody. That was something that demonstrated what an effect the mental part of the game had on the physical part. Jim Landis and I were good friends and my wife was a good friend of his wife, having met down in Puerto Rico. From the mound I would look in to him standing in the batter's box and I guess I said to myself, "God, it would be terrible to hurt him." He was with the White Sox and we were such good friends. He had just adopted this new crouch batting stance, and I couldn't stop looking at his head. I thought it was terrible if I hit him in the head. But evidently, you throw where you look. So I was looking at him and first pitch down he went, second pitch down he went. The third pitch hit his helmet, knocked it all the way back to the screen. I was just having a wild day. Casey came and took me out of the ballgame after that. Gene Freese was the on deck hitter, and later on he told me he grounded into a double play and he laughed all the way to first base, because he faced Bobby Shantz instead of me. That's one of his favorite stories. I think I wound up hitting Landis four times all in all, and I never meant to hit him once.

Jim Landis: *"Well, with about at least a half dozen welts still on my head from Ryne's 100 mph fastball, this is my story: it didn't matter where I stood in the batter's box, or if I thought to duck and hide, it did not matter. Ryne plunked me good in the head. One day, Nellie Fox challenged Ryne on the situation and Ryne swore it was an accidental situation, and I believe him. It is almost fifty years since Ryne and I started our friendship in Puerto Rico during winter ball."*

It was a terrible fear that I had - it would be terrible if I killed somebody. Back home in town ball, I hit one of my best friends that I played amateur ball with, Johnny Beatty, and it affected his hearing, and then in the minor leagues there was a little guy playing for Natchez, Mississippi. He was the leadoff hitter of the game and he got crouched down over the plate, had his head in the strike zone almost. The very first pitch of the game hit him in the head. They brought the ambulance on the field and took him to the hospital. Evidently, he was alright, he was not out solid, and I went on to pitch a good ball game after that

Antagonism between pitchers and batters was always a part of the game. A couple of times in the minor leagues, guys were going to challenge me, but nobody ever got to the mound. One time I had a manager, by the name of Harry Chosen, that jumped out there. He was actually my manager and catcher, and he was catching me and somebody was headed for the mound and he was there in front of him. Then somebody else was going to come out and I think Ellie Howard got in front of him.

I did get involved in several "major league" brawls when I was in the minor leagues. I remember get punched out by an opposing manager who was convinced that I was throwing at his batters.

I don't think anybody ever thought I threw at hitters, I truly don't. I hope that is the case because I didn't, other than when they knew they had to get hit. Now, once in awhile there'd be a ball that would get away from me, and I felt bad about it, but you tend to block those things out of your mind. I was speaking with Harmon Killebrew recently at an alumni dinner and he told me that I hit him once in the elbow, unintentionally, and it still hurts, some forty years later, depending on the humidity. He joked that with one pitch I converted him from a ballplayer into a weatherman.

I was recently playing at a golf tournament and before we were introduced to the other members of our foursome, I walked over to my cart and there was a nice Detroit Tiger bag in the back of my cart, a little old, but you know, of good quality and everything. I looked at the name on it and it said Jim Wilson, so I said to the guy when he came up, "Oh, were you in the Detroit minor league system, or did you know somebody with the Tigers or something?" He says, "You don't remember me do you?" I said, "No, I really don't." He said, "Well, I didn't think you would, but you ended my career." I hit him on the wrist and broke his wrist, and although he tried to make a comeback after that he couldn't throw as well as he had, and he had to retire at an early age. I really apologized, "I'm sorry," I said, "I'd didn't think I ever hurt anybody." So, evidently we tend, as human beings do, to actually put something so deep in our subconscious that we don't find it very easily. I said, "Well, I'm really sorry about that." He said, "No, you know what? I think you did me a favor because had I hung around the game with no more ability than I had I probably would have thrown away a number of years and I wouldn't have had a chance to be in business and have the good life I have now." So he figured he was better off outside of baseball through those years and maybe he's right. If he didn't get any pension time to amount to anything, he may have had a good career in business and he was very happy with his life.

I inadvertently added 30 days to Carl Furillo's career with the Dodgers. On May 7, 1959, the Yankees played a fundraising exhibition game, for Roy Campanella, against the Dodgers in the Los Angeles Coliseum. They said over 93,000 people attended and 15,000 more were turned away, the largest crowd to ever witness a baseball game. There was a candlelight vigil for Roy and it was very touching. However, during the game I hit Furillo in the chest with a pitch and broke a couple of ribs. The Dodgers were going to release him, but had to keep him on the disabled list for thirty days. As it turns out he played on and off that year, totaling only 50 games and the next year the Dodgers finally let him go after he appeared in only 8 games. I remember that I sent Furillo a letter after that happened, apologizing for hitting him. I explained to him that I did not hit him on purpose and was sorry that I hurt him. I also remember explaining that I didn't move off the mound when it happened because I found that to be the best approach, and I hoped he didn't misinterpret that to mean that I wasn't upset, because I was.

It was absolutely standard procedure for the pitchers and coaches to get together and discuss how to pitch to opposition batters before a series. I was a little better student of the game than I got credit for as far as pitching was concerned, I think. In 1963, when I was with the Phillies, Gene Mauch had a meeting before our series with the Giants, and I had had successful outings against them. I had made some pretty good pitches I thought, as far as high and low, in and out, to some of the guys that were pretty difficult. I know I struck McCovey out two or three times in the one start I made against him, and at the time our series against the Giants was to start, he was tearing up the league. So, we had the meeting before the game and Mauch says "Well, what about McCovey?" I said, well one thing that I think is he just gets up there and digs in, you know, like Ted Williams used to, really taking charge and I think somebody ought to just make him lift that back leg out of that hole." During his first at bat I threw an inside pitch to him and it nailed him dead on the shins. He wasn't going to rub it and he just walked down to first base. After he took his lead down there, all of a sudden the fans made a funny noise. I looked over and he had fainted dead away. They took him out of the ballgame. My first pitch to the next batter, Willie Mays, sent him sprawling. When I came up to bat, the San Francisco pitcher, Billy Pierce, hit me with his first pitch. That resulted in the umpire ejecting Giant manager, Alvin Dark. Other than the McCovey thing I don't think I ever got in to having to knock anybody down. And the reason was that probably within the game I would do it two or three times anyway, without trying. I think things like that came up once in a while where you may have to shake somebody up a little bit that's too comfortable up there.

SPEED

Many people have asked me what was the fastest speed I ever threw a ball. I have no idea exactly how fast I throw. One thing that I can tell you, was when I was pitching batters couldn't justify the strikeouts that we do today. At the time that I was pitching guys struck out about half of what they do now. Mickey struck out quite a bit, but other than him there were a few other guys. But today, I think, guys strike out an awful lot more. But I was averaging almost two strikeouts an inning in my relief appearances when guys didn't strike out that much and on some days, not every day but on some days I could throw the ball right by good hitters. That would prompt Mickey or Whitey or the guys to come by and say, "I can't believe the ball can be thrown like that." As I read through some of the newspaper articles recently, I read that through that stretch in 1959 when I had those 31+ consecutive scoreless innings, I had an ungodly amount of strikeouts. I think I averaged over two an inning for let's say 8, 10, 12 innings.

Well, there was some kind of a machine or set-up back when I was pitching that you could throw a ball through and the speed would be electronically measured. Maybe it was a type of radar, I don't know, but they had it around and I never did throw into it. And I don't know if I saw it in some ballpark or something like that. Frank Scott of the Yankees, had talked to NBC and they wanted to have a contest after the Game of the Week, where Dick Farrell and I would throw at these machines and see who could throw the hardest. They were going to give $1,500 to the winner and $1,000 to the runner-up. Well, I thought that was a great opportunity to make some money, because how much was I making then, $10,000 a year, or whatever, $12,000 maybe? But, anyway, the Yankees wouldn't let me do it. Well then we said to them, what if I'm warmed up, and I'm in the bullpen and already warmed up? "Well, yeah, if we've had you up and you're warmed up or you're in the ballgame, then you can go throw at it, but we're not going to

waste an appearance for you to throw at this thing." So Frank
went back to NBC and said yeah we can do it only if ... and
NBC said "No go. We have to advertise it and we want to do it
live." Another opportunity lost.

So, although I was never measured by that machine, or
against Ferrell, I have read an awful lot of comments by the
guys I pitched against, and the catchers I threw to, that I was
one of the fastest pitchers they had ever seen. I will accept their
testimony:

Yogi Berra: *"Ryne may have been the hardest thrower I
ever caught."*

Bobby Richardson: *"I agree with Yogi Berra when he said
Ryne could throw as hard as anybody in baseball."*

Phil Rizzuto: *"I put Ryne Duren in the same class with
Herb Score and Bob Feller. He was tough to hit."*

Jim Kaat: *"Ryne Duren was the standard by how we ranked
hard throwers, for example, we'd say Johnny can throw almost
as hard as Duren."*

Chuck Tanner
**Chuck spent parts of eight seasons in the majors, his best
year being 1957 with the Chicago Cubs. We were teammates
in Los Angels in 1961 and 1962. Chuck went on to have a
successful managerial career with the Chicago White Sox,
Oakland Athletics, Pittsburgh Pirates and Atlanta Braves,
winning the World Series with the Pirates in 1979.**
*"I consider him one of the players God gifted with great
ability. Nobody ever threw the ball harder. Ryne was in the 97-
100 mph range."*

Tommy Lasorda: *"Ryne was an outstanding competitor.
He threw as hard as anybody in the game. He had a great
fastball."*

Lee Thomas: *"Ryne could throw 95 to 100 mph.   He was very unhittable.   In today's game he would be quite intimidating and be making millions of dollars."*

Russ Kemmerer: *"I first faced Ryne in the Pacific Coast League in 1956.   To say he was blazing fast would be an understatement.   I never saw the first pitch; lucky for me it must have been high."*

Joe Ginsberg: *"Ryne was the fastest pitcher I ever caught, along with Virgil Trucks and Herb Score.   We had no speed gun in those days, but I know Ryne threw the ball 100 miles per hour or more.   We used to talk over the hitters before the game. I would say that this guy is a good fastball hitter.   Ryne would say, 'Good, let's see if he can hit mine.'"*

Frank Torre: *"I played against Ryne in the World Series in 1958.   He was a very intimidating pitcher who threw very hard."*

Appendix II
My Major League Career Pitching Record

Regular Season

Year	Tm	Lg	W	L	G	GS	CG	SV	IP	H	ER	BB	SO	ERA
1954	Bal	AL	0	0	1	0	0	0	2.0	3	2	1	2	9.00
1957	KCA	AL	0	3	14	6	0	1	42.2	37	25	30	37	5.27
1958	NYY	AL	6	4	44	1	0	20	75.2	40	17	43	87	2.02
1959	NYY	AL	3	6	41	0	0	14	76.2	49	16	43	96	1.88
1960	NYY	AL	3	4	42	1	0	9	49.0	27	27	49	67	4.96
1961	NYY	AL	0	1	4	0	0	0	5.0	2	3	4	7	5.40
	LAA	AL	6	12	40	14	1	2	99.0	87	57	75	108	5.18
	Tot		6	13	44	14	1	2	104.0	89	60	79	115	5.19
1962	LAA	AL	2	9	42	3	1	8	71.1	53	35	57	74	4.42
1963	Phi	NL	6	2	33	7	1	2	87.1	65	32	52	84	3.30
1964	Phi	NL	0	0	2	0	0	0	3.0	5	2	1	5	6.00
	Cin	NL	0	2	26	0	0	1	43.2	41	14	15	39	2.89
	Tot		0	2	28	0	0	1	46.2	46	16	16	44	3.08
1965	Phi	NL	0	0	6	0	0	0	11.0	10	4	4	6	3.27
	Was	AL	1	1	16	0	0	0	23.0	24	17	18	18	6.65
	Tot		1	1	22	0	0	0	34.0	34	21	22	24	5.55
	Tot		27	44	311	32	2	57	589.1	443	251	392	630	3.83

World Series

Year	Tm	Opp	G	W	L	CG	SV	IP	H	ER	BB	SO	ERA
1958	NYY	Mil	3	1	1	0	1	9.1	7	2	6	14	1.93
1960	NYY	Pit	2	0	0	0	0	4.0	2	1	1	5	2.25
		Tot	5	1	1	0	1	13.1	9	3	7	19	2.03

Key:

W   Wins
L   Losses
G   Games Appeared In
GS Games Started
CG Complete Games
SV Saves
IP Innings Pitched
H   Hits Allowed
ER Earned Runs
BB Bases on Balls
SO Strikeouts
ERA Earned Run Average

Index

Printed in the United States
119250LV00003B/188/A